T0277378

CREATED
IN THE
IMAGE
OF
GOD

CREATED
IN THE
IMAGE
OF
GOD

APPLICATIONS AND IMPLICATIONS
FOR OUR CULTURAL CONFUSION

EDITED BY
DAVID S. DOCKERY
WITH LAUREN MCAFEE

Forefront
BOOKS

Published by Forefront Books (Nashville, TN).
Distributed by Simon & Schuster (New York, NY).

Library of Congress Control Number: 2023901456

Print ISBN: 978-1-63763-172-0
E-book ISBN: 978-1-63763-173-7

Cover Design by Kelly L. Howard
Interior Design by Bill Kersey, KerseyGraphics

With gratitude to those who

faithfully Stand for Life

TABLE OF CONTENTS

PART 3
OUR CULTURAL CONFUSION

INTRODUCTION

David S. Dockery

MEN AND WOMEN are the highest forms of God's earthly creation, indeed the crowning work of God's creative activity. All other aspects of creation have been created for the purpose of serving men and women, whereas men and women are created to serve God and are thus theocentric.

Men and women are complex creatures of God composed of not only a physical body but also an immaterial self, called a soul or spirit, which has been understood in various ways by Christians through the ages. The Bible affirms that humans are more than a material body. We affirm that, in the present life, men and women function as whole persons, though it is a type of conditional unity. We offer this recognition because the material and immaterial aspects interact upon each other in such intricate ways that they are not easily distinguished. Yet, as has been expounded by many in the history of the church, the characteristics of the immaterial (soul/spirit) cannot be attributed only to the physical.

The material and immaterial remain distinct but not separated until death, closely related and interacting with each other. Humans were a unity at creation and will again be a complete unity at glorification, but during the present time, we can affirm a conditional unity brought about by the entrance and effects of sin. The primary reason for the assertion and affirmation regarding the importance of men and women in creation, over against the rest of God's creation, is related to the biblical teaching that men and women are created in God's image (Gen. 1:26–27).

CREATED IN THE IMAGE OF GOD

Genesis 1:26–28, along with a more detailed account in Genesis 2:5–25, relates the scriptural story of the direct creation of the first man and first woman. In the other aspects of the creation account in Genesis 1, we read over and over that "God said, 'Let there be . . . ,'" but in the account of the creation of humanity, we read that "God said, 'Let Us make man in Our image, according to Our likeness'" (NKJV).

Indeed, God has created humans in his image and likeness. At first, such an idea might appear to refer to our physical makeup—that we look like God. This idea, however, is not what the Bible means by the terms "image" and "likeness" of God. Men and women, because they are created in the image of God, have rationality, morality, spirituality, and personality. They can relate to God and other humans while rightly exercising dominion over the earth and the animals (Gen 1:26–28). Moreover, Psalm 8:3–8 (HCSB) says,

> When I observe Your heavens,
> the work of Your fingers,
> the moon and the stars,
> which You set in place,
> what is man that You remember him,
> the son of man that You look after him?
> You made him little less than God

and crowned him with glory and honor.
You made him lord over the works of Your hands;
You put everything under his feet:
all the sheep and oxen,
as well as animals in the wild,
the birds of the sky,
and the fish of the sea
that pass through the currents of the seas.

At first blush, these verses may appear to suggest the insignificance of humans before the marvelous and majestic heavens. Yet, on closer reflection, the psalmist is overwhelmed by the exalted place God has granted to humankind. Moreover, God cares for his own.

This is true because humans have been created in God's image and likeness. Nothing in us is separable, distinct, or discoverable as the divine image. Each person individually and the entire race corporately are the image of God. At creation, men and women were granted spiritual comprehension and a conscience. More than innocence, the first man and the first woman were given intelligence as well as positive righteousness and holiness. The image of God needs to be understood in terms of both *being* and *relation*. We recognize both a substantive and functional understanding of the image. We can grasp God's design for humans by reflecting on the fact that the image of God includes ideas of being, substance, relationship, and function, and perhaps more. In Genesis 1:28, we read that humans were designed to function as vice-regents, exercising oversight of and dominion over God's creation, bringing order and beauty to this world. In addition, we have been given relational capacities, allowing humans to relate to God, to others, to God's created world, and to ourselves. Other contributors to this volume will expand significantly on these ideas.

For our purposes in this introduction, we can say that no single aspect of human nature or behavior or thought pattern can be isolated as the image of God. We want to affirm that in creation, there is a complete equality between men and women; neither sex is given prominence over the other. Again, this equality is related to the fact that male and female are both created in God's image. Also, "in Christ," in our redeemed state, "there is neither male nor female" (Gal. 3:28 KJV). A difference in function between women and men, however, is addressed in Genesis 2:18–25.

SIN AND THE FALL

Even though men and women are created in God's image, the entrance of sin into the world has had great and negative influences on God's creation, especially humans created in God's image. God had created perfect conditions for humanity; everything in this created world was good, and the creation of men and women was very good (Gen. 1:31). As a result of sin, the image of God was not lost or destroyed (Gen. 9:6; James 3:9) but was tainted by sin. The role of exercising dominion (Gen. 1:28) has been drastically disturbed by the effects of sin on humans and the curse on nature (Gen. 3). The ability to live in right relationship with God, with others, with nature, and with ourselves has been marred. All attempts at righteousness fall short in God's sight (Isa. 64:6; Rom. 3:23). Humans are, ultimately, spiritually dead and alienated from God (Eph. 2:1–3). Therefore, we are unable to reflect properly the divine image and likeness as we were designed and created to do (Rom. 1:18–3:20).

It is necessary to see that the sin of Adam and Eve (Gen. 3) was not just a moral lapse but a deliberate turning away from God and rejection of him. The day that the first man and first woman disobeyed God, they died spiritually—which ultimately brought physical death (Gen. 2:17). The consequences were many (Rom. 1:18–3:20; 5:12–21;

Eph. 2:1–3, 11–18). Important among these consequences are the effects upon our wills, the volitional elements of men and women. Sin's entrance has brought a sinful nature in all humanity. People act in accord with their sinful natures. No one ever acts in a way that is contrary to his or her own inner nature apart from regeneration (Gal. 5:16–25; Eph. 4:17–32).

This idea is significant when reflecting on our relationship with God. Because of the entrance of sin into the world and our inheritance of Adam's sinful nature (Rom. 5:12–19), we are constituted as sinners (Rom. 5:19) and are by nature hostile to God and estranged from him (Rom. 8:7; Eph. 2:13). We have wills that do not obey God, spiritual eyes that do not see, and spiritual ears that do not hear because spiritually we are dead to God. While we function as free moral agents, our decisions and actions are always affected by sin. In day-to-day decisions, we have the ability to make free and rational choices, but these choices are always influenced by our sinful nature. In regard to our relationship with God, we do not repent or genuinely turn to God without divine enablement because we are by nature hostile to God.

An awareness of these ideas helps to clarify frequently misunderstood concepts about the nature of sinful humanity. We are depraved, but this does not mean we are as wicked as we can be. Rather the idea of depravity refers to the fact that all aspects of our being are negatively influenced by sin. Men and women still can do and continue to do good and right things as viewed by society, but these thoughts and actions, no matter how benevolent, are sinful if not done for the glory of God. People choose to do good but not the ultimate good, which is the goal of pleasing God and seeking his eternal glory. Thus, depravity involves our total, willful rejection of the will and glory of God.

We are, therefore, totally depraved, but we cannot say that we are totally corrupt. Other factors, such as environment, emotional makeup, heritage, and of course, the continuing effect of our having been created in God's image, influence the degree of corruption. The degree of wickedness, corruption, and deceitfulness differs from individual to individual and from culture to culture, but certainly, some are more noble than others. Still, sin is inevitable because all in this world are estranged from God, but the biblical answer is that Jesus Christ has regained what was lost in Adam (Rom. 5:12–21).

It is important to note that nothing we have said infers that the soul or spirt is the valuable and Godlike part of humans while the body is what brings the soul down to sin and corruption. Both the material and immaterial aspects are valuable and significant to God. The chapter by Gregg Allison in this book particularly makes the case for the importance of embodiment. We celebrate the wonderful truth that the grace of God has provided our restoration and brought about a right relationship with God, with one another, with nature, and with ourselves.

CULTURAL CONFUSION AND OUR HOPE IN CHRIST

Augustine, in the initial sections of his *Confessions*, observes that God has made humans for himself, and we are restless until we find rest in him. At this present time, our culture is indeed restless, and confusion abounds regarding questions about what it means to be human, the importance of life, the significance of relationships, the meaning of human sexuality, the understanding of maleness and femaleness, and the looming questions of artificial intelligence and transhumanism. In this book, the authors seek to address these important matters in accordance with its title: *Created in the Image of God: Applications and Implications for Our Cultural Confusion*. These important issues and questions will be explored from the standpoint of the Christian teaching about creation and the promised eschatological union and fellowship with the triune God for those who have placed their trust in the redemptive work of Jesus Christ.

The confusion in this cultural moment is the result of what some refer to as the human condition, our sinful and restless alienation from God apart from Christ. The overall approach in this book, though distinct and focused in each of the chapters, reflects a consensus understanding that men and women have been created in God's image, that they have fallen and are influenced by sin, that Christ has provided redemption through his vicarious death and resurrection, and that there is hope in the promise of eternal life in Christ. Christ succeeded where Adam failed (Rom. 5:12–21; 1 Cor. 15), allowing those who trust in him to enjoy and glorify him forever.[1]

It has been a joy to have the privilege to work with Lauren McAfee, Elizabeth Graham, and Daniel Darling on this important project. Together, we are thankful for the wise, thoughtful, and insightful contributions from John Kilner, Scott Horrell, Ben Mitchell, Jennifer Marshall Patterson, Scott Rae, Gregg Allison, Katie McCoy, Jacob Shatzer, John Stonestreet, and Robert Stewart. We appreciate the assistance from Wang Yong Lee and the overall support and oversight for this project from our friends at Forefront Books.

We pray that the Lord will use this book for good in the lives of many to bring clarity and guidance in the midst of our cultural confusion as we seek, with God's help, to regain a sense of the marvelous privilege that is ours to be created in the image of God and restored to his likeness in Jesus Christ our Lord.

PART 1

CREATED

IN THE

IMAGE

OF GOD

THE IMAGE OF GOD AND HUMAN DIGNITY

RECOVERING A BIBLICAL TREASURE

John F. Kilner

ALL PEOPLE HAVE DIGNITY because they are created in the image of God.[1] This theological conviction, with its origins in the Old and New Testaments, has long been a liberating force in the world by inspiring people to respect and protect the dignity of all human beings. Yet misunderstandings of it have at times more than neutralized its liberating power.

Accordingly, explaining how humanity's existence "in God's image" can provide an enduring basis for human dignity requires a three-part argument. The first part explains how much is at stake—why a biblically sound understanding of the image of God is crucial. The next part develops a biblical understanding of what it means for people to be in God's image. The final part highlights some of the many ways that biblically grounded human dignity can be upheld.

MUCH IS AT STAKE: AFFIRMATION, LIBERATION, AND DEVASTATION

Is the image of God concept really that important, and does it really matter that much how accurately one understands it? The answer to both is yes.

1. *Affirmation*. The concept of affirmation is important, not because of how many times it appears in the Bible, but because of the particularly significant points in human history where it is affirmed.[2] The first affirmation, in Genesis 1, is at the very creation of humanity, where being created in God's image stands out as a key statement about who human beings are. Extraordinarily, in the space of two verses, there are three statements of the divine intention and action to create humanity in God's image. This is not an incidental matter but something that readers of the Bible are to notice and remember.[3]

The image again appears in Genesis at two other pivotal points in human history. At the start of Genesis 5, the fall has occurred, radically affecting humanity. Also, the genealogies are about to begin, specifically identifying humanity. For humanity again to be freshly identified as being in God's image, at this pivotal point, is particularly significant. Then early in Genesis 9, right after the Flood wipes out virtually all of the human race, and humanity receives a fresh (albeit still fallen) start, humanity's image-of-God status yet again appears to reiterate what is irremovable from who human beings are. This is the place where God most fundamentally addresses the uniquely destructive action a person can take against another human being—murder. God's justification for the serious punishment that murder warrants focuses squarely on humanity's creation in God's image.

A fourth pivotal point in human history is the coming of Jesus Christ as God incarnate. As we will see shortly, not only does the New Testament identify Christ as God's image, but humanity's dignity is also freshly defined in terms of that image. Both Pauline and non-Pauline books of the New Testament reaffirm humanity's creational association with God's image (Col. 1; Heb. 1). Accordingly, the vast amount of Christian literature devoted to the topic of God's image is not surprising.[4] The passages in the Bible that address God's image may not be large in number, but they are huge in significance and warrant careful attention.

2. *Liberation.* Such strategic affirmation of the image of God in the Bible is not surprising because it makes sense of human dignity and can foster great liberation, especially for the poorest and weakest people in society.[5] For example, acknowledging people in need as created in God's image—and Christian service as conforming to the image of Christ—has long been a powerful impetus to help people in poverty.[6] North American Christian leaders, such as Martin Luther King Jr., have demonstrated the power of mobilizing efforts to care for impoverished people by making countercultural appeals to their status as "in God's image."[7]

Meanwhile, from the earliest centuries of the church, Christians have cared for those who are weak because "every stranger in need was a neighbor who bore the image of God."[8] This recognition motivated Christians to refuse to participate in the common practice of infanticide (frequently in the form of abandoning deformed or unwanted infants outdoors).[9] In fact, this notion also spurred the early church to go beyond nonparticipation in infanticide to rescuing abandoned infants and caring for them.[10] More recently it has inspired Christian efforts to care for people with disabilities and for those with socially stigmatized diseases such as HIV/AIDS.[11]

Humanity's creation in God's image has also inspired initiatives to stop people from oppressing other groups, such as

Native Americans, enslaved Africans and their descendants, and women.[12] Consider a few representative examples. Regarding Native Americans, what drove Spanish friars to risk their lives for indigenous peoples was "the abiding confidence that they would not encounter any human being . . . who was not created in the image and likeness of God."[13]

The image of God played a similarly significant role in liberating enslaved Africans and their descendants in the United States and elsewhere. According to Abraham Lincoln: "Nothing stamped with the Divine image and likeness was sent into the world to be trodden on and degraded."[14] Surveying the many arguments made against slavery in the decades leading up to the Civil War, pastor-educator Richard Wills concludes, "More than the secular rationale could admit, freedom had a moral quality that grew out of a theological worldview that sought to articulate what it meant to have been created in God's image. . . . It was this theological idea that rallied the social resistance against the forces of slavery so all those created in God's image might be included in 'We the people.'"[15]

Women have also often discovered that their creation in God's image is one of the most powerful protections against mistreatment. In the words of African theologian Mercy Amba Oduyoye: "Many women have claimed the biblical affirmation of our being created 'in the Image of God' both for the protection of women's self-worth and self-esteem and to protest dehumanization by others."[16] Accordingly, the Asian Women's Resource Centre has named its journal *In God's image.*[17]

This liberating influence has always been in danger of being undermined when people have altered what it means to be in God's image, either consciously or unconsciously, often in order to benefit themselves and to put down others. Some examples will underscore how much is at stake when that happens.

3. *Devastation*. Surprisingly, the devastation caused by misusing the idea of God's image ranges as widely as the idea's liberating effects.[18] Typically, the problem has involved people's tendency to view being in God's image in terms of ways that people presently are most excellent—most like God and most unlike animals. That has commonly involved equating being in God's image with abilities or capacities for relationship, reason, righteousness, rulership, and so on. This way of thinking has encouraged such abuses as mistreatment of disabled people, the Nazi Holocaust, exterminations of Native American groups, oppression of enslaved Africans (and their descendants), and oppression of women.

First, consider people with disabilities, particularly mental disabilities.[19] Various Christian leaders in the history of the church have considered the image-of-God status of mentally compromised people to be "practically nonexistent."[20] The result has been a degrading of people with disabilities—a denial of their dignity.[21] Adolf Hitler recognized that he could use common misunderstandings of what it means to be in God's image to argue that weaker members are mere "deformities" of God's image that ought to be "cleansed" from society.[22] The problem here was understanding God's image in terms of something that can be deformed by sin or other causes, as can any human attribute. That understanding logically invited the conclusion that some people can be less in God's image than others and so warrant less respect and protection.

There were many influences that helped shape Hitler's thinking. One was the government effort in the United States to suppress and exploit Native American people, as portrayed in the novels of Karl May, which Hitler devotedly read.[23] One of the greatest champions of such governmental efforts was Harvard professor Oliver Wendell Holmes. Holmes argued that Native

Americans were not as fully "God's image" as the so-called "white man" was, and so it would be appropriate for the "red man" to be "rubbed out."[24] Native Americans in Latin America shared the predicament of Native Americans in the United States to such a degree that the study *Racism and the Image of God* found image-related misunderstandings to be connected with "the death and enslavement of millions and the imperialistic domination of millions more."[25]

Victims of this massive abuse include not only Native Americans but also enslaved Africans and their descendants. According to the research of Christian ethicist Kyle Fedler, slavery was able to gain a strong foothold in the United States "because many theologians, both northern and southern, held that black men and women were not made in the image of God."[26] Long after the Civil War, the idea of African Americans not being in the image of God was promoted by such influential books as Charles Carroll's *The Negro a Beast*, or *In the Image of God*. Carroll explains that because the protection of being in God's image wasn't involved, "extermination" of black people was reasonable.[27] The Jim Crow Museum of Racist Memorabilia at Ferris State University suggests that the teaching of Carroll's book on the deficiency of God's image in African Americans did, indeed, turn out to play a significant role in fostering the thousands of lynchings of African Americans between 1882 and 1951.[28]

Against this backdrop has arisen the so-called "Christian Identity" movement, which developed significant and increasing popularity during the latter half of the twentieth century through such groups as the Ku Klux Klan; Aryan Nations; and the Covenant, the Sword, and the Arm of the Lord (CSA).[29] As CSA puts it, only white people "walk in [God's] image upon this earth."[30] From such a view, atrocities like Klan lynchings and Aryan Nations's celebration of racially motivated murders readily follow.[31]

Demeaning and oppression of women has similarly resulted from misunderstanding what it means to be created in God's image. Men have supposed that they are the true images of God due to their supposedly superior reasoning and rulership.[32] As Yale professor Margaret Farley observes, "Numerous studies have already documented the tendency of Christian theology to ... [refuse] to ascribe to women the fullness of the *imago Dei*."[33] This recurs from Tertullian to Augustine to Aquinas to Calvin and far beyond.[34] It is no wonder that Julia O'Faolain and Lauro Martines titled their book about women in the last two millennia *Not in God's Image*.[35]

If being in God's image is indeed rooted in current human attributes—in anything that can vary among people because it is changeable due to sin—history teaches an important lesson. The idea that humanity is created in God's image will not just be a source of great liberation, it will continue to invite terrible devastation. It will be fair to say regarding this idea what some have said regarding religion in general: it is "high voltage; it can energize much or electrocute many."[36]

Accordingly, looking carefully at what the Bible teaches about humanity in the image of God is important for the preservation and promotion of this concept's liberating power.

A BIBLICAL UNDERSTANDING OF BEING IN GOD'S IMAGE

1. *Christ Is God's Image*. Defining God's image has more to do with who God is—it is, after all, the image *of God*—than about who people are. The clearest definitional statements about the image of God in the Bible are those that straightforwardly state that Jesus Christ is the image of God (2 Cor. 4:4; Col. 1:15; cf. Heb. 1:3).

The New Testament reveals that God's purpose all along has not been for humanity to develop into some sort of generic

"God's image," but to conform specifically to the image of Christ. "For those whom [God] foreknew [God] also predestined to be conformed to the image of [God's] Son, in order that he might be the firstborn within a large family" (Rom. 8:29 NRSV). However, since Christ *is* God's image, conforming to the model of who Christ is and what Christ does is tantamount to conforming to God's image. It is the fulfillment of God's determination in the beginning that people would be created "in" or "according to" God's image, living and growing in reference to God's standard for humanity. That image or standard is Christ, whose God-given glory—evidence of being God's image—was present "before the beginning" (see John 17:5; cf. Jude v. 25).

If today's discussion took place at a time before the New Testament was available, then it would make sense to begin with an analysis of Genesis. However, that is not our point in history. Since Genesis indicates that people are "in" or "according to" God's image, we would do well first to obtain as much clarity as the entire Bible provides on what God's image is. We can then examine what it means for humanity to be "in" or "according to" that image.

When the Bible talks about something being an "image," that means it (1) has a *connection* with something else in a way that (2) often also involves a *reflection* of it. Being the image "of God," in particular, means having a special connection with God as well as being a substantial reflection of God. Having a special connection is significant, since that means when one mistreats the image, one is mistreating the original. Being a substantial reflection is significant, since that means the image displays attributes (capacities, traits, abilities, and so on) of the original.

"Image" is the most common translation of the Hebrew word *tselem*, which appears in various biblical passages addressing humanity's creation in the image of God. Why the Old Testament employed this term for "image" most likely has to do, not with the term's precision, but with its flexibility and range. In the Old Testament, the range of meaning of *tselem* extends all the way from the very physical to the completely nonmaterial. As such, it works well in reference to people who have physical form but are more than material.[37]

The idea that an image signifies a special *connection* is evident, for example, in Daniel 3, which reports Babylonian King Nebuchadnezzar erecting a large *tselem* in the province of Babylonia. Anyone who spurned the image was to be thrown into a blazing furnace (v. 6)—a threat that Nebuchadnezzar acted on in the case of Shadrach, Meshach, and Abednego (v. 21). The purpose of this image was to represent the original in a way so closely connected to it that to honor it was to honor the original, and to dishonor it was to dishonor the original.

As in Daniel 3, kings in the ancient Near East would periodically erect an image (*tselem*) in order to establish their presence as rulers where they were not physically present.[38] Evidence exists of this practice in Mesopotamia, the setting of Daniel 3.[39] Images representing rulers also occurred in Egypt, as when Pharaoh Ramses II had his image hewn out of rock on the Mediterranean coast, north of Beirut, as a sign of his rule there.[40]

While images could directly represent human rulers— reminding people of the rulers they represented—images could just as easily have a god as the reference point. This concept of an image representing a god, common in the ancient Near East,[41] surfaces in Amos 5:26 (cited in Acts 7:43), where even the house of Israel appears to be worshiping Mesopotamian gods by worshiping their images (*tselem*).

The other element often present in an image is the way that it provides a *reflection* of certain attributes of the original. In Old Testament times, images often displayed something about a king. In Daniel 3 the great height and gold surface of the image reflected the king's grandeur and wealth. Similarly, the image of Ramses II in Egypt (like that of Ashurnasirpal II in Mesopotamia) appears to have been fashioned to look like the ruler, with size or attached words impressing the observer with some of the ruler's noteworthy attributes. Accordingly, the biblical authors would reasonably have assumed the core ideas of connection and reflection as the reader's basic understanding of the term.

Not surprisingly, the primary Greek translation of *tselem* in the Greek Old Testament, *eikon*—which is also the primary word for "image" in the New Testament—can have as wide a range of meaning as *tselem*. In the New Testament, *eikon* most often refers to physical representations, but what an *eikon* represents is far more than physical in nature.[42] Furthermore, the idea that the original is closely connected with or somehow present in the image—already suggested in the term *tselem*[43]—becomes even more evident in the term *eikon*.[44] This renders the latter a particularly appropriate term for talking about Christ's identity as the image of God.

A good place to begin an investigation of Christ as the image (*eikon*) of God is Colossians 1:15. There Paul straightforwardly affirms that Christ "is the image of the invisible God" (KJV) signaling both special connection and substantial reflection. The special connection is striking. As the image of the invisible God, Christ gives people the opportunity actually to see God. Moreover, Jesus is a substantial reflection of God—someone who can be seen, in contrast with the "invisible God." When people look at Christ, they see an expression of all the divine attributes in a way that reveals who God is and models how God intends for people to be in the world.[45]

The second of the two New Testament verses that explicitly identify Christ as "the image [*eikon*] of God" is 2 Corinthians 4:4.

Here the idea of close connection is also present, again to the ultimate degree in which two are really one. Whereas in verse 4, the focus is on "the glory of Christ, who is the image of God," verse 6 explains that this glory is the "glory of God in the face of Jesus Christ" (NKJV). Because Christ is God's image, God and Christ are so closely associated that the glory of one is essentially the glory of the other. As the image of God, Christ is the expression, revelation, and very presence of God. Yet the close association of glory (*doxa*) with image suggests that being God's image involves more than connection. The image reflects the splendor of the very attributes of God. Many of those attributes in Christ provide the standard for who people were always meant to be and still can become if they will conform to Christ (Rom. 8:29).[46]

One example of such attributes is God's *reason*, more commonly spoken of as God's wisdom. Christ's wisdom is not merely abstract, but it ultimately provides concrete guidance for godly living. To "learn Christ" is to develop minds that are not futile or darkened (Eph. 4:17–18, 20). A second example is *righteousness*. When Paul lifts up Christ as God's image (2 Cor. 4:4), according to which believers are to be transformed (2 Cor. 3:18), it is in terms of a particular manifestation of glory—right standing with God (2 Cor. 3:9).

A third example of Christ's image-related attributes involves *rulership over creation*. Following language early in Hebrews 1, which echoes Christ's image-of-God status, Hebrews 2:8–9 indicates that God's intentions for people's rulership since the beginning have not come to fruition—"but we do see Jesus."[47] Christ demonstrates what rulership can be when sin no longer has control. One final example involves *relationship*. In Romans 8:29, Christ is the firstborn in a loving family. According to Colossians 3:10–11, when Christ serves as the image according to which Christians are renewed, that renewal does away with prioritizing people on the basis of their being Greek or Jew, circumcised or uncircumcised, slave or free.

2. *Setting the Stage.* If Christ is God's image, then how does that help explain who people are? The best way to answer that is to set the stage with several observations regarding how the Bible speaks about people and the image of God:

- people are "in" or "according to" God's image;
- God's image is undamaged by sin;
- not only are individuals in God's image but humanity as a whole is as well;
- God's image has to do with people as a whole rather than with particular human attributes.

Regarding the first observation, in various parts of the ancient Near East, people considered kings, priests, and monuments to *be* images of gods or kings, as we have seen. The biblical writings adopt the general concept but adapt it in various ways to fit the biblical message—for example, by applying it to all people.

Another important adaptation of the biblical authors is their preference to not affirm that people *are* the image of God.[48] Rather, these authors insert a preposition indicating that people stand in some relationship with God's image.[49] Whereas Christ simply *is* the image of God (no preposition; 2 Cor. 4:4; Col. 1:15), people are created "in" or "according to" God's image. All of the image-related passages in Genesis (1:26, 27; 5:1; 9:6) consistently insert a preposition—and not always the same one—between people and the image. Image-related passages in the New Testament directly or indirectly referring to Genesis (e.g., Col. 3:10; James 3:9) also insert a preposition.

It is not plausible that in each of these passages the author is simply saying that people *are* God's image, as if there were no prepositions there and no need to add them.[50] In fact, prepositions such as "in" or "according to" make quite a difference. Saying that someone *is in* the water is quite different from saying that someone *is* the water. Saying that a violin *is (made) according to* a paper blueprint is quite different from saying that the violin *is* a paper blueprint.

The biblical authors use prepositions to distinguish the rest of humanity from Christ. With Christ not overtly in view as a reference point in the Old Testament, the recognition there would simply have been that people are not yet God's image but are created "according to"[51] the standard of who God is (in order to reflect God's attributes to God's glory).[52] In the New Testament, it would become clearer that Christ as God's image is the standard to which people need to conform completely. James 3:9 is particularly significant on this point since it conveys a New Testament author's summary of how the Genesis idea should be understood—not just as reinterpreted in Christ but in its own right applying to all people. In the words of James, people are made *kata* (according to) the likeness (image) of God, just as Paul explains that people need further making *kata* (according to or toward) the image of their Creator (Col. 3:10).

There are two New Testament books that comment on the image status of both Christ and people, and they consistently distinguish between Christ, who is God's image, and people who need transformative growth according to the standard of that image. In Colossians 1, Christ straightforwardly *is* the image of God (v. 15). However, two chapters later, when people are in view, they are not God's image but need renewal *according to* God's image in Christ (3:10).[53] Similarly, according to 2 Corinthians 4:4, Christ *is* God's image. Yet, four verses earlier (3:18), when people are in view, they need transformation *into* the divine image.[54]

Failing to take seriously the distinction between Christ being God's image and humanity being *in* God's image has contributed to overlooking a second important observation—that sin has damaged *people* but not God's image. If people were God's image, then by damaging people, sin would plausibly damage God's image. However, if people are created in (i.e., according to the standard of) God's image, there is no damage done to the standard just because people are at some point damaged.

There is ample discussion and documentation in the Bible regarding the destructive impact of sin on people. Yet, at the same time there is every indication that people remain "in God's image"—that no harm has been done to this status or to the image on which it is based. People retain a special connection with God (though their relationship with God is badly damaged), and God still intends for people to reflect likenesses to God (though in actuality they largely fail to do so). The image of God is the standard of who people are created to be—embodied in the person of Christ—and that standard is not diminished in any way because of sin.

The image-of-God passages in Genesis 1, 5, and 9 all affirm that people are created in God's image. Although people subsequent to the fall in Genesis 3 are sinful, there is not the slightest indication of any damage to God's image. In particular, the rationale for punishing murder in Genesis 9:6 depends on even the worst people continuing to be in God's image.

The closest New Testament parallel to Genesis 9:6 is James 3:9. That passage similarly grounds a current standard of moral conduct directly in humanity's creation as being according to the image of God. The point that James is making requires the affirmation that all human beings have the status of being in God's image. Long after the author of Genesis 9 employed this affirmation to forbid murder, James heard Jesus teach that if murder (angry action) is wrong, so are angry words (Matt. 5:21–22).[55] So James appropriately updates the image-of-God teaching of Genesis. In order to explain why his readers are not to curse human beings, he must affirm who even the worst human beings are today. They are specially connected with God by virtue of being made in God's image.

If God's image is a crucial basis for human significance, and that basis is damaged, people cannot help but have less respect for the "least lovely" among them, as history has shown.[56] It is, therefore, no wonder that the biblical authors never even hint that the image of God has been damaged.

Acknowledging that the biblical writings recognize no damage done to God's image does not weaken or question the gravity of sin and its devastating effect on the human race and beyond. If anything, sin is all the more heinous because of the way it causes people to contradict who their Creator intends them to be.

Is a damaged image restored then, or are damaged human beings restored? It is important to read the texts carefully and not to read into them ideas that are not there. In Romans 8:29, no language indicates that any sort of image is changing. Rather, God is changing people, and the image of Christ (God's image, who is Christ[57]) is that to which people are being conformed. If anything, it is the constancy of that image that provides a sure goal for humanity.

Again in 2 Corinthians 3:18, the image does not change; people do. Here and elsewhere, a different term—*glory*—signifies what changes. People are transformed "from one degree of glory to another." Discussions of God's image often confuse or conflate the terms "glory" and "image," resulting in the biblically unsound assumption that God's image can be damaged or lost and then restored, the way that glory can be. Colossians 3:10 conveys an outlook similar to that of the Romans and 2 Corinthians passages. The new humanity that characterizes Christians "is being renewed in knowledge according to the image of its creator" (v. 10

NRSV). The image is not being renewed; people are. The image is the standard or goal according to which people are being renewed.

A third observation to make regarding how the Bible speaks about the image of God concerns who exactly is in God's image. Is it particular people, humanity as a whole, or both? Genesis 1:26 introduces the creation of humanity using a singular noun, *adam*, to which verse 27 refers by using both a singular and a plural pronoun. In other words, humanity is both a singular entity and a plurality of members. The members and the entity as a whole are in God's image. Contemporary readers can easily miss the corporate dimension if they are located in societies like the United States, which emphasize individuals, personal freedom, and autonomy.

At the same time, other passages such as Genesis 9:6 and James 3:9 more directly suggest that particular people do have "image" status with all of the protections that should afford because it is *individual* people who are at risk for being killed or cursed. Connecting God's image both to humankind as a whole and to each of the humans who constitute that "kind" guards against destructive overemphasis on individuals or collectives.

A fourth and crucial observation about the biblical image-of-God idea is that being in God's image has to do with people as entire beings (whether humanity as a whole or its component members are in view). There is no suggestion that being in God's image is constituted only by particular attributes (e.g., abilities, traits, capacities) that people have or have had. Select attributes (even if Godlike) are not what are in God's image; persons as a whole are.

In Genesis 1, 5, and 9, each image statement is simply about "humanity" (*adam*) per se, not a particular aspect of *adam*, as being in God's image. James 3:9 (NIV), which states, "With the tongue we praise our Lord and Father, and with it, we curse men, who have been made in God's likeness," reflects a similar outlook. James identifies those who apparently warrant cursing most—those with the least Godlike attributes—as those who are in God's image. The understanding that God's image has to do with people in their entirety, rather than with their most attractive attributes, has been heralded as "a new consensus."[58]

Viewing attributes (likenesses to God or differences from animals) as the basis of human worth opens the door to reductionism—focusing only on those characteristics of people that one thinks are most important. Such an outlook in turn can all too easily lead to devaluing those who do not manifest those characteristics sufficiently. From that flows logically (though perhaps unconsciously) the demeaning and oppression of particular groups of people who are seen as not as much in God's image as others are.[59] Defining "being in God's image" in terms of people's reason (or other mental or spiritual capacities), righteousness, rulership over creation, or relationship all fall short on this score.[60] As Martin Luther King Jr. once observed, "There are no gradations in the image of God."[61]

3. *Creation and Renewal of People in God's Image*. Stating that something is "in God's image" is actually an abbreviated way of referring to the biblical idea of being "in God's image and likeness." Because two terms ("image" and "likeness") are involved here, some people have mistakenly thought that they refer to two different ideas. However, there is ample biblical and extrabiblical evidence to confirm that there is a single idea (with two aspects) here that falls within the range of meaning of each term. Either term alone is sufficient to refer to this idea. For example, Genesis 1:26 indicates that God intended to create humanity according to the divine "image" (*tselem*) and "likeness" (*demuth*). Nevertheless, the author considers *tselem* alone to be sufficient to describe that standard in Genesis 1:27 and 9:6 and *demuth* alone sufficient

in Genesis 5:1. At the same time, the idea to which either term can refer throughout the Bible does have two aspects, related to *connection* and *reflection*.

First, some sort of special *connection* between God and people is in view here. Understanding who people are is not possible without recognizing this connection. Passages about God's image do not define "image," but they do suggest something essential about it. According to Genesis 9:6, for instance, murdering human beings is forbidden not simply because God forbids it but for the deeper reason that people are connected with God in a profoundly significant way: they are created in God's image. When one destroys a human being, one is affronting God. According to James 3:9, not just murdering but even cursing a person is wrong because a person is in the image of God.[62] Cursing people is tantamount to cursing God.

People are not (yet) the image of God. Rather, they are made *in* the image of God—created to become God's image. That alone gives people a close connection with God. It identifies them with God. Christ as the standard of what that image entails was not revealed per se until the New Testament. Yet even the Old Testament acknowledged that humanity is profoundly connected with God by virtue of God's eternal purposes for humanity. It affirmed that people are not just stone statues the way that so many ancient images were—created in the final form of the image they were intended to be. Rather, people are living beings who must grow before they are what the Creator intended them to become. Perceiving this and altering the ancient Near Eastern concept to communicate it is one of the great contributions of the Old Testament.

The primary way that the biblical account adds the aspect of growth is by joining the idea of "likeness" to "image" in a distinctive way. The term "image" indicates the presence of a connection between an image and an original. However, an image may or may not have anything to do with being like (i.e., sharing the traits or other attributes of) the original. Including "likeness" with "image" communicates that the kind of image in view here somehow has to do with likeness to the original.[63] It ensures that *reflection* and connection are a part of the concept.

Whenever the "likeness" term appears in reference to humanity and God's "likeness-image," it is explicitly in the context of how God created people to be. There is a verb and a preposition. People are created "in" or "according to" the likeness of God. That is not the case where "likeness" appears elsewhere in the Bible. Elsewhere one thing is simply stated to be a likeness of something else. It is not just created with the *intention* that it be like it. It simply *is* like it. By contrast, in Genesis 1:26, God's intention for humanity is at the heart of what creation in the likeness-image of God entails. Later references to people created in God's likeness in Genesis 5:1 and James 3:9 not surprisingly mention the same creational intention since that is an important context for understanding the meaning of the term.[64]

Humanity's creation, then, in God's "likeness-image" (often in Scripture simply "image" or "likeness") means the following. All people are created according to "God's image," which the New Testament identifies as Jesus Christ. From before the beginning of creation, God intended that humanity should conform to the divine image, to Christ. So God created humanity well along the way toward that end. Even before the fall, humanity had further to go before becoming a full reflection of Christ, with a transformed spiritual body and imperishability (not able to die).[65]

However, after the fall people lost most of their ability to reflect God. They, nevertheless, continue to be in God's image, unique among creation as those whom God intends and will enable to become conformed to the divine image. No image has been damaged, for God's image is Christ—it is the standard of what God has always intended humanity to become. Even "being in" God's image has not been damaged, for to be in God's image is to be created according to that image, accountable to that standard. People are no less accountable simply because they reject God's standard.

In other words, the tremendous significance of human beings is completely secure, rooted in God's unwavering intentions rather than in variable, current human capacities. Even with their many limitations, all people have a special connection with God, and all people are created and intended to be a meaningful reflection of God. Christians are a community of people who are on a transformative journey mapped out for humanity by their Creator. They are inspired by a destiny that others do not see and a dignity that others cannot adequately explain.

Being in God's image is not unrelated to the actual capacities, relationships, and functions that people have. Having those things is what normally flows from being in God's image but is not what defines it. People who lack those things are not any less "in God's image" than anyone else because of what it means to be "in" (i.e., "according to") God's image. It means that God's image (revealed to be Christ in the New Testament) provides the standard for their existence and their growth. To whatever extent they fall short of fulfilling that standard and are able to grow, God intends for them—and offers them the means—to grow into more of what actually being God's image entails.

God provides everyone with the opportunity for transformation according to the image of God that is Christ (i.e., according to the image of Christ). Humanity gains a dignity even now simply by being the recipient of such an amazing offer. God does not want anyone to perish (2 Pet. 3:9). In that sense, God intends for all to reflect God-glorifying attributes.[66] God has created all according to the divine image and wants all actually to become God's image in Christ.[67] The offer they receive to be renewed according to (Col. 3:10), conformed to (Rom. 8:29), and thus transformed into (2 Cor. 3:18) God's image in Christ means that all are loved by God even with their many shortcomings. For all we know, any particular person's renewal according to God's image may begin this very day. They should be viewed and treated accordingly.

UPHOLDING HUMAN DIGNITY

The implications for how best to view and act toward people are extensive. As we noted at the outset, these implications are not merely theoretical but have been lived out in history. They are the evidence of the inspirational potential of the idea that all people are in God's image. People matter precisely because they are in the image of God.

Human existence itself has great significance on these very grounds. Many people use some term such as "dignity" to describe the special significance that comes from being in God's image.[68] This is not the dignity that varies according to circumstances but the dignity that necessarily accompanies being human. To reflect that distinction, some people refer to the latter form of dignity as "natural" or "inherent." The danger of such language is that it can imply that dignity is intrinsic to humanity without any necessary reference to God. Such is not the case with the dignity resulting from creation in God's image. This dignity is literally God-given.[69]

People receive dignity as a gift of God's grace. However, it does not come without requirements. So in that sense, it has an element of loan as well as gift to it. There is something that must in some sense be accounted for or repaid (though not in kind).[70] Being created in God's image has great benefits, but it comes with God's great expectations. The dignity of all who are in God's image neither depends on particular human attributes nor diminishes due to sin. Human limitations cannot weaken it. This dignity is as unshakable as God.

Just as humanity is not merely a collection of separate people but is also an interrelated whole, so humanity's status as created in God's image has implications for the whole together. God has a connection with humanity as a whole, just as God intends divine attributes to be reflected in humanity corporately and not just in particular people. For example, God intends justice to be a hallmark of human society, as it is of God's own character. Just treatment of all requires taking account of personal and societal relationships in which people live, rather than merely viewing people as individuals. Where there is injustice, freedom from that oppression is what humanity's status in God's image mandates.

While people never warrant less than what justice requires, they frequently warrant more, namely, love. Love is God's ultimate intention for relationships of people with one another and with the natural world as well. Love involves giving more than the required minimum and entails more than utilitarian maximizing of social benefit. It generates true solidarity, fellowship, interdependence, inclusive community, and unified mission. Again, the reason that people warrant love is not that people are so lovable in themselves, but that love is the appropriate way to treat those in God's image—whether they be friend or enemy.

There are many arenas where treating people correctly as created in God's image is particularly important in light of historical abuses.[71] The existence of all humanity in God's image offers a potent rallying cry for respecting and protecting even the weakest and most marginalized of human beings. God would have people attend to the needs of those who are impoverished, for example, precisely because they are in God's image. Similarly, people with special needs due to disabilities warrant special care and welcome. They have an image-based dignity that does not waver, regardless of their ability or potential ability.[72]

Slavery is a particularly outrageous example of making unwarranted distinctions among people. It is a violation of how God intends one person in the divine image to behave toward another and is thus an offense against God. Affirming humanity's creation in God's image is a powerful way to mobilize the church to oppose racism in word and deed. With due appreciation for the extent of evil involved in racism, Christians will not be satisfied with bandaging the wounded but will insist on transforming the social practices and structures that perpetuate racism. The same goes for overcoming the oppression of women. People, male and female alike, are created in God's image—not because women and men have all the same attributes but because of God's connection with them and the divine reflection God intends them to be.

The implications for pastoral care, counseling, and evangelism are immense. Even the weakest person—morally, emotionally, spiritually—has a special connection with the God of the universe. Moreover, God intends for that person increasingly to become a meaningful reflection of God en route to a glorious eternal life as the image of God in Christ. People's existence as created in God's image can give them meaning and hope even in the depth of despair. The special connection and intended reflection that constitute being in God's image are God's enduring promise to them that so much more is possible if they are willing to let God break the power that sin has over them.

In light of the huge potential for a biblically sound understanding of God's image to uphold human dignity in many arenas, Christian education can and should play a major role here.[73] Christian education upholds human dignity by equipping people both to grow in their reflection of God and to appreciate their connection with God.

As explained above, God's creation of humanity in his image entails that God intends for people increasingly to reflect all the attributes of God that people are created to reflect, as modeled in Christ's humanity. For example, effective education can foster better knowledge (reason), stewardship (rulership), and relationships. It can encourage the pursuit not only of personal righteousness but also of societal righteousness (justice). After all, being in God's image and intended to reflect his attributes is as true of humanity as a whole as it is of every member of humanity.

At the same time, being in the image of God is as much about connection as it is about reflection. Christian education also upholds human dignity by equipping people to appreciate their connection with God, with substantial implications for how they relate to others as well as how they see themselves. The Bible itself is explicit that, since every person is created according to God's image, we cannot kill or curse anyone. In other words, we are not to jeopardize human life or dignity in any way. The Genesis 1 context of the introduction of the image of God concept in the Bible suggests that any living being who is human (as opposed to a plant or another kind of creature) is created in God's image. That means every human, from conception to death, falls into this category, so their lives and dignity are to be respected and protected.[74] Moreover, recall that humanity as a whole and not just individual people are created according to God's image. That means, where particular people or societal structures have violated the life and dignity of certain groups, there is an obligation for them to stop and normally to provide restitution.

Creation in God's image also has profound implications for how people should see themselves. There is no firmer foundation for a person's sense of self-worth than to know that they have a special connection with God, created in order to reflect God's attributes to the world. Nevertheless, as great a blessing as it is to be created according to God's image—according to Christ—it is essential that people understand it to be a responsibility as well. Yes, our dignity ought to be respected. But whether or not it is, we must respect and protect the dignity of every other person because of who God has made them to be. They have a special connection with God and are intended to be a meaningful reflection of God. What profound dignity is that!

"PERSONS" DIVINE AND HUMAN

THE CONCEPT OF PERSON IN AND BEYOND NICAEA FOR TODAY

J. Scott Horrell

THE GREATEST QUESTION OF THE TWENTY-FIRST CENTURY is "What is a *human being*?" More precisely, beyond the material *Homo sapiens*: Who am I?[1] and What am I? What does it mean to be a *person*? A *human person*?[2]

Doubtless the question of what a person is has always been part of universal discourse (Ps. 8:4), even as the word *person* itself slowly evolved in Greek and Latin use. The idea of person particularly took on importance within trinitarian theology. Through the centuries, non-biblical worldviews—whether animist, polytheist, pantheist, or Buddhist—conceive of the human being as part of an ascending hierarchy of person-like beings or, again, as a finite entity to be transcended ultimately into an apersonal Ultimate. Conversely, contemporary Western atheism increasingly reduces *Homo sapiens* to DNA and extraordinary evolutionary luck. Advancing theories of evolutionary psychology, genetic engineering, and transhumanism dominate human sciences today. Among a growing cohort of futurists, Yuval Noah Harari declares that today the *Homo sapien* is becoming its own intelligent designer, gods stepping beyond the constraints of evolution to transcend our limited capacities[3]—what he terms the greatest revolution in the history of life. Lev Grossman boldly announces the merger of the human being with artificial intelligence, per the cover of *TIME* magazine: "2045: The Year Man Becomes Immortal."[4]

The contemporary enigma of self-consciousness raises as never before questions regarding human definition, particularly in the sense of what is a *person*? The existential cry of "Who am I?" must evoke from Christians the decided response that we come to understand who we are, not by looking within, but by looking up to the tripersonal God of the Bible.

On the one hand, theologians are rightly guarded in ascribing the personalistic descriptions of God univocally to humankind. Certain biblical descriptions of God soar far beyond human comprehension (Rom. 11:33–36; 1 Tim. 6:15–16), as both rabbis and the earliest fathers were quick to discern. When interpreting the Bible, the place of anthropomorphism must be recognized. On the other hand, the God of the Bible almost always comes to us in blatantly personal terms, from our creation as *imago Dei*, to various theophanies of the Old Testament, to the incarnation of the "Son" ("truly God, truly man") who invites us to call God "Father," to a Spirit who can be grieved and insulted, to a physical return of Jesus Christ, who will reign over an earthly kingdom of redeemed humanity. Arched high, the bridge from God to human personality stands remarkably wide, sturdy, and eternal. Nonetheless, in recent discourse the insights of a past generation of social and relational trinitarian theologians have been largely ignored by those who prefer to emphasize divine transcendence and oneness—this at the loss of the abundant self-revelation of the Father, Son, and Holy Spirit as *persons*.

I suggest that within trinitarian studies a plurality of perspectives regarding the highest mystery of Christian faith seems far wiser and humbler than selective dogmatic strands drawn from Christian history. The Nicene-Constantinopolitan Creed (AD 381) serves as the doctrinal box outside of which lies heterodoxy yet within allows room for various efforts to better fathom the meaning of the trinitarian God today. One would expect a cornucopia of riches forever to be explored within divine revelation and mystery. From Augustine's *De Trinitate* to Vern Poythress's multi-perspectival approach,[5] to greater global multicultural appropriations,[6] a diversity of complementary descriptions of the divine Being points toward the comprehensibility yet ultimate incomprehensibility of the triune God.

One example of this need for a plurality of trinitarian lenses is that the often insisted upon "one undivided will" of the Godhead must be complemented by recognizing the "distinct wills" of the Father, Son, and Holy Spirit, each loving the other and relating together within the economy. Either option if taken alone—an absolute singular divine will (modalism) or three harmonious wills (tri-theism)—truncates and distorts the greater biblical (and historical) witness. The three divine persons, as Vladimir Lossky argues, while of a singular divine nature, cannot be reduced to that nature alone, rather in some sense each person remains unique and beyond the undivided *ousia*.[7] We may rest and explore within the mystery of the one and the three.

This chapter proposes to strengthen the definition of the term *person*—the human person—by drawing parallels with the Christian Godhead. In one sense, any definition of what constitutes a person remains elusive and multi-dimensional, as an enormous amount of literature attests.[8] This effort makes no attempt to provide a final definition of *person*, but I will explore several aspects of personhood, divine and human, that may be constructive in seeking to understand the nature of what constitutes a person. First, I will give a brief (admittedly simplistic) overview of Western history's definition of *person* from pre-Christian Greek philosophy into the evolving trinitarian theology of the early centuries, later still into the Enlightenment, and up until today. Concepts of *person* continue to develop after Nicaea-Constantinople, Chalcedon, and Boethius, with insights and dimensions in later history that help fill out the meaning of person for us today. Second, I explore five parallels between divine and human personhood based upon (1) the one nature of God (and the one nature of humankind), (2) the "I" and "I Am" of each divine person, (3) the I-Thou of trinitarian relations, (4) the perichoretic structure and relations of the divine persons, and (5) the self-givingness of the triune God, each person to the other and toward creation. For sure, responses to what is a person transcend simple categories, but these five divine-human parallels serve as a family of characteristics that hedge in and help define Christian anthropology, and specifically human personhood.

THE EVOLUTION OF *PERSON* IN WESTERN THOUGHT

Hans Urs von Balthasar observes that "few words have as many layers of meaning as *person*," which in one sense denotes merely a "countable" individual within humanity but, in another sense, one who is entirely unique, one of a kind, and "therefore cannot be counted."[9] Human beings cannot deny their consciousness, thoughts, feelings, dispositions, and personalistic relations/activities with others, but with the advancement on nearly all sides of the human sciences, ironically, defining what is a *person* has become increasingly elusive.

1. *Earliest Biblical Uses of Person*. Certainly, all the elements of personhood are visible in the Old Testament, from the creation of the first man and woman to the personalities of Abraham, Sarah, Moses, and David. Even more, the New Testament reflects fullness of personhood supremely in Jesus Christ. But the meaning of the word *person* as employed later in Christendom is somewhat foreign to both Testaments. To be sure, a plurality of terms refers to the human being in the Bible, but as Walter Taylor observes: "There is no independent reflection on anthropology . . . dealing with humanity's qualities, constituent parts, or nature, and therefore little definition of terms and no standardization of their usage. Rather *anthropos* is always understood in terms of the relationship with God."[10] As Christians, what we are as human beings (*imago Dei*) is directly related to who God is, that is, to our concept of the divine Being.

Found as early as Homer, the Greek *prosōpon* derives from the preposition *pros* ("to, toward") and the root *ophis* ("sight"), denoting "that which lies opposite one's sight," such as another person's face, appearance, or mask. *Prosōpon* is found over 1,230 times in the Septuagint, often used for "face" (Heb. *pānîm*), sometimes as a preposition ("in front of, before"), or with compounds describing, for example, Sarah's beautiful appearance (Gen. 12:11). More generally in the LXX, *prosōpon* communicates simply a physical "face," "nose," or "brow" (e.g., Gen. 3:19) yet may also reflect human emotions or attitudes. As does the Hebrew *pānîm*, so *prosōpon* may denote someone's presence, even the "presence" of God (Exod. 33:14, lit "my face will go"; cf. Isa. 63:9).[11] Yet the meaning of *person* as developed later in history, i.e., in the *Definitio Fidei* of Chalcedon (AD 451), is at best inferential from the Old Testament.

The New Testament employs *prosōpon* about seventy-five times. The term generally denotes external appearance, face, countenance, even surface (of earth, sea, and so on), but the word in its plurality of expressions sometimes intimates a deeper reality behind the outward appearance. The term can carry the idea of pretense toward others (Gal. 6:12) or of showing partiality (Gal. 2:6; James 2:9). Paul draws the analogy of Moses's veiled face reflective of God's presence to the now unveiled, radiant face of Christ in which "we all, who with unveiled faces [prosōpō] contemplate the Lord's glory" (2 Cor. 3:18[12]). Again, he speaks of "God's glory displayed in the *face* of Christ" (2 Cor. 4:6; italics added). In these texts, "face" (*prosōpon*) suggests what is behind outward appearance, that is a person's entire being.

Closely related to the Greek *prosōpon*, the Latin *persona* finds its roots in the Etruscan *phersu*, designating an actor's mask, thus also a role, part, character, or person represented by the mask. The expression *ex persona* denotes an actor speaking in the role of someone such as the goddess *Persephone* (*phersu*).[13] Only in the third century AD did the Latin *persona* take on the idea of an individual legal entity.

2. *Person in Early Christian Theology.* If in embryonic form in earlier usage, the concept of person began to develop as appropriated for the Christian Trinity. By the time of Tertullian, the Latin *persona* could designate not only a character in the theater but also in Roman law: "An objective individual capable of having property or substance (*substantia*)."[14] Arguing against Sabellius and other modalists, Tertullian famously defined the Trinity (*trinitas*) as *una substantia et tres personae*, "one substance and three persons." Interpreting Matthew's baptismal formula—"in the name of the Father and of the Son and of the Holy Spirit" (Matt. 28:19)—the Latin terms *substantia* and *personae* came to prevail in the West, as did the Greek *ousia* and *prosōpa* in the East.[15] A particular point of contention was whether the Son was equally God in nature (*ousia*) or something lesser and created.

But that both the Father and the Son were distinct *personae* was undisputed by early trinitarian fathers, however ambiguous the word remained. As third-and fourth-century theology advanced, increasingly central to emerging orthodoxy was the insistence on the undivided *substance* (nature, essence) of God—a point theologians rightly emphasized to exclude Arianism.

  3. *Nicene-Constantinopolitan Personhood*. At the Council of Nicaea (AD 325) the key Greek term *homoousios* ("same nature") was set forth as dogma. The term *prosōpa* ("persons") was not. If the oneness of nature is made absolute, however, one must ask if adequate difference is attributed to the three divine persons? Uncomfortable with the modalistic implications of the Greek *prosōpon* (as "mask," "role"), by the 370s, the Cappadocian fathers were popularizing the term *hypostasis* to more deliberately distinguish the three persons.[16] In 381, the Council of Constantinople reinforced the Nicene *homoousios* ("same nature") yet coupled it with more emphatic affirmation of the uniqueness of each divine person: The Son is "eternally begotten of the Father ... begotten, not made, of one Being with the Father" and the Spirit is "the Lord, the giver of life, who proceeds from the Father. With the Father and the Son, he is worshiped and glorified."[17] Nonetheless, neither the term *prosōpon* nor *hypostasis* was formalized in the trinitarian creeds themselves.

  Regarding the emerging Cappadocian concept of *person*, Orthodox scholar Khaled Anatolios draws several continuities between the biblical narrative and Eastern patristic understanding of the Trinity that inform our conception of personhood today:

  • Father, Son, and Spirit are *persons* inasmuch as the scriptural narrative presents them in conversation with one another that cannot be reduced to a mere monologue without destroying the intelligibility of that narrative.

- Father, Son, and Spirit are *persons* inasmuch as the biblical narrative presents each of them as a distinct agent, a possessor of active intentionality, even though they together constitute a single unified agency in relation to creation.
- Father, Son, and Holy Spirit are *persons in communion*, not only in the minimally ontological sense that they all share in the divine nature, but also inasmuch as the biblical narrative indicates that the mutual relations by which they share in the divine substance may be appropriately characterized according to the interpersonal categories of delight and mutual gratification.[18]

4. *Augustinian Ambiguity*. Slightly later in the Latin West, Augustine reaffirmed divine unity but preferred to describe the three divine persons as "subsistent relations." Augustine rightly perceived real differentiation between the Father, Son, and Holy Spirit, yet he expressed unease with the Latin term *persona*.[19] When asking "Three what?" he opines that no language is adequate for speaking of persons within the transcendent God. Putting his formidable philosophic skills to use, he believed God to be utterly outside space and time, the one, truly simple Being—in one sense not unlike the Neoplatonic philosophy against which he sometimes argued.[20]

If God is truly infinitely simple, then how is the personalistic language of Scripture to be understood? Lewis Ayes responds, "This is for Augustine partly a discipline of the mind in which we learn to remove from our interpretation of Scripture's logic any temporal or material qualifications, and it is a search for correspondences between Scripture's language and metaphors and the divine realities signified by that language."[21] That is, the explicit, relational language of the Father, Son, and Holy Spirit in

Scripture and in part affirmed by the Greek fathers must finally be transcended. Augustine would argue that what can be known of God's internal relations is revealed in the *missions* of the Son and Spirit in creation and redemption. The *ad extra* missions of the Son and the Spirit point back to the timeless, internal, subsistent relations within the simplicity of God—that is, to the eternal *generation* of the Son and the eternal *procession* of the Spirit (*Trinitate* 4.20.27–21.32). To Augustine's credit, his multiple analogies of the Trinity as in *De Trinitate* remind us of the usefulness of various perspectives in describing the infinite, personal God. However, biblicist as he was, he generally presupposed as primary the transcendent, timeless, one God. Within a Platonic "metaphysical architecture of reality,"[22] trinitarian personal relations were not easily explained.

5. *Chalcedon's Definitio Fidei* (AD 451). As historic orthodoxy developed, the language of *person* was formally included in Chalcedon's *Definitio Fidei*. Focused on "the one and same Son, our Lord Jesus Christ," the creed declares Christ as *homoousios* with the Father as to his deity and *homoousios* with us as to his humanity, "sin only excepted." The two natures of Christ are unified, "without confusion, without change, without division, without separation—the distinction of each nature in no way annulled by the union. Rather the characteristics of each nature are preserved and come together to form one person [*prosōpon*] and being [*hypostasis*], not parted or separated into two persons [*prosōpa*] . . . ." The *Definitio Fidei*'s terminology uses both *prosōpon* and *hypostasis* for the one person and being of Christ or, more properly, for the divine person of the Son, who fully assumed a human nature. The Greek *hypostasis* reinforces the unique personal "being" of the Son-become-man, and the same term extends to each unique member of the Trinity.

6. *Boethius and Beyond*. Seventy years after Chalcedon, Boethius's *Opuscula Sacra* defends Augustinian trinitarianism and Chalcedonian Christology—interlaced with significant Platonic and Aristotelian thought.[23] Boethius famously thought of a *person* as an individual substance of a rational nature. *Nature* is the general category of being that enables individual rational thought. That is, the individuation of that rational nature is a person. Thus, the essence of personhood (divine and human) is rationality: through reason (philosophy/theology) the soul attains knowledge of the vision of God. Boethius's definition of *person* dominated Western thought for over a millennium, shaping Scholasticism and flowing into the Enlightenment. Theologians over the centuries both appropriated and struggled with Boethius's definition—Anselm, St. Richard of Victor, Bonaventure, and Thomas Aquinas to name a few.

Yet questions arise: Is a person essentially a rational individual being? Are we more personal and more Godlike through greater exercise of reason? Are those lacking rational abilities (infants, those with dementia, or anyone during hours of sleep) disqualified as persons?

7. *Descartes, the Enlightenment, to Modernity*. In popular history, René Descartes's declaration "I think, therefore I am" is often heralded as foundational to the Enlightenment and Western philosophy (specifically rationalism). A person can be sure they exist because they exercise reason. A Creator may be out there, but the human being exists as an autonomous agent in deducing truth. Descartes assumed that a person is a compound of rational soul and body ("Cartesian dualism"), whereas animals (with bodies) have no soul or capacity for mental reasoning. The empiricist John Locke soon contended that God created humanity with minds as blank slates, but with the onus or urge to learn: a *person* is "a thinking intelligent Being, that has reason and

reflection, and can consider itself as self, the same thinking thing in different times and places."[24] Albeit with different philosophic structures, both rationalists and empiricists largely concurred with Boethius's definition of a *person* as an individual substance of a rational nature.

If in classical Christianity various integrations of theology with the Platonic One served as the metaphysical backdrop to faith, in post-Enlightenment modernity a unified universe was no longer presumed. From the eighteenth to twentieth centuries, the assertion of human autonomy increasingly dominated Western thought.[25] In the academy with the continuing demise of Christianity and Deism, no longer could a cosmic Creator be assumed. On the one hand, the existence of some kind of transcendent principle continued as seen in Immanuel Kant's probable moral Being, Frederick Hegel's *Geist*, and Rudolf Otto's Holy Other. On the other hand, with Auguste Comte, Ludwig Feuerbach, Karl Marx, Charles Darwin, and Friedrich Nietzsche, the belief in the Transcendent was eliminated. Entering the twentieth century, nihilism (Nietzsche's rejection of all absolutes and moral principles) and secular existentialism abandoned rationalism and redefined the essence of personhood as self-authenticating acts of the will: "I *will*, therefore I am." Philosopher John Macmurray observes, "Modern philosophy is characteristically egocentric. . . . it takes the Self as its starting point, and not God, or the world or the community; and that, secondly, the Self is an individual in isolation, an ego or 'I', never a 'thou.'"[26] Definitions of *person* dissipate amidst multiple academic disciplines.

8. *Postmodernity and Today*. Most contemporary scholars continue to emphasize the place of the will for subjective self-authentification, whether within the philosophic setting of atheism or that of a hazy pantheism/panentheism in which the

individual comes to terms with his or her finitude in a transient world. In *Giving an Account of Oneself*, Judith Butler writes:

> My account of myself is partial, haunted by that for which I can devise no definitive story. I cannot explain exactly why I have emerged in this way, and my efforts at narrative reconstruction are always undergoing revision. There is that in me and of me for which I can give no account. But does this mean that I am not, in the moral sense, accountable for who I am and for what I do?[27]

Writers in the humanities yet seek to affirm the self as meaningful, moral, and free. The late Ronald Dworkin introduces *Religion Without God* by asserting that "religion is deeper than God. Religion is a deep, distinct, and comprehensive worldview: it holds that inherent, objective value permeates everything, that the universe and its creatures are awe-inspiring, that human life has purpose and the universe order."[28] Others such as Jordan Peterson affirm a semi-Christian theism that posits a meaningful, moral world,[29] but with little definition of how or why that might be possible.

For others in the "hard sciences," although the word *person* may be variously appropriated, it increasingly appears as the "monotheistic myth," the ghost in the machine, the illusion of that we call the *self*, the *soul*, the *me*. Peter Singer famously ascribes *personhood* to animals but not necessarily to severely handicapped human beings.[30] Thought-magus Harari declares, "There is zero scientific evidence that in contrast to pigs, Sapiens have souls." He then adds, "The very idea of soul contradicts the most fundamental principles of evolution."[31] Floundering without definition, the term *person* itself is disappearing in the academy. The United Nations' Declaration of Human Rights stands in

increasing tension with biological assumptions of what constitutes a *human being*—all the more when a nation like Argentina
grants juridical human rights to an orangutan named Sandra
(2014), and New Zealand does the same for a river and forest in
deference to Maori indigenous beliefs.

The ways of defining personhood through the centuries into
modernity and postmodernity are complex.[32] Today, the term
person dissipates in common usage. If once defined by reason, or
later by the will, today the word *person* has become a vacuous,
social term without substance. The question of "What is a
person?" is the greatest enigma of humanity today.

TOWARD A TRINITARIAN UNDERSTANDING OF PERSON

The following proposes a framework for defining *person*, human
and divine, drawn from trinitarian revelation. Our starting point
is Genesis 1:26–27, with male and female created in the image
of God. While the word *person* is not used in Scripture in the
modern sense, nevertheless the *concept* of person proves canon-
ically rich.[33] Although the divine "Let us make mankind in our
image, in our likeness, . . . male and female he created them" of
Genesis 1 (vv. 26–27) may not be explicitly trinitarian, the earliest
church fathers often perceived it to be so (as do I). We begin by
asking, if human beings are the *imago*, then what is the *Dei*?
From trinitarian revelation in Scripture emerges tracings of a
basic ontology of "person" informed by five dimensions: nature,
self-consciousness, I-thou relationality, perichoretic capacity
(indwelling by another), and self-giving.

Two caveats are important. First, by human *person*, the
definition intends the *ideal* human being as God designed. This
is seen preeminently in Jesus Christ.[34] In the midst of a broken
world, for those redeemed through God's grace, this ideal might

be glimpsed in daily Christian life, but only in the life to come will we experience the fullness of being conformed to Christ's image. Second, within the conceptual framework of Nicaea, my proposal suggests only several ways for interpreting personhood in light of the Godhead. The mystery of the triune God exceeds our comprehension and our limited doctrinal formulas. Therefore, the five correspondent likenesses between divine and human personhood must be understood as correspondent in some but not all respects (i.e., analogically). The similarities between the Trinity and human personhood pale in light of our Lord's transcendent otherness. But similarities they are, and these parallels of personhood serve as a collection of characteristics that help ground what we are (and can be) as *imago Dei* in light of the tripersonal God.[35]

1. *Nature, Substance Unity*. The "divine attributes" describe the essence of God, the substance or infinite reality of the divine Being. The *incommunicable* attributes exist as God's alone: aseity, eternality, omniscience, omnipotence, omnipresence, and so on. Descriptions of the incommunicable attributes derive from biblical and philosophical language pointing toward a God absolutely beyond us, one who transcends creation. Conversely, God's *communicable* attributes invite the participation of personal creation; these include love, holiness, righteousness, wisdom, goodness, and so on. By inviting the participation of finite, created persons, God's communicable attributes imply the exercise of these primary attributes within the Trinity itself.[36] Different from Islam's Allah, the triune God *ad intra* experiences what he beckons us to experience with him *ad extra* and with one another.

As the Father, Son, and Holy Spirit share fully and equally in the one divine nature, so humanity shares in a distinct yet common human nature. *Homo sapiens* are united by a unique "material" reality which diversifies in gender, race, and a multitude of other features. All of us are "essentially" human, yet no one of us is identical to another. As God's reality is defined by the divine essence, so at the moment of conception, we are created with an innate human essence—a nature designed to flourish in a world seemingly created for our physical bodies,[37] even though now subjected to fallenness. For this reason, Christians defend the inherent dignity of every human being, whether undeveloped, broken, or deformed—this from conception to death. In one sense, but outside of time, as the Son is generated and the Spirit proceeds within the divine essence, similarly within our time-space dependent existence, our conception as finite human beings is genetically coded for diversity with a plurality of features that makes each of us unique. Assuredly, the Trinity's oneness of essence is uncreated and eternal, unlike our common human nature, but the parallels are instructive. By virtue of creation as *imago Dei*, all human life by very *nature* is given dignity.

2. *Self-consciousness*. In the divine ideal, a "person" is characterized by self-consciousness. In the Bible, God defines himself as the "I AM" (*Yahweh*), a perfect divine consciousness. Yet, Scripture likewise records the Father's "I AM," the Son's "I am," and the Spirit's speaking in first-person terms "I" and "me" (e.g., Acts 13:2). While each is entirely God, the trinitarian persons reflect distinct personal consciousness in relation to the other.

As finite human beings, our existence begins embryonically (i.e., biologically), yet our human nature is designed to develop self-consciousness. At birth every newborn cries out, "I am," as she or he comes into the world, soon loudly announcing, "I am hungry," for a mother's nurture. Self-consciousness integrates the whole of our individual reality: we scrape our knee and cry; our hearts are happy in morning sunshine; we wonder at the natural world around us; we feel sadness or guilt in failure; we are fearful of dying. Moreover, our physical bodies are designed to contribute to self-understanding[38]: one body has breasts, another a penis; one flexes youthful muscles, another sits wrinkled with age; one reflects brown skin, another beige. Yet, unifying all humankind is the inner structure of who we are as persons. That we think, speak, will, and feel is finally anchored in a trinitarian God, who in Scripture also reasons, speaks, wills, and feels. Even though the transcendent God surely differs from ourselves in such activities, the New Testament language ascribing self-conscious personhood to each member of the Godhead is striking.

God further defines himself as everlasting, exercising lordship, abundantly creative, the acme of righteousness, and so on. To be *imago Dei*, then, gives reason for our sense of immortality, our role as vice-regents of creation, our desire to master skills and disciplines, our inclination toward creativity, and our moral compass regarding right and wrong. Our common human realities find moorings in God himself. As a consequence, when our self-understanding is tethered to the knowledge of the divine—I AM—we move toward being more genuinely *personal* ourselves, reflective of and authentic to our innermost being. In truth, we are an integrated whole of body and immaterial self, shaped by a myriad of factors.[39] Nonetheless, in a day when the concept of person has been reduced to chemicals and conditioning, classical Christianity proclaims that the self-consciousness of human beings is neither illusion nor a quirk of chance in an absurd universe. Rather, as *imago Dei*, our "I" reflects the genesis of the Creator's "let us."

3. *I-Thou Relationality*. Especially visible in the Gospels, Jesus' relationship with God the Father led the early church to confess both the Son and the Father as God. The two persons stand in I-Thou communion, yet not as two Gods but one God (John 1:1–2). Classical theology insists that the Father has ever been the Father of the Son who has ever been the Son. The Son further describes

the Spirit as "another advocate" (John 14:16), one like himself yet personally distinct from himself and the Father. Each member of the Godhead is defined not only as a distinct person but also by eternal I-Thou relationship.[40]

We have seen that the Nicene-Constantinopolitan Creed (AD 381) declares the eternal *generation* of the Son and eternal *procession* of the Spirit. All orthodoxy affirms the trinitarian relations of origin, but the West has often been loath to ascribe to each member of the Trinity distinct personal initiative and communion with the other.[41] Describing the reasoning of Basil of Caesaria, Anatolios explains, "The unity of activity among the persons does not at all preclude that each is in himself an intentional agent. Indeed, it is precisely the fact that each is in himself an intentional agent that is the basis for the unity of the operation among the three."[42] That is, a self-sufficient God must in some way experience *internal* fellowship, joy, and the giving-receiving of glory if this same God delights in these activities with his creation. We rejoice in fellowship with God because the Holy Trinity *ad intra* rejoices in fellowship in measure far beyond what we can fathom.

Because God the Father is eternally defined as Father in relation to the Son, and vice versa, the definition of *person* is not only individual but also social. Analogous to how each member of the Trinity is defined by (1) the divine nature, (2) distinct self-consciousness, and (3) I-Thou relationship, so our identity derives from our material human nature, self-awareness, and the I-thou relationships around us, and this at every point in our lives. Thus, different from eternal God, as finite beings we are continually shaped within in our changing social milieus and personal interactions with others including God himself.

Within the broad horizon of anthropology, neither the individualism of the West nor the self-transcendence (or non-self) of Eastern thought captures the complexity of what we are as persons, i.e., as finite images of God. In fact, our identity as persons derives from both our ontology as *imago Dei* and our relationships with others. Our "I" and the other's "thou" create mutual acknowledgement of acceptance, status, roles, and boundaries (or rejection of such relations). In the case of friends, the I-thou consciousness draws forth reciprocal attraction and engagement. For human beings, our relationships with one another are ever changing, from birth to death. The Christian's communion may fluctuate also with the triune God, but through the grace revealed in Christ, her position as daughter of God is ever sealed (Eph. 1:3–14).

As the intra-trinitarian relations from all eternity are constituted, in part, by each divine person loving the other, so the *imago Dei* of Genesis 1 unfolds immediately in Genesis 2 with the man and woman each uniquely created and defined by their relationship to the other. Adam's loneliness finds satisfaction in Eve, his counterpart. "Far from being a mystical loss of selfhood, the appropriate union between embodied creatures is the union of presence."[43] The I-thou sexual differences enable them to become one flesh and so to obey the mandate to populate the earth with their offspring. Adam and Eve's marriage in the garden, through love's consummation, generates the human race. Each "I am" is fortified and flourishes through the "I-thou" with the other.

4. *Mutual Indwelling*. The I-Thou within the Christian Godhead suggests a greater depth of unity. Jesus declares, "I am in the Father, and the Father is in Me" (John 14:10 NASB; cf. 10:38)—a mutual spiritual indwelling or reciprocal habitation. In each context Jesus clearly distinguishes himself as Son from the Father. Equally impactful, Jesus invites and prays that believers also participate in this habitation by the Son and the Father "that all of them may be one, Father, just as you are in me and I am in you. May they also be in us so that the world may

believe that you have sent me. . . . that they may be one as we are one—I in them and you in me" (John 17:21–23; cf. 14:20). In similar language, the Savior speaks of the Spirit, who comes forth from the Father, is sent by the Son, and "will be *in* you" (14:17; cf. 15:26). In Christian tradition, the Greek term *perichoresis* was initially adopted to describe the coinherence (without confusion) of the two natures of Christ.[44] With time the Eastern fathers, notably John of Damascus, appropriated *perichoresis* for the full mutual indwelling of the three persons in the one being of God. Along with their inseparable union in the divine nature, implicit likewise is the dynamic and reciprocal cohabitation of each divine person in the other.[45]

While major categorical differences exist between the *perichoresis* of the three infinite persons of the Trinity and God's indwelling of finite, imperfect Christians, the parallels are intriguing. As each person of the Godhead mutually indwells the other, so we as *imago Dei* are structured to be indwelt by God (1 Cor. 6:19). Actual divine indwelling, owing to sin, is not innate to our human condition. Rather, the grace of God concedes this great honor. Through regeneration, believers enter an analogous perichoretic relationship with the Father, Son, and Spirit, experiencing the habitation of God within. Yet we do not become God. Our human personhood is not overwhelmed or obfuscated by the divine presence. To the contrary, God's indwelling enables us to be all the more the unique persons we were created to be while simultaneously being conformed to the image of Christ (Rom. 8:29; 2 Cor. 3:18).[46]

5. *Self-giving.* The Holy Trinity may rightly be denominated by the self-giving God, the one who freely created and sustains the entirety of creation by grace. In the New Testament, this self-giving manifests particularly in the love between the Son and the Father. The Father gives to the Son all judgment, all authority, "all

things" (Matt. 28:18; John 5:22; 13:3). Yet, after Christ conquers all enemies and establishes his kingdom, then he, the Son, will hand over "everything" to the Father, "so that God may be all in all" (1 Cor. 15:28). God's glory is a shared glory, even as each person of the Trinity works within creation in distinctive ways (John 17:1–5).

The divine invitation to self-giving extends to the Christian life. "We love because he first loved us" (1 John 4:19). Ephesians 5:1–2 directly summons us to "be imitators of God, as beloved children. And walk in love, as Christ loved us and gave himself up for us" (ESV). Paul warns against any hint of sexual immorality (5:3) and admonishes believers to "submit to one another out of reverence for Christ" (5:21). In the weightiest passage on marriage in the Bible (5:22–33), Paul then exhorts husbands and wives to give of themselves to one another. This self-giving expresses itself in both similar yet different ways by husband and wife, the husband as Christ and the wife as the church—sacrificer and responder. Admonitions to the local churches are much the same—pastors, presbyters, all (Eph. 4:11–15; 1 Pet. 5:1–5). We imitate the Trinity by giving of ourselves in different ways to those around us.

By nature, and by communal disposition, the Holy Trinity is love. The Creator has no obligation to give to creation. Yet, this triune God has so structured human beings in the *imago Dei* that we *must* give of ourselves to others to be filled with God's life. Within every maturing person—Christian or non-Christian alike—exists an onus, a spiritual imperative, to actively do good, to give of oneself to others. Jesus, the perfect image of God, declares, "For whoever wants to save their life will lose it, but whoever loses their life for me will save it" (Luke 9:24 NIV). In imitation of the Savior, humans have an ontological necessity to freely give of themselves to God and to others. Self-giving fills a believer with divine life. There is no other way to be fulfilled, no other way for the Christian to radiate the life of God.

CONCLUSION

In the modern and then postmodern world, the concept of person has slowly melted into individual drops of arbitrary self-assertions with little if any substance remaining. Questions of *"Who* am I?" and *"What* am I?" lie silently at the core of noisy internet culture, without God and without meaningful response.

The burden of this chapter is that a developed Christian anthropology grounded in the tripersonal God of the Bible is of incalculable worth as the foundation for human life. Not that the mystery of person, divine and human, has been fully resolved. But within the Nicene framework characteristics of the trinitarian relations shed light on the nature of humanity created in the image of God. Arching out beyond the Nicene fathers, the greater biblical view of *person* reminds us that who we are is directly related to who God is.

This work began by presenting an overview of the evolving definition of *person* in pre-Christian and then trinitarian history. Although rejecting pagan Greek notions of an impersonal transcendent One, Christian tradition especially in the West tended to locate the divine persons within the one divine essence. The arguments for *homoousios* strengthened the case against Arians and Eunomians but weakened the relational trinitarian testimony of Scripture. The Cappadocian approach in the East showed greater appreciation for the personal agencies of the Father, Son, and Holy Spirit. But definitions of *person* remained unclear.

Boethius's definition of *person* as an "individual substance of a rational nature" served as a template for much of Western theology up through the Enlightenment, when it was rearticulated by Descartes's "I think, therefore I am." Through the centuries, however, modernity abandoned belief in a unified universe and later the idea that the concept of person could be defined by a rational nature. Reason was replaced by existential self-authenticating *will* or alternative orientations. Today, with physicalist assumptions, definitions of *person* are hard-pressed for any foundation or structure.

The second half of this essay suggests that beginning with the biblical relations of the Father, Son, and Holy Spirit, the concept of person gains meaning through Christian history and, in part, may be freshly articulated today. The Nicene-Constantinopolitan Creed invites many lenses with no single perspective adequate to capture the abundant implications of the tripersonal God. This is not to say that the New Testament intra-trinitarian relations are identical to the divine transcendent reality. But while we recognize the analogous nature of language in speaking of Trinity, rather than dissolving the personal distinctions, instead our language may fall short of the infinite richness of the trinitarian communion.

The Christian doctrine of the Trinity helps reorient us as to what it means to be persons, with five similarities between the Godhead and humans as *imago Dei*. First, as the Trinity equally shares the infinite, single divine nature, so all *Homo sapiens* universally share a unique finite human nature. From conception to death, our "material" nature is coded to develop, ideally, into fully functional human persons. Therefore, all human life is sacred with no exceptions. Second, as each member of the Godhead speaks in the first person reflecting distinct personal consciousness, so a human being exists as an integrated whole with self-consciousness—an "I am." Personhood finds ontological grounding in the personal God. Third, as each member of the Trinity is defined in eternal relation to the other, so time-space bound human persons are defined by their I-thou relations. Our self-identity is defined and conditioned by relationships with others—not the least being the I-Thou relationship with the triune Creator. Fourth, as each member of the Godhead inhabits the other, so God designed human beings to be indwelt by his presence. Whereas divine *perichoresis* has multiple dimensions, as *imago Dei* humanity has been structured to experience a similar indwelling by God, both in this life (through regeneration and filling) and all the more in the life to come (through glorification and God's full presence). And fifth, as the triune God freely and gracefully gives each to the other and to creation, so human persons are called to give of themselves to God and to others. In so doing we are filled up with the life of God and, as Jesus admonishes, we save our souls.

Within the Nicaean framework multiple perspectives enable us to better comprehend the infinite splendor of the triune God. No singular definition captures the lushness of the biblical testimony regarding who is God or what is a human person. Nevertheless, reappreciating God's self-revelation as irrepressibly personal and relational enables us to better understand who we are created to be as *imago Dei*.

WHAT IT MEANS TO BE HUMAN

C. Ben Mitchell

Christianity is almost the only one of the great religions which thoroughly approves of the body—which believes that matter is good, that God Himself once took on a human body, that some kind of body is going to be given to us even in Heaven and is going to be an essential part of our happiness, our beauty, and our energy.
C. S. LEWIS, *MERE CHRISTIANITY*

WHILE CARING FOR MY FATHER who suffered from dementia, I have reflected on what it means to be human. Being with Dad every day for several years gave me a lot of time to think about what it means to be human. His final few weeks gave me even more opportunity to reflect on our common humanity. Because he was, and always shall be, my father, I realize my perspective is biased. So it will be helpful to begin to think about what it means to be human in a slightly different way, which will hopefully be less biased by personal experience but no less informed by it.

Two pervasive perspectives on the question linger: the standard Enlightenment model and the standard medical model. They are at a contrast to what I believe is a more consistently biblical way of understanding what it means to be human.

THE STANDARD ENLIGHTENMENT MODEL

We begin with the Enlightenment model of human personhood because it is the most pervasive view in Western culture. We can find ample evidence of this claim in many places, from Charles Taylor's magisterial volume *A Secular Age* to Carl Trueman's more recent *The Rise and Triumph of the Modern Self*. Two historical examples will suffice to map the contours of this perspective.

In his brief but in some ways disproportionally influential treatise of 1690, *An Essay Concerning Human Understanding*, English philosopher and physician John Locke (1632–1704) defines what it means to be a human person in the following way. To be a human person is to be . . .

> . . . a thinking intelligent Being that has reason and reflection and can consider itself as itself the same thinking thing in different times and places which it does only by that consciousness which is inseparable from thinking, and as it seems to me essential to it.[1]

Every adjective is important. The criteria for personhood include existence as a thinking, intelligent being possessing self-consciousness in a variety of times and places. To put it another way, for Locke, a human person is an individual, rational self who is consciously aware of her conscious awareness as a thinking self over time.

Add to this definition Immanuel Kant's (1724–1804) criteria for human personhood. At the heart of Kant's moral philosophy is the idea that human persons are rational, autonomous agents. That is, they are thinking, willing selves. In his *Groundwork of the Metaphysics of Morals,* he says:

> Every rational being, exists as an end in himself and not merely as a means to be arbitrarily used by this or that will . . . . Beings whose existence depends not on our will but on nature have, nevertheless, if they are not rational beings, only a relative value as means and are therefore called things. On the other hand, rational beings are called persons inasmuch as their nature already marks them out as ends in themselves.[2]

Those beings which are rational beings, then, are ends in themselves and should not be treated as means to someone else's ends, *but* those beings which are not autonomous, rational individuals are neither persons, nor do we have the same duties toward them. They are merely "things" and may be treated instrumentally. Kant famously argued that the duty not to harm animals unnecessarily was only an *indirect duty.* Animals should not be harmed capriciously because doing so might desensitize us, tempting us to harm rational, autonomous beings, and thereby treating them as means to our own ends rather than ends in themselves. In his 1798 *Anthropology from a Pragmatic Point of View,* Kant declares:

> The fact that the human being can have the representation "I" raises him infinitely above all the other beings on earth. By this he is a person . . . that is, a being altogether different in rank and dignity from things, such as irrational animals, with which one may deal and dispose at one's discretion.[3]

Of the many good things Lockean and Kantian thought have bequeathed to the West, I worry that their anthropology has not been entirely salutary and beneficial. In fact, I would argue that the view of the human person as an autonomous, rational, expressive individual has been extremely detrimental in politics, culture, education, health care, and religion—from creation care, to discipleship, to liturgy. This perspective is the air we breathe and the water in which we swim.

In biology and medicine, for example, we have seen this perspective threaten vulnerable human beings at what the late Princeton ethicist Paul Ramsey called "the edges of life" in his Bampton Lectures and subsequent volume, *Ethics at the Edges of Life*.[4] What do we say of the unborn human being who has not yet developed "reason and reflection and cannot consider himself or herself the same thinking thing in different times and places," as Locke says? Or what of the human being who is in a chronic coma and has lost "the representation 'I'" according to Kant?

Quite apart from the preborn or the PVS patient, what happens in the case of dementia when, as Scottish theologian and registered nurse John Swinton puts it, "one can no longer remember either self or God?" What do we Christians say of the person who "can no longer contemplate God?" asks Swinton. Are they persons? What care do we owe them? Did my Dad cease to be a human person as his dementia progressed?

When debates about abortion emerged in the late 1960s in America, the question posed was "When does *human life* begin?" Now, through a variety of means including genetics, embryology, ultrasonography, and 3-D imaging, everyone knows that the unborn human embryo is both a human and a life. Every honest observer must agree that human life—at least one human life—begins at conception. Today the question has become, "When does human personhood begin?" The Enlightenment model is often employed in one way or another to justify abortion, infanticide, assisted suicide, euthanasia, and other harms to persons. This leads to the standard medical model.

THE STANDARD MEDICAL MODEL

Briefly, the standard medical model affirms that what makes human beings distinct from other animals is "higher cortical function." The standard definition of dementia, for instance, is "a syndrome due to disease of the brain, usually of a chronic or progressive nature, in which there is a disturbance of multiple higher cortical functions, including memory, thinking, orientation, comprehension, calculation, learning capability, language, and judgment."[5] Notice that this description defines dementia as a pathology of the brain. And that the pathology results in diminished or diminishing *higher* cortical function.

John Swinton suggests that the language used to describe the phenomena is very important:

> Here we must note that to indicate that acquiring dementia includes losing one's higher cortical functions is a much deeper and altogether more alarming statement than it might at first appear to be. Hidden in the midst of this apparently objective and scientific statement is the subliminal suggestion that people with dementia are losing those aspects of being human which are perceived as more important than the other capacities humans might have. They are losing that which society prizes. Receiving such a diagnosis puts people in a tricky position which has both neurological *and* social implications. Definitions are not value neutral. Often they are value-forming.[6]

According to Swinton's argument in his book *Dementia: Living in the Memories of God*, this approach "proposes that there is a straightforward, linear connection between brain pathology and the behaviors and experiences that we choose to name as dementia."[7]

While there is not space to unpack all of Swinton's helpful insights here (and there are many), one of those germane to our topic is that Western liberal cultures, including the institution of medicine, imbibe the notion that "a life which is truly valuable and worth living is fundamentally defined by the ability to function effectively on the level of intellect and reason"—or what ethicist Stephen Post has described as "hypercognition."[8]

When combined, the Enlightenment model and the scientific model lead to a definition of what it means to be human as "the rational, self-determining, expressive, individual, higher functioning brain in a vat."[9] On this materialist model, the human person is little more than a meat machine of a particular sort. This is what Christian philosopher James K. A. Smith calls "thinking thingism" in his book *You Are What You Love*.[10] Human beings are just thinking things.

If one is to think Christianly about what it means to be human, one will need another model. The Christological model is a better vantage from which to answer the question, "What does it mean to be human?"

1. *The Christological Model*. Students of the Bible often begin their thinking about what it means to be human from the Genesis account. After all, it is Scripture's first revelation of when and how God made humanity. Let me say clearly that I think it is good and right to begin there, and the chapter by John Kilner in this volume is a very good place to start.

We learn from Genesis 1 that human persons are made in the image and likeness of God, but we are not told much about what that means. In his *Systematic Theology*, James Leo Garrett Jr., the late distinguished professor at Southwestern Baptist Theological Seminary, points out that there are no fewer than eight different notions of the content of the *imago Dei*: (1) humankind's erect bodily form; (2) human dominion over nature; (3) human reason; (4) human pre-fallen righteousness; (5) human capacities; (6) the juxtaposition between man and woman; (7) responsible creaturehood and moral conformity to God; and (8) various composite views.[11] Doubtless there are more than eight views by now and who knows how many ways they can be combined into composites?

Many of those perspectives describe various *functions* of personhood. Offered this way they seem to suggest that they are the communicable attributes of God. But if we take seriously our critique of the Enlightenment and medical models, what do we say of those living members of the species *Homo sapiens*—such as human embryos or Alzheimer's patients—who either have never possessed or have lost those functions? Are they human persons on those accounts? Is this just another version of thinking-thingism?[12]

There is another way for Christians to understand what it means to be human. Someone has wisely said that Christology should inform anthropology.[13] That is, the clearest lens through which to see what it means to be human may not be Genesis but Jesus. That is by no means to disparage the Genesis account, but rather to exalt the God-Man, and better understand the importance of his incarnation.

2. *Humans Are Necessarily Embodied*. In the January 2000 issue of the medical journal *Pediatrics*, a team at the Boston University Division of Behavioral and Developmental Pediatrics reported on a study they had performed with thirty mothers and their newborn infants regarding pain. They divided the infants into two groups.

Half of the mothers held their babies in whole-body, skin-to-skin contact while doctors performed a standard heel stick procedure to draw blood samples. The other half of the babies were wrapped in receiving blankets while the blood was drawn. Babies in contact with their mothers grimaced 65 percent less than the swaddled babies in the bassinettes, and get this, their crying time was a remarkable 85 percent less.

Embodiment (and touch) matters. And it matters at the other end of life too. The nursing literature is replete with references to "therapeutic touch." It is hard to imagine that something so palpably human as touch is now seen as a therapy. Yet on reflection, it all makes perfect sense. No other part of *us* makes contact with something that is *not us* but the skin. Our skin weighs between six to ten pounds and is the largest organ of the body, covering an area of about twenty-two square feet. And it renews itself about once a month.

Our skin imprisons us, but it also gives us shape, protects us from invaders, and cools us down or heats us up as needed. And think about how many metaphors in our common language are steeped in the metaphor of touch. We say something "touches" us. Or we say, "My, he was touchy." Problems can be thorny, ticklish, sticky, or need to be handled with kid gloves, or be only skin deep. These metaphors point to a deeper reality.

The reality of the human, embodied God was codified in the church's early confession at Nicaea (AD 325):

We ... believe in one Lord Jesus Christ,
the only Son of God,
begotten from the Father before all ages,
God from God,
Light from Light,
true God from true God,

begotten, not made.

of the same essence as the Father.

Through him all things were made.

For us and for our salvation

he came down from heaven;

he became incarnate by the Holy Spirit and the

virgin Mary,

and was made human.

He was crucified for us under Pontius Pilate;

he suffered and was buried.

The third day he rose again, according to the Scriptures.

He ascended to heaven

and is seated at the right hand of the Father.

He will come again with glory

to judge the living and the dead.

His kingdom will never end.

The humanity of Jesus of Nazareth sacralizes the embodiment of every human being.

The necessity and gift of embodiment is also clear from the apostle Paul's letter in 2 Corinthians 4–5:

> But we have this treasure in jars of clay, to show that the surpassing power belongs to God and not to us. We are afflicted in every way, but not crushed; perplexed, but not driven to despair; persecuted, but not forsaken; struck down, but not destroyed; always carrying in the body the death of Jesus, so that the life of Jesus may also be manifested in our bodies. For we who live are always being given over to death for Jesus' sake, so that the life of Jesus also may be manifested in our mortal flesh. So death is at work in us, but life in you . . .

For we know that if the tent that is our earthly home is destroyed, we have a building from God, a house not made with hands, eternal in the heavens. For in this tent we groan, longing to put on our heavenly dwelling, if indeed by putting it on we may not be found naked. For while we are still in this tent, we groan, being burdened—*not that we would be unclothed, but that we would be further clothed, so that what is mortal may be swallowed up by life. He who has prepared us for this very thing is God, who has given us the Spirit as a guarantee.*

So we are always of good courage. We know that while we are at home in the body we are away from the Lord, for we walk by faith, not by sight. Yes, we are of good courage, and we would rather be away from the body and at home with the Lord. So whether we are at home or away, we make it our aim to please him. For we must all appear before the judgment seat of Christ, so that each one may receive what is due for what he has done in the body, whether good or evil. (4:7—5:10 ESV)

The apostle did not long for some disembodied state as a rational, autonomous, expressive, conscious self. He was anticipating a resurrection *body*! There is only one way to be human, and that is to be embodied. And if we are embodied, we are also finite.

3. *Human Persons Are Necessarily Finite.* Finitude and its entailment, limitation, is one of those aspects of being human that tends to annoy us. Most uses of—and most synonyms for—the word *limitation* are disparaging. Consider: restriction, impediment, obstacle, deterrent, clamp down, imperfection, flaw, defect, failure, and shortcoming. The reality is that human persons are necessarily finite beings. As Lutheran theologian and

ethicist Gilbert Meilaender has put it in the title of his book on human dignity, we are *Neither Beast Nor God*.[14] But we want to be God. And we want to live lives without limitations. And we often try. Yet we are finite, particular, and located in time and space. Finitude is not a sin. In his incarnation Jesus limited himself, identifying with us in his full humanity:

> he became incarnate by the Holy Spirit and the
> virgin Mary,
> and was made human.
> He was crucified for us under Pontius Pilate;
> he suffered and was buried.[15]

In his extraordinary volume *You're Only Human: How Your Limits Reflect God's Design and Why That's Good News*, theologian Kelly Kapic explores (among other things) the work of one of the great African theologians in the past, Tertullian of Carthage (ca. 155–220) and his essay against the Marcionites, "De carne Christi (On the Flesh of Christ)." "Let us examine," requests Tertullian, "our Lord's bodily substance, for about His spiritual nature we are all agreed."[16] Divine embodiment was one of the most important questions the early church faced: "What does it mean to confess that God was made human?" For us the question must be, "What do we learn from the incarnation about ourselves?"

What *shall* we say of our Lord's bodily substance? Well first, that Jesus was embodied from conception in Mary's uterus. We know that fact now more clearly than ever through technology, but they knew it in Jesus' day too. Jesus was born a helpless baby who longed to be held against his mother's body, skin-to-skin. Jesus was limited in time and place—in his earliest days in a cattle stall in Bethlehem. Jesus had human flesh, a vascular system, and cardiac function with a blood pressure and pulse.

Later, Jesus worked with his hands, human hands. Jesus cut himself, got splinters, and bled human blood. He sweated, human sweat, and got tired over time. He got hungry. He needed sleep. He went fishing. He experienced puberty. He grew facial hair and began to smell like other teenage boys, human teenage boys. He had bad breath, human bad breath.

Surely this is at least part of what St. John means when he exclaims, "And the Word became flesh and dwelt among us" (John 1:14 ESV), and why in the same Gospel account the people questioned his deity and asked, "Is not this Jesus, the son of Joseph, whose father and mother we know?" (John 6:42). They could not question Jesus' humanity because he was limited by his embodiment just like they were. To our own detriment, we treat these limits as if they are either obstacles or extraneous to our humanity rather than necessary to it.

Kapic says,

> The odd thing is that, even when we run into our inevi-table limits, we often hang on to the delusion that if we just work harder, if we simply squeeze tighter, if we become more efficient, we can eventually gain control. We imagine we can keep our children safe, our incomes secure, and our bodies whole. When I complain about getting older, my wife sometimes laughs and says to me, "You have two options: either you are getting older or you are dead." Denying our finitude cripples us in ways we don't realize. It also distorts our view of God and what Christian spirituality should look like.[17]

And not just distorts our view of what Christian spirituality should look like, but what our very humanity should look like. "I think," says Kapic, "we have a massive problem, but it is not a time-management issue. It is a *theological* and *pastoral* problem."[18]

I am convinced that only when we have grasped the implications of the humanity of Jesus will we be able to properly assess our own humanity. The doctrine that the Word became flesh means that God himself affirms our flesh as good, and that affirmation liberates us from apologizing for our creaturely limitations. If we believe that Jesus, who was free from all sin, was fully human, then this means that he considered creaturely restrictions to be part of his good creation and not evil at all. It means that we must not apologize for what the Son of God freely embraces.[19]

Finally, if we are embodied, we are finite. And if we are finite, we are dependent.

4. *Human Persons Are Necessarily Dependent.* We are, of course, dependent on God "in [whom] we live, and move, and have our being" (Acts 17:28 KJV). No theist would deny that. Even within the realm of the human community, however, we are not independent, self-determining creatures any more than the infant Jesus was independent of Joseph and Mary's care, expressing his autonomy by changing his own diapers, or by offering informed consent for and determining his own post-procedure care plan after his circumcision. The Enlightenment autonomous self is a mythical creation of the human imagination. God himself said, "It is not good that the man should be alone; I will make him a helper fit for him" (Gen. 2:18 ESV)—a companion in a relationship of dependence on God and interdependence one with the other.

Kapic continues:

Our bodies, with all their needs and dependencies, were made good. And part of the intrinsic good of our bodies is that they are an ever-present reminder of our creaturely needs: to be human is to be dependent on the Creator Lord, dependent on other human creatures who provide their presence and love, and dependent on the earth, which provides for our physical needs, from oxygen to lettuce, from shade to springs of water. This dependence, when recognized and remembered, raises serious questions about the emphasis on self-generated identity that is so often assumed and encouraged in our modern world. As embodied finite creatures, do we have a purely self-generated identity? How do I value my particularity without ignoring the countless ways my identity is given as much as it is self-created?[20]

Did Adam have a bellybutton? I do not know (and you do not either), but I am fairly certain Jesus did. He was human, and in his humanity, he was dependent on God and on Mary's body during gestation and, unless she used a wet nurse, after his birth. His dependence on Mary was not a result of Adam and Eve's independent decision to disobey God, it was a necessary aspect of his humanity.

"Nothing is quite as ontologically revealing as our belly button," say Stanley Hauerwas and William Willimon. "It's our body's way of reminding us that we are not self-made people, we are not separate islands, we are not merely rugged individuals."[21]

This reminder of our dependence has huge implications, not only for understanding our humanity, but for understanding our interdependence.

Kapic tells the story of one of his sociologist friends and colleagues at Covenant College, Matthew Vos, who has developed an exercise for his freshmen students to help them think about their interconnectedness.[22] He has two students stand up—one male and one female—and asks them to introduce themselves. Simple, right? Here's the catch. They must not mention in their introduction any groups in which they hold membership. One student offers his name. Oops! That membership in a family. Oh, and you're speaking English. That's membership in a language group. "I like pizza" is membership in the group that likes pizza, especially college students. Even "I'm just me!" involves membership in the group of living things.

You get it, don't you? We are more the product of things and people outside us than we are our own isolated, autonomous selves.

Again, the implications of our dependence and interdependence are huge. A few examples will have to suffice:

1. The values of the family unit
2. Teaching ethics to seminarians in China
3. The importance of the common good over the individual good
4. The reality that some dependences and obligations are not chosen

Some human dependencies and duties are *not* voluntary and *not* assumed by my autonomous, expressive, individual self. I was reminded of this fact while caring for my dad. Although I am grateful to be his son, I did not volunteer autonomously to be the offspring of Warren and Irma Mitchell. Nevertheless, I felt responsible as a son to care for my father. Doing so was an extension of the Pauline exhortation from the law to "Honor your father and your mother, as the Lord your God commanded you" (Deut. 5:16 ESV; also Eph. 6:2 and echoed throughout the Bible).

CONCLUSION

In addition to being imagers of God, what it means to be human necessarily means being embodied, limited, and dependent. Given the Enlightenment model and the medical model, we are tempted to think that advancing in health and maturity means that we grow out of these attributes—we become more cerebral, freer, more independent. It is a half-truth that can lead to a whole lie.

"So teach us to number our days that we may get a heart of wisdom" (Ps. 90:12 ESV).

PART 2

APPLICATIONS
AND
IMPLICATIONS

HUMAN BEINGS CREATED IN AND FOR RELATIONSHIP

Jennifer Marshall Patterson

RESEARCH IS REVEALING MORE AND MORE about the significance of relationships for human well-being. For example, the relationships around a child shape all aspects of her development, even the growth of her brain.[1] Throughout the life cycle, the bonds formed through family, church, friendship, and voluntary groups serve as important sources of meaning and purpose for individuals and sources of social health for communities.

Even as evidence about the importance of relationships grows, the experience of basic human bonds has diminished in recent decades in the United States. Marriage has declined while the number of children living with only their mother has grown.[2] A greater share of people are living alone, and reliance on friends has waned. For example, more than a quarter of adults over the age of sixty live alone.[3]

Human beings are created in and for relationship. This inescapable reality matters tremendously for human flourishing. To be equipped to give and to receive in the context of relationships calls for particular virtues. We need generosity and compassion to serve others, and we need humility and patience at times when our limits make us depend on others. Responding effectively to those experiencing hardship in our communities includes working to restore relational well-being.

This chapter will discuss human nature, created in the image of God and made to flourish in relationship. This leads to consideration of the relational dimensions of human need in three different contexts. These include solidarity with mother and child at the beginning of life, effective compassion toward those in hardship during the course of life, and the grace of receiving at the end of life.

CREATED TO FLOURISH IN RELATIONSHIP

Human beings are relational because God is relational. The Father, the Son, and the Holy Spirit have their being in perfect "self-giving and self-receiving."[4] The three persons of the Trinity share completely and eternally in the same being, knowledge, and activity.

Creation is the self-communication of this triune, relational God. In creation, God forms and then fills spheres of the cosmos: the heavens, the seas, the dry land. Then God makes human beings in his image to cultivate his creation. God commissions humanity to follow the pattern he set in creation: forming and filling. That task could only be pursued in community, beginning with the relationship of male and female, and extending to the whole of humanity.

God created human beings, male and female, in his image both individually and together "in mutual relation," writes Herman Bavinck, a Dutch theologian writing at the beginning of the twentieth century.[5] "God made two out of one, so that he could then make the two into one," he explains. "The two-in-oneness of husband and wife expands with a child into a three-in-oneness," with the family together "unfolding the one image of God."[6] Bavinck continues: "From conception onward, a human being is a product of fellowship; every person is born from, and in, fellowship; persons are cared for and nurtured in the context of fellowship, and continue in some kind of fellowship throughout life, all the way to one's final breath."[7]

God's design for human flourishing is structured around the fellowship of four essential relationships: communion with God, peace with self, harmony with others, and nurture toward the created world. True human flourishing is wholeness and harmony in these four relationships.

Sin distorts each of these relationships, however. It produces alienation from God, self, others, and the world. It sets up a rival vision of flourishing in which the path to fulfillment is paved by autonomy and control. It resists the givenness and limits of the human condition and our dependence on one another. "Expressive individualism" is the phrase that a number of writers have used to describe this vision of human fulfillment.[8] This is a path by which each person is on a quest to discover reality *for himself, from within himself*, in order to project his self-understanding *outside himself* to the world.

Notre Dame law professor O. Carter Snead argues that expressive individualism is the default assumption about human beings at work in our culture and law today. Because this outlook puts such a priority on autonomy and control, it neglects entire dimensions of our human existence.[9] The irony is that expressive individualism disregards the very things that produce the capacity to exercise self-control and autonomy. None of us was born with the capacity for autonomy, after all. Every human child enters the world completely dependent on others—most immediately, on a mother. Beyond infancy and for the better part of two decades, a child needs extensive help to survive and to become capable of exercising self-control and independence.

What produces those capacities in a young person? Parents know well from vast firsthand experience. It takes countless hours of investment over years to nurture a child's ability to make his own way in the world. It requires constant care for the child as a whole person: for his physical, intellectual, psychological, relational, and spiritual development. Parents do not keep a timecard. Theirs is a round-the-clock, multi-decade investment of giving. For the child's part, the degree to which a young person is able to fully benefit from all this giving on the part of parents depends on the gradual emergence of gratitude for what they have received.

The significance of this giving and receiving has been overlooked too often by the law's definition of what it means to be human. Why? Because public policy has prioritized the self-directed will, says Snead in his book *What It Means to Be Human: The Case for the Body in Public Bioethics.* As a result, policy has neglected the importance of the body in human flourishing and the relationships that are essential to our existence and well-being as embodied beings.[10]

Human embodiment is not only a biological reality. It is also a relational reality. Because we are embodied, human life goes through seasons of vulnerability, weakness, sickness, and incapacitation. This is always true at the beginning of life, often true at the end of life, and occasionally true for periods of time throughout the course of life. In certain cases of serious illness or disability, it is true throughout the whole of life.

Because we are embodied, we need relationships characterized by what Snead calls "uncalculated giving and graceful receiving" to make our way through life.[11] That begins with recognizing the limits and vulnerabilities we all face as human beings.

Accepting the givenness of our embodied existence prepares us to pursue relationships marked by grace in giving and gratitude in receiving.

To be equipped for such relationships, we need both active and passive virtues.[12] We need to pursue "active" virtues of solidarity and hospitality, which make us approach others with care, compassion, and generosity. We need also to learn "passive" virtues of humility, patience, and wisdom, which reconcile us to our limitations and make us ready to receive others' giving in our own seasons of need. As we respond to those in need around us, the relational aspects of human flourishing are critical to keep in mind. To be effective, compassion must work to restore relationships with God, self, others, and the created world.

SOLIDARITY, COMPASSION, AND THE BEGINNING OF LIFE

The concept of "person" has a long and complex history, even though it has a very straightforward definition: every human being is a person. That raises the question, "What does the concept of *person* add to the idea of *human being*?"

Person is like a family name, suggests German Catholic philosopher Robert Spaemann. It is the name shared by all the individuals making up the whole of humanity. Each member of the human family bears the name *person*.[13]

In a family, multiple people bear the same surname. That does not mean, however, that the individuals who share that family name are interchangeable parts. To the contrary, each person in the family has a unique place within it. You can see this visually in the form of a family tree. That picture, often in the shape of an actual tree, represents the different lines and layers of relationship that exist within a family. Each member occupies a unique place within the family tree. If you were to describe one person's location in the family tree, you would describe it differently from that of every other member of the family.

The uniqueness of each family member is why, in the tragic circumstance of the death of a child, that family's loss can never simply be replaced by the birth of another child, as welcome and joyful as that new birth may be. That new child is a new family member who will form a new set of relationships within that family. Likewise, the death of a parent or spouse can never be erased by remarriage.

We are not interchangeable parts in our family, or in the family of humanity. As Spaemann wrote, "The family name assigns a particular place in the family structure to each one who bears it. In the community of persons, similarly, each person has a place forever uniquely defined as his or hers."[14] Persons "form a system of relations in which each is uniquely situated in relation to every other."[15] To be a person is to have a place reserved in the grand procession of humanity that extends throughout all history. It is a distinct location within the human race that cannot be replaced, repeated, or erased.

Sometimes we hear appeals to respect others because, as human beings, we are "all the same." That is true, but only if we understand that it does not mean that we are interchangeable. To say we are "all the same" or someone is "just like me" is not a comment on the similarity of our features. What such comments actually point out is something much more profound than height or sense of humor. What we share is an utter uniqueness. What each of us has in common is a dignity that cannot be exchanged or replaced.[16]

Herman Bavinck wrote beautifully about humanity created in the image of God. He taught that God had designed the whole person to image him. God made male and female individually and together to extend his image on earth. "The image of God is much too rich for it to be fully realized in a single human being," he writes. "It can only be somewhat unfolded in its depth and riches in a humanity counting billions of members." The many-faceted fullness of the image of God can only be seen in the whole of humanity extending throughout the world and through all generations. "Only humanity in its entirety ... is the fully finished image, the most telling and striking likeness of God," concludes Bavinck.[17]

With that picture of the whole of humanity in mind, it is staggering to contemplate that more than sixty million unborn children have had their lives snuffed out by abortion in the United States since the *Roe v. Wade* decision fifty years ago. These lives took their place for a moment but were never allowed to unfurl as a part of the banner of humanity extending through time. They were treated as though outside the protection of personhood.

To recognize personhood implies moral responsibility. *Person* is not a merely descriptive term, says Spaemann. To call someone a person has normative significance. "It is to make a demand."[18] What it demands of us is to show solidarity in recognizing others as persons and to extend hospitality in welcoming them within the human family. It compels us to exercise the duties of care and compassion toward one another. It commits us to seek the flourishing of others.

In the case of the unborn child, rather than treating her as a person toward whom we have responsibility, abortion policy took a much different view in the half century after *Roe v. Wade*. As Carter Snead points out, the anthropology of *Roe* treated the unplanned pregnancy as a conflict between two "atomized strangers [who] are isolated in their vulnerability."[19]

There are indeed two vulnerable persons in the midst of an unplanned pregnancy. But, as Professor Snead reminds us, "They are not strangers."[20] Their human embodiment situates them in a relation of mother and child, and the flourishing of the child depends entirely on the mother. For her part, the mother's carrying her unborn child is already the beginning of a relationship of incalculable giving.

A pregnant mother and her unborn child are vulnerable, but they are not strangers to one another, nor should they be isolated from others. Their vulnerability calls for compassionate care, most immediately for the pregnant mother. She needs a community of support for her holistic needs, especially relationally, before and long after the birth of her child.

The US Supreme Court's 2022 reversal of *Roe* presents a new opportunity to expand recognition of the humanity of the unborn in culture and law. This is an occasion to consider anew how more and more women could be emboldened to choose life with the respect and support of those around them. Christians have a responsibility to declare the truth about life made in the image of God and to come alongside those in need to serve them through relationships and resources on the path of life.

EFFECTIVE COMPASSION THROUGH RESTORING RELATIONSHIPS

One of the central ideas in Bavinck's work is that "grace restores nature." In other words, God's grace restrains and overcomes the effects of sin to restore creation toward what it was intended to be. Bavinck uses the biblical metaphor of leaven to explain how the Christian faith influences every dimension of life. A Christian worldview serves as a leaven, a catalyst that enables everything to develop toward its full created potential.

Grace restores nature with respect to the four essential relationships of our human existence. God designed us for right relationship with him, with self, with other people, and with the created world around us. Sin harmed each of these relationships, but God's grace operates to restore and renew them. The challenges that individuals and communities face today can be traced to brokenness in one or more of these relationships. Child poverty, for example, is highly correlated with the absence of a father. Most long-term poverty occurs in homes headed by a single parent.

Christian responses to challenges like poverty, homelessness, or drug addiction should consider how to rebuild relationships. Flourishing is about more than material need and more than individualistic self-determination. Our concern in serving others must be for the whole person. The framework of these four essential relationships—with God, self, others, and the created world—helps us stay focused on true human flourishing as we approach social issues.

Social entrepreneur Bob Woodson worked for more than four decades with neighborhood leaders around the country to tackle poverty, gang violence, addiction, and homelessness. In 2021, he wrote *Lessons from the Least of These* about what he has learned over the years about what changes lives and communities.

Trust is foundational to Woodson's teaching. The kind of trust that can lead to transformation comes through personal presence. "Relationships are the necessary condition for transforming others, and trust is the common currency," writes Woodson. Relationships of trust can only be built by being available to those facing hardship, even when it is not convenient.[21]

One of the projects Woodson has helped organize over the years is a program to prevent youth gang violence. It aims to change the culture of a community by changing the character of young people. Like Woodson said, that requires presence, relationships, and trust. For adult mentors like Vincent and Dawn Barnett, a husband-and-wife team who lead a community center in Milwaukee, Wisconsin, this means the teens in their program have their cell phone numbers so they can call them any time of day or night when they find themselves in the midst of a crisis. The Barnetts are investing in young people today, with the hope that they in turn will take part in renewing their community in the future.

Effective compassion is relational, and relationships require investing of time. Effective compassion requires long-term commitment to those in need, through face-to-face relationships that build trust. The local church, in particular, should have every reason to take this personal, relational approach to mercy ministry. The church exists because of the reconciled relationship made possible through Jesus Christ. Of all people, Christians should recognize the importance of relational outreach that addresses the whole person made in the image of God. But because material need is often most obvious and urgent, churches can fall into the trap of focusing narrowly on physical resources and overlook caring for the needs of the full person, especially rebuilding relationships.

This realization prompted leaders at First Baptist Church of Leesburg, Florida, to make a dramatic change in their mercy ministries years ago. They came to recognize that the outreach they were doing through a soup kitchen and shelter had made the mistake of responding to material needs while neglecting the broader needs of the whole person. Each day, the same men would show up. Ministry leaders realized that these men needed more than a meal and roof over their heads. They needed to tackle deeper issues, especially substance abuse. The church started a residential rehabilitation center for men, which could provide holistic help. As a residential center, it provided men with the relational support they needed to be restored. It gave them the opportunity to find freedom in Christ, overcome addiction, and gain practical skills through programs like financial-literacy education and job training.

This model is not one that every church is called to follow. But every congregation can make sure that its mercy ministries build relationships that seek to serve the needs of the whole person, from the spiritual to the emotional to the physical. Meeting material needs does not need to be at odds with responding to relational needs. To address the whole person requires both. Pastor Chris Sicks makes the point in his book *Tangible* that tackling material needs can contribute to building relationships. As he says, our mercy ministries ought to "demonstrate and declare God's compassion for bodies and souls."[22]

We are designed to grow in the interdependence within a family and to weave lives of mutual support with neighbors. We are created to connect with others as we work to provide for our households and to solve social challenges together. Thick networks of relationships are the best kind of social insurance for the unexpected developments of family life.

THE GRACE OF RECEIVING AT THE END OF LIFE

In an age that defines human flourishing in terms of autonomy and control, the end of life and declining capacities that come with it are an ominous cloud gathering on the horizon. Because of that, physician-assisted suicide has emerged, ostensibly as a way to maintain autonomy and control in the face of terminal illness. Carried forward by the fear of losing independence and becoming a burden on loved ones, physician-assisted suicide has been legalized in several states in recent years.[23]

Brittany Maynard became well-known as an advocate for physician-assisted suicide after she was diagnosed in early 2014 with terminal brain cancer and was told that she had six months to live. She moved to Oregon so that she could use doctor-prescribed drugs, as she explained, in order "to die on my own terms."[24]

Across the country, in Connecticut, Maggie Karner was diagnosed around the same time with the same form of brain cancer. Maggie was an advocate for life-and-health policies for the Lutheran Church Missouri Synod. Brittany and Maggie shared the same terminal diagnosis.

Maggie wrote an open letter to Brittany Maynard in October 2014, days before the date Brittany had announced she planned to take her own life. In that letter, she appealed to Brittany to remember the unique presence and beauty her life gave to the world. Maggie asked her to consider the gift she could give her family by remaining "to squeeze every drop out of life" during the unknown number of her remaining days.[25]

Maggie's letter talked about her own family's experience decades earlier when her father was paralyzed from the neck down after a serious accident. Her father was unable to do anything for himself and needed hospice care for the remaining five months that he lived. But he was able to talk, and that was what he and his children did.

Maggie wrote to Brittany, "I never had that kind of candor and intimacy with my dad before those days. My brothers and sisters and I—we learned more about ourselves and each other than we ever could have in any other way. We grew as a family, and we learned about sacrifice and love. Each of us became wiser and better people through that whole experience."[26]

Maggie looked back on those days as a gift, and she encouraged Brittany to let her family give to her through all the remaining days of her "cancer journey." Brittany chose to take her own life on November 1, 2014. She was twenty-nine.

For her part, Maggie accepted to walk the full path of suffering. Her remaining days were filled with giving and receiving in the company of her family. She died September 25, 2015. She was fifty-two.

Many centuries ago, Augustine observed that growing old and nearing death point us toward an eternal Sabbath rest as described in Hebrews.[27] That future rest is the ultimate calling of those in Christ, and aging is a preparation for it, says Autumn Alcott Ridenour. Her book, *Sabbath Rest as Vocation: Aging Toward Death*, gives us a much different outlook than the prevailing perspective on aging today.

The limits of aging and death teach us to depend on God and make us recognize the reality of our finite identity in relation to him.[28] Recognizing limits, in turn, makes us value the days at hand differently. It encourages us to prioritize and make commitments to people and projects with an eternal perspective in mind.[29] We are to accompany one another in times of need and vulnerability, particularly in our passage through old age.[30] As Ridenour writes, aging teaches us that we are "limited, time-bound creatures made for transcendence." This "transform[s] the experience of aging and death as one of interdependence, giving, receiving, and vocation before God and one another."[31]

Augustine reminds us in his great work *The City of God* that rightly ordered love pursues the right objects of love, *and* it seeks them with the right terminus in mind. The full human flourishing we long for will not be reached in this world.

"The City of Man" has always set its sights too low. Its horizon is too short for its aspirations. Its vision only extends as far as the temporal, but its longings reach for more. Reconciling transcendent longings and temporal reality lies beyond us. If we are united with Christ, we can accept limits in this life because we know we will one day transcend them through communion with our Creator and Redeemer.

Accepting the givenness of our human, embodied existence allows us to keep our sights set on transcendence. As we make our way toward that horizon, relationships characterized by grace in giving and gratitude in receiving carry us through this vale of tears. The fluctuation of our interdependence in those relationships makes us lean alternately on the active virtues of compassion and care and on the passive virtues of humility, patience, and wisdom. This is the path by which we reach our eternal Sabbath rest.

CULTIVATING RELATIONAL VIRTUES AND RESPONSES

Family, church, and Christian education are particularly suited to nurture the relational wholeness human beings were designed by God to enjoy. The family is the first school of virtue. Here children learn and parents grow in the habits of self-sacrifice required for relationships of "uncalculated giving and graceful receiving." The commitments we make to family are more than private promises. They have public implications as they provide the context for addressing our deepest needs, particularly at the beginning and end of life. A biological father's commitment to the mother of his unborn child or an adult child's faithfulness to an aging mother are profound at a personal level. They are also consequential at a community level—a reality that becomes clear especially in their absence.

Alongside the family, the church has a significant role to play in helping us focus on the fullness of human flourishing, including spiritual, relational, and material aspects. Church ministries can model this as they uphold the dignity of human life made in the image of God. The post-*Roe* moment offers churches the occasion to evaluate their holistic support for life. Resources for doing so are available from Her Pregnancy and Life Assistance Network (Her PLAN). Her PLAN is building a network to provide a safety net of medical, social, and material support for mothers and their children during and after pregnancy. Her PLAN helps churches to assess how well they are responding to these needs and to expand their efforts in support of mothers and children.[32]

Church mercy ministries as a whole should reflect the relational nature of the image of God as they seek to serve their communities. Responding to poverty and hardship requires more than material support. The Chalmers Center at Covenant College in Georgia provides resources for deacons and other ministry leaders to evaluate how they can respond to needs relationally. Helping Without Hurting is a series of books by Brian Fikkert, director of the Chalmers Center, and Steve Corbett to guide individuals and churches who want to grow in serving others.

Christian education has a particular responsibility and opportunity to shape engagement in these areas. Both curriculum and culture matter in this regard. Schools should consider how to nurture virtues like compassion and generosity, which extend support to others, as well as those virtues like humility and patience, which are ready to receive help.

In Christian higher education, a particular curricular challenge is to pursue disciplinary specialization without losing sight of the holistic nature of human flourishing. Practitioners across academic fields can keep that end in view by considering how the methods and content of their study shed light on the relational, embodied nature of humanity. A wide range of disciplines can add insights about cultivating the thick networks of relationships that provide social support and are essential to flourishing. At the same time, Christian higher education is equipping students who are about to enter the prime of life. They will make critical, life-shaping decisions in their twenties and thirties. Campus culture plays an important role in fostering the virtues required for healthy relationships both during and after college.

CONCLUSION

Human beings are designed for relationship. Communion with God, peace with oneself, harmony with other people, and nurture toward creation are all aspects of what it means to flourish fully as human beings created in the image of God. Sin harms, but grace restores each of these relationships from the effects of sin.

Brokenness in one or more of these connections is typically at the root of the challenges that individuals and communities experience today. Restoring relationships should be a priority in Christian responses to challenges like poverty or opioid addiction. To serve the whole person includes caring for relational well-being.

We need certain virtues to enable us to give and to receive in relationship. These include generosity and compassion as well as humility and patience. Family, church, and Christian education are especially equipped to form their members in the virtues needed for "uncalculated giving and graceful receiving." Such relational qualities are essential to welcome new human life, to support one another through the hardships of life, and to exhibit the grace of receiving at life's end.

A THEOLOGY OF HUMAN EMBODIMENT

Gregg R. Allison

> *The* LORD *appeared to Abraham at the oaks of Mamre while*
> *he was sitting at the entrance of his tent during the heat of the*
> *day. He looked up, and he saw three men standing near him.*
>
> ~GENESIS 18:1–2 CSB

THE NARRATIVE OF GENESIS 18 IS INTRIGUING for several reasons. It wonderfully presents an ancient cultural expression of hospitality (vv. 1–8). It provides choreographic details about the positioning of the Lord, Abraham, and Sarah, as God challenges Sarah about her denial of laughing at his (seemingly) ridiculous promise that she would bear a child in her old age (vv. 9–15). It recounts a daring conversation between the Lord and his covenant partner, Abraham, concerning the fate of desperately wicked people (vv. 16–33).

Our focus is another matter. Though the narrative characterizes the visitors as three "men" (vv. 2, 22), we readers know that one of the three is "the LORD" (e.g., vv. 1, 10, 17, 33). Furthermore, in the subsequent narrative, we learn that the other two visitors are actually "angels" (19:1, 12, 15). Strangely, then, these three "men" are actually one divine being and two angelic beings. As for the first strangeness, theologians use the term *theophany* or *Christophany*: a highly unusual appearance of God or, given the insistence of other biblical passages that "no one has ever seen God" (John 1:18 CSB),[1] more probably a preincarnate, temporary manifestation of God the Son.[2] As for the second strangeness, theologians employ the term *angelophany* and insist that angels are properly immaterial beings that can, on occasion, take on human shape and appear as "men."[3] Consequently, the narrative of Genesis 18 is strange because it features three beings—God (or the preincarnate Son) and two angels—who, though usually and properly immaterial, have taken on human-like physicality.

Does such strangeness pertain also to Abraham and Sarah? We readers give no second thought to these protagonists being embodied people, one a male embodied human being and the other a female embodied human being. They share every possible human characteristic with us readers, including embodiment. There is not one strange thing about these two characters. As far as I can recall, theologians never use the word *anthropophany*.

This point leads to the thesis of this chapter: embodiment is the proper state of human existence. Whereas God's existence as embodied is strange, and whereas angels' existence as embodied is strange, human existence as embodied is natural and normal. Indeed, God has designed and creates human beings to be embodied. This is the embodiment thesis.

EMBODIMENT: A DEFINITION[4]

In *Embodiment: A History*, Justin Smith defines *embodiment* as "having, being in, or being associated with a body."[5] Human nature is complex, consisting of both an immaterial aspect and a material aspect; so "the body is a biological, material entity."[6] There is a second definition of "embodiment." As a discipline of study, like biology and psychology, embodiment is "an indeterminate methodological field defined by perceptual experience and the mode of presence and engagement in the world."[7] From a theological perspective, human embodiment intersects with a host of other important theological concerns:[8]

(1) an understanding of God's creation of human beings and his design for human flourishing (thus, the theology of creation); (2) the constitution of human nature (thus, theological anthropology); (3) the somatic effects of the fall and sin (thus, hamartiology); (4) the nature of the incarnation (thus, Christology); (5) the Holy Spirit's indwelling of, and divine action through, redeemed human beings (thus, pneumatology and soteriology); (6) the strangeness of disembodiment in the intermediate state and the completion of God's redemptive work through the general resurrection (thus, eschatology); (7) numerous contemporary moral and social issues such as heterosexuality and homosexuality, transgenderism and gender dysphoria, and body image and body modification; and (8) an exposé of the devastating impact of Gnosticism/neo-Gnosticism on the America society and church.[9]

To advance a theology of human embodiment, I will offer some biblical and theological considerations, then turn to a discussion of the debated statement "I am my body." I will then present an entailment of human embodiment—genderedness—and conclude with several applications of gendered embodiment.

BIBLICAL CONSIDERATIONS

Genesis 1:26–28 (ESV) underscores this fact of human embodied existence:

> Then God said, "Let us make man in our image, after our likeness. And let them have dominion over the fish of the sea and over the birds of the heavens and over the livestock and over all the earth and over every creeping thing that creeps on the earth."
>
> So God created man in his own image, in the image of God he created him; male and female he created them.
>
> And God blessed them. And God said to them, "Be fruitful and multiply and fill the earth and subdue it, and have dominion over the fish of the sea and over the birds of the heavens and over every living thing that moves on the earth."

Following the divine deliberation (v. 26), God created human beings in his image, specifically male image bearers and female image bearers (v. 27). To these gendered embodied beings, God gave what is popularly called the cultural mandate, that is, the duty to build human society for the flourishing of its citizens. This responsibility consists of reflecting God, in whose image they are made, and representing God through procreation ("be fruitful and multiply and fill the earth") and vocation ("subdue it, and have dominion over" the rest of the created order).

A moment's reflection leads us to affirm the essential embodiment of these human-beings-as-divine-image-bearers.[10] When we readers first come upon the word "man" (v. 26), we think immediately of the race of people who are embodied. We would never think of this embodied condition of human creation as strange (remember Genesis 18). Moreover, because sex or gender (almost completely) maps onto embodiment, the actualization of the divine purpose means that embodied image bearers are either male or female (v. 27). We would never consider this gendered embodied condition of human creation as strange. Furthermore, the cultural mandate about procreation and vocation demands embodied people to accomplish these. We would never envision a flourishing human society with embodied men and embodied women multiplying children and engaging in work as strange.

Embodiment is the proper state of human existence by divine design and creation. The embodiment thesis is supported.

The next few chapters of Genesis rehearse the beginning of the fulfillment of the cultural mandate. It starts in the garden of Eden: "The Lord God took the man and placed him in the garden of Eden to work it and watch over it" (Gen. 2:15 CSB). While Adam and Eve's mutual task of "Edenizing" the world through procreation and vocation was horribly complicated by their fall into sin they, nonetheless, carry out their responsibilities as (now fallen) image bearers:[11] "The man was intimate with his wife Eve, and she conceived and gave birth to Cain [procreation]. She said, 'I have had a male child with the Lord's help.' She also gave birth to his brother Abel [procreation]. Now Abel became a shepherd of flocks, but Cain worked the ground [vocation]" (Gen. 4:1–2). This divinely designed duality of procreation and vocation repeats itself over and over again as "she conceived" and he "fathered" along with city building, tending livestock, musical artistry, and tool making (4:17–22). Obedience to and fulfillment of the divinely given task of building human civilization is necessarily carried out by embodied image bearers.

Embodiment is the proper state of human existence, by divine design and creation. The embodiment thesis is supported.

THEOLOGICAL CONSIDERATION

One of the devastating results of the fall was the divine decision to punish sin with death. Whereas before their fall Adam and Eve were not susceptible to death, after their catastrophic collapse, not only did they become liable to death, but the entire human race did as well. Importantly for our purposes, death is not only the cessation of the physiological functioning of the material aspect of human nature. It is also the separation of that material element from the immaterial element, often called the soul or the spirit. At death, the deceased person's body is sloughed off, laid in a grave or entombed or cremated, and begins to decay. Still, the person herself continues to exist in a disembodied state, with this important distinction: disembodied believers go immediately into the presence of the Lord in heaven and disembodied unbelievers go immediately into conscious torment in hell. Theologians refer to this as the intermediate state, the condition of deceased people between their death and the return of Jesus Christ (accompanied by bodily resurrection).

The obvious questions arise: If human existence is possible in a disembodied state, how can I maintain my embodiment thesis? If deceased human beings can exist without their bodies, isn't it better to define the proper state of human existence as immaterial yet with the usual but not necessary material component?

On the contrary, this condition of temporary disembodiment supports the embodiment thesis. The apostle Paul describes death, the intermediate state, and the resurrection with startling metaphors:

For we know that if our earthly tent we live in is destroyed, we have a building from God, an eternal dwelling in the heavens, not made with hands. Indeed, we groan in this tent, desiring to put on our heavenly dwelling, since, when we are clothed, we will not be found naked. Indeed, we groan while we are in this tent, burdened as we are, because we do not want to be unclothed but clothed, so that mortality may be swallowed up by life. (2 Cor. 5:1–5 CSB)

First, Paul presents death as the tearing down of our earthly tent, a dissolution of or separation from our body. Second, he gives assurance of our bodily resurrection, which involves a divinely prepared, eternal building, or re-embodiment with an incorruptible, strong, glorious, and Spirit-dominated body (1 Cor. 15:42–44). Third, Paul quakes at what lies between the two events: the intermediate state, in which we will be "naked," or "unclothed," that is, disembodied. If the condition of disembodiment in the intermediate state is a horror to dread, we should not allow this abnormal situation to define human existence. Indeed, during life on earth, human existence is embodied. Following death, the intermediate state, and the resurrection, human existence will be embodied. Thus, the temporary condition of disembodiment does not overthrow the thesis that the proper state of human existence is embodiment.

It should also be called to mind that if Adam and Eve had not fallen, they would not have died as a punishment for sin. They would not have experienced the intermediate state; that is, they would never have been disembodied. Thus, the condition of disembodiment in the intermediate state is foreign to human experience as divinely designed. Though it is "natural" in the sense that it is common to all human beings after the fall, it is not "natural" in the sense that it is not the way it is supposed to be. Therefore, it should not be allowed to contradict the embodiment thesis.

Thus, embodiment is the proper state of human existence. Whereas God's existence as embodied is strange, and whereas angels' existence as embodied is strange, and whereas human existence as disembodied in the intermediate state is strange, human existence as embodied is natural and normal.

A DEBATED STATEMENT

This theology of embodiment prompts me to make the following statement: "I am my body." So as to avoid confusion, it should be noted that I have not formulated the statement as "I am *only* my body." Though I have only briefly mentioned it, human nature or constitution is complex, consisting of both an immaterial aspect and a material aspect. Though my discussion has focused on the latter, bodily aspect, I by no means deny the immaterial aspect, which many call the soul or spirit (or, according to some, the soul *and* spirit).[12] Moreover, as noted above, the intermediate state demands the ongoing existence of human beings as disembodied people; thus, some type of immaterial existence is necessary for life after death. Thus, "I am *only* my body" is a false affirmation.

To focus on human embodiment, I frame the statement as "I am my body." As expressed by the Russian philosopher Vladimir Iljine: "Without this body I do not exist, and I am myself as my body."[13] Again, the affirmation of this statement applies to my earthly existence; to dismiss the statement because it is false in regard to the intermediate state misses the point of reference. Also, to disagree with the affirmation on the theoretical basis that I could exist with a different body is highly problematic, because with a different body—say that of my wife or that of my best friend—I would be a different person, a different "I."

Indeed, that idea is the point of the second phrase: "I am myself as my body." Change my embodiment, and I am not *my*self but a *different* self. Once again, now expressed as a question, "Am I who I am principally in virtue of the fact that I have the body I have?"[14] Exchange my body with that of another person, or in the case of my body struggling to pass a kidney stone as I write this chapter, I am not who I am in virtue of the fact that I have a different body or that I have the same body that does not implicate me in renal pain and sleeplessness.

The statement "I am my body" runs counter to prevalent views that have been expressed historically and in our contemporary context. As a first example, Plato played "a decisive role in the history of philosophy in establishing body and soul as a pair wherein the latter is superior to the former.... We see him minimizing the body's participation in human life by defining it in simple terms as a tool and by isolating its care from the care of the soul."[15] To take another example, Aristotle, in *On the Soul*, classified "body" as matter (*hulē*), the substratum or "substance that is *not* a this."[16] In contrast, he classified "soul" as form (*morphēn*), the shape "in virtue of which a thing *is* called 'a this.'"[17] Additionally, matter is potentiality and form is actuality; thus, "soul is 'form and actuality of a natural body able to have life' .... As actuality, form acts as mover and body as matter and potentiality is moved, or acted upon by form."[18] Clearly then, for Aristotle, the soul is primary, the body is secondary. Indeed, according to Aristotle, when it is engaged in contemplation of eternal things (in this way, thinking like gods think), the human soul (with particular reference to the intellect) briefly experiences thinking that is both proper to soul and that is "perfect activity, free of body or matter." Such disembodied freedom of the soul is the "highest excellence" of human beings.[19]

In the early church, these and other influences resulted in prioritizing the soul over the body. In his development of the concept of the image of God, for example, Tertullian explained that the nature of the soul includes "rationality, sensibility, intelligence, and freedom of the will."[20] Coming close to identifying the image of God with the human soul, Justin Martyr offered, "In the beginning [God] made the human race with the power of thought and of choosing the truth and doing right."[21] And what of the body? The *Letter to Diognetus* rehearsed the tension between the lofty soul and the miserable body:

> To sum up all in one word—what the soul is in the body, that are Christians in the world. The soul is dispersed through all the members of the body, and Christians are scattered through all the cities of the world. The soul dwells in the body, yet is not of the body; and Christians dwell in the world, yet are not of the world. . . . The flesh hates the soul, and wars against it, though itself suffering no injury, because it is prevented from enjoying pleasures; the world also hates the Christians, though in nowise injured, because they abjure pleasures. The soul loves the flesh that hates it, and [loves also] the members; Christians likewise love those that hate them. The soul is imprisoned in the body, yet preserves that very body; and Christians are confined in the world as in a prison, and yet they are the preservers of the world.[22]

The soul-destroying activity of the body should prompt Christians to desire death, at which point the soul is released from the body:

> The flesh, since it is earthly, and therefore mortal, draws with itself [drags down] the spirit linked to it, and

leads it from immortality to death. . . . The flesh hinders the spirit from following God. . . . But when a separation shall have been made between the body and the soul [at death], then evil will be disunited from good; and as the body perishes and the soul remains, so evil will perish and good be permanent. Then man, having received the garment of immortality, will be wise and free from evil, as God is.[23]

Thankfully, at times the church has pushed back against this far too common disparagement of the body and sought to emphasize the intimate connectedness of the soul and the body. As an example, Patrick Lee and Robert P. George rehearse Thomas Aquinas's argument against Plato's notion of the body-soul relationship:

1. Sensing is a living, bodily act, that is, an essentially bodily action performed by a living being.
2. Therefore, the agent that performs the act of sensing is a bodily entity, an animal.
3. But in human beings, it is the same agent that performs the act of sensing and that performs the act of understanding, including conceptual self-awareness.
4. Therefore, in human beings, the agent that performs the act of understanding (including conceptual self-awareness, what everyone refers to as "I") is a bodily entity, not a spiritual entity making use of the body as an extrinsic instrument.[24]

Thus, Lee and George, building on Aquinas, make a strong case that what most theologians consider to be the classical faculties of the "soul" (e.g., thinking, understanding, intellectually apprehending) have "an intrinsic need and functional orientation to matter or the body."[25]

To oversimplify, the church has perennially struggled to overcome the influence of Gnosticism and its contemporary expression in neo-Gnosticism, both of which privilege the immaterial element of human nature over the material element. Popular expressions of these positions include George MacDonald's "You don't have a soul. You are a soul. You have a body."[26] This instrumentalist view of human embodiment demeans the material aspect of human nature or at least considers it to be of less importance than the immaterial aspect. Some even take their rejection of embodiment to a disconcerting extreme. C. S. Lewis quipped that "the fact that we have bodies is the oldest joke there is."[27] Rejecting this perspective, I affirm to the contrary, "I am my body."

Yet Luke Timothy Johnson notes that MacDonald's and Lewis's position is not completely wrong: "Whereas there is some truth to the claim that I *have* a body, since I can in fact dispose of it in a number of ways, there is at least equal truth to the claim that I *am* my body. I cannot completely dispose of my body without at the same time losing myself. In strict empirical terms, when my body disappears, so do I."[28] Adjusting Johnson's view slightly, I aver that the statement "I *am* my body" is the ground for the statement "I *have* a body." As I've written elsewhere:

> Let me illustrate Johnson's point. Because I *have* a body, I can sacrifice certain parts of it for the sake of others. For example, I can donate one of my kidneys so that someone whose kidneys are failing may, by organ transplantation, live. But if I sacrifice too much of my body, which I *have*—for example, if I donate both kidneys for the sake of others— then I (and I *am* my body) no longer exist (that is, I'm dead). Thus, "I *am* my body" is the ground for "I *have* a body."[29]

GENDEREDNESS: AN ENTAILMENT
OF HUMAN EMBODIMENT

Without developing it at length, I draw attention to the fact that embodiment entails genderedness.[30] Simply put, a fundamental given of human existence is maleness or femaleness. Physiologically and genetically, gender maps almost completely onto (correlates with) embodiment. In rare cases "a child is born with an ambiguous gender, and it is not clear whether the child is male or female. One form of this is known as intersex. Ambiguous gender results from a genetic abnormality."[31] Because the condition of intersex affects from between .04% to 1.7% of the population and is a matter of genetics, its exceptional nature prevents me from including it as part of this discussion. Bracketing that condition, God's design for his image bearers is that they are gendered as either male or female.

Maleness and femaleness are well supported from the opening pages of Scripture. Following the divine deliberation to "make man in [God's] image," the narrative continues: "So God created man in his own image, in the image of God he created him; male and female he created them" (Gen. 1:26–27 ESV). The divine plan to create beings who would be more like God than any other creatures results in human image bearers who are embodied and gendered. As noted above, God gives to both the cultural mandate to build society through procreation and vocation (Gen. 1:28).

In terms of specific creative action, as for the first embodied male, "the Lord God formed the man of dust from the ground and breathed into his nostrils the breath of life, and the man became a living creature" (Gen. 2:7 ESV). God then took Adam and placed him in the garden of Eden (Gen. 2:8–9, 15–17); the first man was embodied and emplaced. Next, God formed the first embodied female: "So the Lord God caused a deep sleep to fall upon the man, and while he slept took one of his ribs and closed up its place with flesh. And the rib that the Lord God had taken from the man he made into a woman and brought her to the man" (Gen. 2:21–22). Out of Adam's physicality, God fashioned Eve, whom Adam enthusiastically recognized as the divinely promised helper fit for him—with an emphasis on her embodied and gendered correspondence: "This at last is bone of my bones and flesh of my flesh; she shall be called Woman, because she was taken out of Man" (Gen. 2:23). The first woman was embodied and emplaced, joining Adam in the garden. "Together and indispensably, they begin to engage in the cultural mandate involving procreation and vocation for human flourishing. They are able and obligated to carry out the mandate to build society because of, and only because of, their complementary genderedness. Adam and Eve are embodied human beings, and as such, they are fundamentally male and female."[32]

The binary pattern used in the creation of Adam and Eve did not differ from the pattern of binary creation that is narrated in Genesis 1 and 2, as seen in the following: heaven and earth; light and darkness; day and night; evening and morning; waters above and waters below; dry land and waters; two great lights (sun and moon); creatures of the sea and birds of the air; work and rest; two trees (of life, of knowledge); good and evil. That God created human beings as male or female is an application of the pattern of binary creation he employed leading up to the apex of his creation of his image bearers. Thus, a fundamental given of human existence is maleness or femaleness. God did not create an agendered being and then add on a secondary characteristic of maleness or femaleness. God did not create a superior male image bearer and then secondarily derive out of him an inferior female image bearer.

Specifically, and contra Megan DeFranza, I do not believe the Genesis narrative portrays a spectrum of human genderedness that is patterned after the spectrum of other created things.[33] According to this idea, "night" and "day" (for example) are two terms that represent the two poles or ends of the spectrum of created temporality. Within these two poles, the spectrum features intermediate created realities that the biblical narrative does not mention (for example, dusk and dawn in between night and day) but that nonetheless exist. Following this spectrum of creation, then, human genderedness includes not only the male and female poles mentioned in the biblical text but other varieties between them as well: androgynous, pangender, transgender male, transgender female, demigender, two spirit, and many more.[34]

What DeFranza seems to overlook is the biblical language of "separation" and "kinds." In terms of the first matter, God separated light from darkness (Gen. 1:4), the waters from the waters (Gen. 1:6), the day from the night (Gen. 1:14), and the light from the darkness (Gen. 1:18). Difference or distinction, not a spectrum of intermediate realities, is emphasized textually. As for the second matter, God created vegetation, plants, fruit trees, great sea creatures, other watery creatures, winged birds, livestock, creeping things, and land beasts "according to their kinds" (Gen. 1:11–12, 21, 24–25 csb). To many of the creatures in this latter category, God gave the command to "be fruitful and multiply" (Gen. 1:22 esv). This duty could only be carried out by species that are binarily male and female, not a spectrum of intermediate realities. Accordingly, the biblical language of "separation" and "kinds" underscores difference and distinction, not the spectrum of intermediaries that DeFranza's position highlights.

Human beings are either male or female by divine design. Indeed, God's assessment of the creation newly brought to completion was "it was very good" (Gen. 1:31). This judgment included the goodness of human image bearers who were male and female. What was pleasing to the Creator and what was certainly pleasant to the original image bearers, Adam and Eve, continues to be pleasant to the vast majority of people today. According to Frederica Mathewes-Green:

> For large segments of the world, gender differences are pleasant, appealing, and enjoyable, and practical application of theory—reproduction itself—is hardly a chore. (The subtitle of a Dave Barry book put it winningly: 'How to make a tiny person in only nine months, with tools you probably have around the home.') Yes, most cultures note and highlight gender differences, because most people find them delightful, as well as useful in producing the next generation.[35]

APPLICATION OF ENGENDERED EMBODIMENT

This theology of human embodiment, with a particular emphasis on genderedness, can be helpful in our discussions about what constitutes a human person, our interactions with those who experience gender dysphoria, our theologizing about transgenderism/transageism/transracialism/trans-speciesism, our pastoral care for those wrestling with problems of heterosexuality and homosexuality, our condemnation of dehumanization and objectification, our counseling of those struggling with body image, and more. A theology of embodiment does not ease the pain that the people we are interacting with face. Nor does it substitute for the compassion that we are called to express toward them. But it does provide a foundation on which to build our counseling and care ministries.

Engendered embodiment also compels us to reconsider our view of and posture toward men and women. First and foremost, our theology underscores that all human beings are image bearers, whose gender (almost always) maps onto their embodiment. All women and all men are divine image bearers and, as such, are worthy to be accorded respect and treated with dignity. We do not have the right to interfere with other image bearers and/or to detract from their image bearing and/or to destroy the purpose for which God created them. As divine image bearers who exist in community, we do not have the right to be isolated from others nor to isolate others from us; to refuse help to others nor to refuse to be helped by others; to deface the image bearing of others nor to permit being defaced by others. Moreover, in terms of redeemed image bearers, women and men are called to love and honor one another: "Love one another with brotherly affection. Outdo one another in showing honor" (Rom. 12:10 ESV). Scripture often employs familial images to help us envision how to express our relationships with one another: "Do not rebuke an older man but encourage him as you would a father, younger men as brothers, older women as mothers, younger women as sisters, in all purity" (1 Tim. 5:1–2). The metaphor of siblingship has a prominent place in the New Testament to instruct us how female believers and male believers are to relate to one another.[36] Admittedly, the church has a long way to go to embrace and actualize this vision. A theology of gendered embodiment can serve this transformation.

This theology also challenges us to reconsider how we view our own embodiment. Do we live the reality that "I am my body," or do we consider our body in instrumentalist terms, as something to be used or managed or stewarded like we do our time, money, gifts, and other resources? Such a perspective of our own embodiment shows up in statements like "I need to feed my body only certain types of foods in order to keep it tuned up like a fine car" or "I must exercise incessantly so that my body will perform at peak performance." Certainly, proper nutrition and regular exercise are important for us as embodied beings, but such statements belie an instrumentalist view of embodiment, as if our bodies are somehow outside of ourselves or different from ourselves. As my theology of embodiment proposes, this perspective, though widespread and entrenched in our mindset, is not the right way to consider our bodies. God's creation of us to be his embodied image bearers stands against this view. As Frederica Mathewes-Green offers, "The initial impression that we stand critically apart from our bodies was our first mistake. We are not merely passengers riding around in skin tight racecars; we are our bodies. They embody us."[37]

Embodiment is the proper state of human existence.

THE SANCTITY OF HUMAN LIFE

Scott B. Rae

WITH THE *ROE V. WADE* DECISION BEING OVERTURNED by the United States Supreme Court in June 2022, questions around the sanctity of human life came to the forefront of public discussion again. The Court's decision placed the matter of abortion rights back into the state legislatures for the people's representatives to decide (and, at this point, the states are split roughly 50/50 in terms of allowing or restricting abortion). Abortion opponents celebrated the protections now available to the unborn, while abortion proponents lamented the loss of a woman's essential reproductive freedom.

What has been somewhat surprising about the protests and counter protests in the aftermath of the Court's decision is *the relative silence about the sanctity of life of the unborn*. In this chapter, we will apply the notion of the image of God to the arena of bioethics, namely the ethical issues that arise at both the beginning and end of life. But perhaps a word of caution is in order at this point, one which I often give my philosophy students who are considering bioethics as a field. God, in his providential sense of humor, has seen fit for my field of bioethics to "follow me home." As a result, these are not merely academic discussions, as interesting as they may be. They are the conversations we have had with my (at times extended) family around the dinner table and at the hospital bedside. For example, my initial foray into this field was in the area of reproductive technologies, including IVF and surrogacy. It was not too long after I began looking at the ethical issues involved in these arrangements that my wife and I began a painful four-year journey through infertility. Similarly, when the legalization of assisted suicide was up for serious discussion (and the first ballot initiative appeared in my home state of California), my wife and I began the first of three journeys through terminal illness and the end of life with our parents. These are not only serious theological and philosophical discussions, but they have a significant pastoral component, since they touch people's lives at some of their most vulnerable points, when they are also most open to the spiritual side of these issues.

The previous essays in this volume, particularly those from John Kilner and Ben Mitchell, underscore an important point for bioethics: that the image of God is fundamentally a matter of *status*, not *function*. That is, the image of God is not dependent on a person's ability to perform a specific set of nonnegotiable functions. Rather the image of God is a status bestowed on human beings that gives them their essential dignity. For if the image of God is related to one's ability to perform a set of functions, such as self-consciousness, rationality, relationship, and so on, then, since those functions are degreed (we have more or less of them), that would suggest that the image of God is a degreed property. Biblically, it is nothing of the sort. It is an all-or-nothing property. The clarity that those essays bring to the image of God and bioethics is critical when we move into questions of personhood at both the beginning and ending edges of life.

For the past fifty years, at least since *Roe v. Wade*[1] became the abortion law of the land, in much of the West there has been a gradual erosion of respect for essential human dignity. Of course, in the atheistic regimes of the communist world during the Cold War era where there was no such doctrine as the image of God that gave human beings their dignity, the erosion of respect for human dignity was much more sudden and more pronounced. In the West, living in what Nietzsche called the "cut flower civilization," in which formerly Christian cultures have become more cut off from their religious roots, the erosion of human dignity, especially at the edges of life, has crept more slowly but surely.

ESSENTIAL HUMAN DIGNITY
AT THE BEGINNING OF LIFE

Nowhere can this erosion be seen more clearly than at the beginning of life. Since 1973, there have been roughly one million abortions annually, a figure that has remained consistent over that period, but hope appeared on the horizon, with the *Roe* decision being overturned in June 2022.[2] The reactions to this decision were interesting—the pro-choice side reacted as though the sky was falling, and the pro-life side acted as though the battle was over. Neither of those things are true. This is because the Court placed the decision back into the domain of the states, giving them the power to make laws on abortion, which reflect the wills of their voters, as expressed through their elected representatives. This is parallel to how the Court addressed the issue of physician-assisted suicide (PAS) in 1997.[3] There, the Court ruled that the states in question could prohibit or allow PAS, and in doing so, they could place whatever restrictions on it that could win the support of voters. They did what critics of *Roe* thought the Court should have done in 1973—turn it over to the states for their legislatures to decide the matter. At this point, roughly half the states have passed laws restricting abortion in some fashion, while the other half have passed laws that would leave abortion access virtually unchanged. Some states may end up passing laws that would allow for abortion with restrictions that would previously have been unconstitutional under *Roe*.

What is new in this area is what has come to be commonly called the DIY (do-it-yourself) or the OTC (over-the-counter) abortion. This is what has been known as the "abortion pill" or RU-486 or some other chemical means of inducing abortion, which a woman can do in the privacy of her home. It is projected that in the next decade this will become the method of choice for abortion and will constitute up to 75 percent of all abortions, essentially replacing surgical abortion as the primary means of ending a pregnancy. As this is practiced today, it is legal (in many states) to obtain the necessary medication to induce abortion without a prescription and without a physician's involvement or follow-up. This is the area at the beginning of life where respect for essential human dignity is most under siege and most difficult to detect, since it can be done in private without a physician (though in many cases, some sort of surgical follow-up is needed).

Over the past one hundred years, attitudes toward abortion have changed dramatically, but since *Roe* they have remained remarkably stable.[4] Most extreme views of abortion (total restriction or total allowance) are not common, but most people in the United States have some sort of practical (not necessarily principled) nuance to their views. This may reflect some cultural ambivalence about what kind of a thing an unborn child actually is. For example, the celebrated case of Scott and Laci Peterson in 2004 is an example of this ambivalence. Laci was eight months pregnant when she and her baby were killed by her husband. He was charged and convicted of *two* murders, even though Laci could have legally aborted the child under the law at that time (appealed to the California Supreme Court in 2005). The difference there seems to be the degree of wantedness for the child on the part of the mother, a shaky foundation for the right to life, to say the least.

Part of the reason for this increasing nuance in people's views has to do with the advances in prenatal technology that enable physicians to look more closely and clearly into the womb. This has been a significant benefit to those defending the personhood of the unborn because it makes it less plausible to hold that that unborn child is simply a clump of cells or something analogous to a piece of tissue, as opposed to a separate entity who is dependent upon the woman's body but not a part of it. This has actually caused a bit of a shift in the pro-choice argument for abortion rights. Increasingly, abortion rights advocates are conceding the personhood of the unborn, and at the same time, they are making the case that the pregnant woman has the right to end the life of her full-person unborn child. This marks a troubling turn in the abortion rights discussion and signals a further erosion of respect for the essential dignity of the unborn. Abortion foes have long argued that once the personhood of the unborn was established and agreed on, the debate over the morality of abortion would be over, but that optimism has proven shortsighted.

Another area of concern where respect for essential human dignity is eroding at the beginning of life is in the increasing acceptance of infanticide, especially at the academic and philosophical level. This view was espoused by Peter Singer in 1985,[5] though he was considered an outlier for some time. But with the publication of a symposium in the prestigious *Journal of Medical Ethics* in 2013,[6] the justification in academic circles by philosophers and even some theologians is something new. Essentially, the philosophers who support infanticide are taking the pro-choice argument for abortion to its logical conclusion, which is why the new euphemism for infanticide is the "after-birth abortion." In addition, the incidence of infanticide is becoming more widely known, as is seen by the infamous case of the Philadelphia abortionist Dr. Kermit Gosnell, who was convicted of several counts of infanticide, even though it was clear from grand jury testimony that it was routinely practiced in his clinic.[7] Both abortion and infanticide have become more clearly linked to the population control movements of the 1960s and 1970s, seen as important means of controlling the explosive population growth during that time in the developing world.[8] Rather than continue trying to get the desired sex (mostly boys), couples could use ultrasound to detect the sex of the child, and if not the desired sex, they could abort or leave the child to die of exposure, another form of infanticide. Calling this "gendercide," *The Economist* magazine estimates that since 1970, roughly 100 million baby girls have been aborted or been victims of infanticide.[9]

ESSENTIAL HUMAN DIGNITY AT THE END OF LIFE

At the other edge of life may be the area where essential human dignity is most under siege today. Physician-assisted suicide (PAS) is legal in a growing number of states in the United States (currently ten states and the District of Columbia) and has recently been made legal in three of six Australian provinces, including New South Wales, Victoria, and Western Australia. PAS refers to the prescription of legal medication to be self-administered by the patient, whereas euthanasia refers to deliberate, direction of causation of death by a physician. Both PAS and euthanasia are legal in eight countries across Western Europe and Canada, and they are technically against the law across the rest of Europe, but such laws are rarely enforced. In some places euthanasia is loosely legal without the explicit consent of the patient, and it is practiced more commonly than most people imagine.

This constitutes an assault on the dignity of the elderly and terminally ill, arguably the most vulnerable among us, especially in a time in which there is a demographic landslide in most of the Western world. In the next decade or two, Western countries will have the largest ever percentage of their populations over the age of sixty-five, with a shrinking younger demographic supporting them. It is estimated that the average person in the US will spend roughly 50 percent of their lifetime health care expenses in the last twelve months of their lives, when it will arguably do them the least amount of good. The pressure this will place on its citizens to reduce health care costs for this demographic will be immense, and some have argued that allowing for PAS/euthanasia is the best and most plausible way to control what will be exploding health care costs in the years to come.

The Nazi notion of a life not worth living has reemerged in the debate over the legalization of euthanasia as the elderly and terminally ill are increasingly viewed as "throwaway people." The Bible is clear that the taking of innocent life is prohibited, including taking one's own life, which leaves no room in a Christian worldview for the acceptance of euthanasia. In recent years well-publicized organizations, such as the Society for the Right to Die (formerly the Hemlock Society) and Compassion in Dying, have worked strenuously for the legalization of assisted suicide. A variety of resources provide detailed instructions on how to be released from the torments of a terminal illness with or without professional medical assistance.[10]

In this area at the end of life, it is possible that there is some misunderstanding and misapplication about what exactly is meant by the sanctity of life. Clearly the starting point for this discussion is that human life is God's sacred gift (by virtue of human beings made in the image of God as we have seen from Genesis 1:26–27). As a result, innocent human life is not to be taken, since it is God who ultimately determines the timing and manner of a person's death (Eccl. 3:1–2). The emphasis on *innocent* human life leaves room for the possibility of taking life in the death penalty (Gen. 9:5–6; the life-for-life principle is connected to the image of God), in taking the life of combatants in a just war, and in taking life in self-defense (Exod. 22:2). In addition, the Bible is clear about the obligation to care for the most vulnerable among us, which clearly includes the elderly and seriously or terminally ill.

To be more specific, in Scripture, death and dying came into the world as a result of the general entrance of sin, occasioned by the fall of Adam and Eve. Death and dying were not part of God's original design for human beings, but the Bible is clear that death and dying are a normal and natural part of human experience on this side of eternity, which is what is meant by the phrase "under the sun" in Ecclesiastes (2:14–16; 3:19–21; 5:15–16; 9:1–6). Of course, when the broader culture speaks of death and dying as a natural part of being human, they often mean it in a morally neutral way. The Bible, however, does not treat it as such. Death is an enemy *and* a normal part of life this side of eternity, and both are true at the same time. The reason that death and dying are a normal part of human experience is precisely because of the pervasiveness and universality of sin.

But thankfully, that is not the end of the story. Death is, after all, *a conquered enemy*, vanquished by the cross and resurrection of Jesus (1 Cor. 15:50–57). What follows from that is critically important for our understanding of the sanctity of life at the end of life. Since death is a conquered enemy, *it need not always be resisted*. That is, under the right circumstances, it can be morally acceptable to say "enough" to medicine and allow the disease to take its natural course. In doing this, we essentially entrust the patient back to God to extend or shorten his or her days as the Lord sees fit. In the right context, it is biblically consistent with the sanctity of life to stop taking medicine or refuse treatments, especially what are traditionally called "life-sustaining treatments" such as ventilator support and feeding tubes.

I will never forget wheeling my father-in-law out of the hospital for the last time. He had had surgery for a bladder tumor at age eighty-eight. Predictably, complications ensued and what should have been a three-to-four-day hospital stay turned into three weeks. His mental state deteriorated, and physically, he was never the same after that. As I was taking him out of his hospital room down the corridor in a wheelchair, he motioned to me to come close so he could whisper something to me, which was all the voice he had at that point. What he said to me was stark and attention-getting—he said, "Don't ever bring me here again." What he meant by that was that he was done with doctors, hospitals, tubes, treatments, and technologies that had seriously compromised his quality of life. Though I am not sure he could articulate it quite this way, I believe he was saying that he would accept from the hand of God whatever remaining days the Lord saw fit to give him, without the interventions of medicine.

The conditions under which it is morally and theologically acceptable to say "stop" to medicine are critically important. First, under the law, if a competent adult patient says to stop, physicians must stop, or they are vulnerable to the charge of battery. The exceptions to this are when the patient is not competent, which occurs when heavily sedated, unconscious, neurologically compromised such that they cannot make their own decisions, or in an emergency. Minor children are also not considered competent to make their own decisions. Usually competent adults, either orally or in writing in some sort of legally recognized advance directive, want medicine to stop when one of the following two conditions are met: if the treatment is futile (that is, it will not reverse a downward spiral toward death), or if the proposed treatment is more burdensome than beneficial.

For example, a case that came to a hospital ethics committee with which I worked involved a ninety-four-year-old man, who weighed about ninety-four pounds, who was being prepped for a colonoscopy to help treat end-stage stomach and colon cancer. The nurses came to the ethics committee and asked pointedly, "Why are we torturing this poor man?" The family was unable to appreciate the burdensome nature of the treatment they were authorizing since they would not be at the bedside when the treatment was being administered. Eventually, they agreed that the treatment was more burdensome than beneficial and allowed the physicians to stop aggressive treatment. The patient was then moved to a regimen of palliative care, the goal of which is to keep the patient comfortable as he lives out his last days. The family later realized that they were authorizing the treatment, not for the patient's benefit, but for theirs, since they were having an understandably difficult time letting go of their loved one. Morally speaking, it is almost always wrong to impose burdensome treatments on a loved one for someone else's benefit—a point which they eventually understood.

The reason that saying "stop" to medicine under the right conditions is not necessarily a violation of the sanctity of life is because earthly life is not the highest good, theologically speaking. Our eternal fellowship with God is, which makes earthly life a *penultimate* good—not the highest good but close to the top of the list. If the sanctity of life means that we as a society are obligated to keep everyone alive at all times and at all costs no matter what, what we are saying in essence is that earthly life is the highest good, which is theologically not the case. I have often been tempted to say to believing families, "Do you all really believe what you say you believe about resurrection and eternity?" Because the way that families hold to earthly life for their loved ones sometimes seems to suggest that they do not.

The other reason that saying "enough" to medicine under the right conditions does not violate the sanctity of life is that the underlying disease is the cause of the patient's death, not the decision to stop the treatments. Therefore, stopping treatments in this way is not "playing God" with your loved one's life. The term "playing God" refers to human beings usurping prerogatives that belong to God alone, such as the taking of innocent human life. If stopping treatments is not killing the patient, but rather allowing him or her to die, then it is not playing God nor is it a violation of the sanctity of human life. In fact, using medicine to extend life artificially and thereby delay someone's homecoming can also be a case of playing God, rather than entrusting the patient to God to live out the rest of their days without the interventions of medicine.

This also holds in the case of supplying medically provided nutrition and hydration using feeding tubes. It's called "medically provided" nutrition and hydration for a reason—that it's medically provided, by licensed medical personnel, in licensed medical facilities, and frequently covered by medical insurance.[11] Food and water are no more basic to life than air to breathe, yet we seem to have little issue with removing ventilator support (medically provided air to breathe) under the right conditions. Withholding medically provided food and water is no more starving someone to death than removing ventilator support constitutes suffocating someone to death.

Note that the notion of suffering being redemptive does not play a role at the end of life. In Scripture, the emphasis on the value of trials and suffering is for refining our character on this side of eternity, since on the other side we will be like him, with our character fully refined. It seems that some if not most suffering at the end of life is so close to the end that it is hard to see how it could have redemptive value in the sense in which the Bible describes. This is especially true if the patient has lost consciousness or is significantly neurologically compromised.

EUGENICS AND THE SANCTITY OF LIFE

With the rise of genetic testing and technologies and gene splicing, the prospect of "designer children" is closer than we once believed. I remember repeatedly telling my bioethics students that it's unlikely we'll have anything like designer children in our lifetimes, though it does occur in crude and unreliable ways through the choices made about sperm and egg donors. With the advances in genetic technologies, eugenics has returned from the ashes of the Nazi experience in World War II, with its distinction between a human being and human person and the notion that there is such a thing as a life not worth living. What makes eugenics such an assault on human dignity—human beings made in the image of God—is the widespread use of prenatal genetic testing.

Couples who have undergone genetic testing for their unborn child and have gotten bad news back on these tests will likely tell you that the physician and nurses presumed that they would end the pregnancy. Some will even say that they were pressured to end the pregnancy. My neighbors, after having two perfectly healthy children, learned they were carrying a child with Down syndrome. They spoke repeatedly of the pressure they received to end the pregnancy and how bewildered the staff was at their decision to keep the pregnancy. At the least, the burden of explanation has shifted for the parents. If a couple is carrying a healthy child, and they choose to end the pregnancy, it's not uncommon to wonder why they wanted to end the pregnancy. The burden of explanation is on the couple for the abortion decision. Conversely, if the couple is carrying a genetically anomalous child, the burden of explanation shifts, and most people wonder, if not ask, why they want to continue the pregnancy. That is, the pressure is on the couple to justify the continued existence of their child. I maintain that having to justify the continued existence of their child is inconsistent with the child having intrinsic dignity and a right to life.

What makes this so problematic is the assumption that often accompanies the decision to end these pregnancies. That is, the parents of the child with Down or some other genetic problem often assume that disability and unhappiness necessarily go together. But that assumption is often, if not normally, false. Though it is true that some genetic abnormalities do cause significant suffering for the child, increasingly the symptoms of these diseases can be managed. For example, medicine has made significant progress in treating the symptoms of cystic fibrosis and has lengthened the average life span of those with that disease. In addition, the experience of Down syndrome exists on a wide continuum, with some very serious cases and others in which the children live relatively normal lives. To assume, however, that unhappiness necessarily goes with disability is presumptuous. I suspect if you asked a group of kids with Down syndrome if they think they would be better off never having been born, they would think it a very odd question to ask. When making the assessment about the burden, both on the child and the parents, we should at least be honest that the burden on the parents often figures significantly into the decision about ending or continuing the pregnancy.

One other area where human dignity is under siege has to do with a curious application of genetic technologies—that is, using these technologies to select *for* a disability. Not to select so that disabilities are removed, but to ensure that they occur. For example, deaf adults have used genetic technologies to give them the best chance that their child will also be deaf.[12] Part of the reason for this is that those in the deaf community do not consider deafness a disability to begin with. But further, for a deaf couple to raise and parent a fully hearing child presents its own set of significant challenges. What is interesting is to listen to a secular culture provide reasons for their intuitions that such selection is harmful to a child and thus the wrong thing to do. Based on our autonomy-driven culture, it's very challenging to find substantive reasons to explain why this is a morally wrong thing to do to a child.

WHO IS A MEMBER OF THE HUMAN COMMUNITY?

The key question in our understanding of the image of God and how it plays out in the broader culture is this: Who is included as a member of the human community, and on what basis? To make it more theologically explicit, Who is counted in the group that is made in the image of God? To be clear, theologically and philosophically speaking, if human beings are not made in the image of God, then the notion of human dignity is an oxymoron, and there is no adequate grounding for anything like the idea of human dignity. Yet cultures around the world tenaciously hang on to the idea that human beings have essential dignity, a notion that is suspended in philosophical midair. If governments can bestow human rights and human dignity, then they can just as easily take them away. The history of the twentieth century is replete with examples of what happens when government takes away rights and dignity.

From a commonsense view of a person, without invoking explicit biblical or theological categories, we can agree that there is a difference between *being* a person and *functioning* as a person. What earlier chapters in this volume by Kilner and Mitchell are defending is a view that philosophers call a "substance view" of a person, where there is a dynamic interaction between body and soul. In addition, there is an immaterial essence to a human person, which gives human beings a continuity of personal identity through time and change. This suggests that a human person is more than a conglomeration of parts and properties; each one has an internal defining essence. This commonsense substance view of a human person is actually the basis for our notions of moral responsibility and criminal justice. If human persons are nothing more than our parts and properties, it would not be far-fetched for a criminal to make the argument that if they committed a crime, went on the lam for twenty years, underwent significant physical changes, and were later captured and brought to trial, that he or she has become a different person than the person who committed the crime and thus cannot be held responsible for his or her actions. Believe it or not, that has actually been tried and was immediately dismissed, precisely because our judicial system assumes a substance view of a person, the view that there is something essential and immaterial that gives persons a continuity of personal identity through time and change.

One way to make the case for the personhood of human beings is to start not with Scripture but with science. That is not to say that fundamentally, human personhood is a scientific question, which it most certainly is not. It is fundamentally a philosophical issue, to which science can contribute but is not determinative. To say that it begins with science is to start with the fact that both fetuses and embryos are living human beings; that is, they are both living and human and scientifically verifiable. For the one who distinguishes between a human being and a human person, this does not settle the question of when they become persons. Of course, what we have been maintaining throughout this volume is that there is no distinction between human beings and human persons and that a human being and a human person are the same entity.

A second building block in the case for the unborn being full persons comes theologically and is relevant primarily for the audience that takes the Scriptures seriously. That is, biblically speaking, abortion stops the handiwork of God in the womb (Ps. 139:13–16). For the person who takes the Bible seriously, this should be sufficient to cast great moral skepticism on most elective abortions. In fact, one does not have to come to a determination that the unborn is a full person and that abortion is the taking of innocent, vulnerable life, both of which are true. For the theologically rigorous pro-life advocate, the fact that abortion stops the handiwork of God in the womb is enough to make the case that abortion should not be undertaken.

We recognize, however, that most people in the broader culture do not find the biblical witness to be persuasive. So a third building block attempts to answer this question: if not at conception, precisely when does the fetus become a person? On the continuum between pregnancy and birth, any attempted "decisive moment" that draws a line delineating a person has come into being (as opposed to merely a human being) is entirely arbitrary and is no necessary commentary on what kind of a thing a fetus or embryo is. For example, both implantation and birth are merely changes in location with no metaphysical significance. Further, viability is more a commentary on the state of medical technology than it is on the ontological nature of the unborn. Any other proposed "line in the sand" suffers from the same arbitrariness, and none of the other decisive moments have any significance as to the moral status of the unborn. Even something such as brain activity, on the parallel with the brain death criteria for death, is far from an exact parallel. At death, brain activity is irreversibly lost, while at the beginning of life lack of brain activity is not only temporary but it is stage-of-maturity appropriate. Further, from the point of conception, the unborn has all the capacities it needs to mature into an adult. Simply because they are not yet actualized does not mean that they are not possessed.

Some will acknowledge that there is indeed no decisive moment along the continuum described above. Instead, they look to particular functions that are nonnegotiable indicators of personhood, such as self-consciousness, awareness of one's environment, capacity for relationships, and elementary rationality.[13] Many of the supporters of the morality of infanticide hold this functional view of a person. But as we maintained earlier, functioning as a person and being a person are two different things, and being a person is metaphysically prior. In addition, one can imagine temporary states for adult persons in which those functions are not possible. Take, for example, the person in a reversible or induced coma, or under general anesthesia. Of course, the objector could retort that these are merely temporary, and the person will have those functions restored when the anesthesia wears off or that person comes out of the coma. But that is also true of the unborn: being without those functions is also temporary and developmentally appropriate.

Some will further concede the unborn are persons, yet the pregnant woman still has the right to take the life of her full-person unborn child. Once this is conceded, then, not only does the unborn have the right to life, but an even stronger claim can be made—that the unborn has a claim on the mother's body for what he or she needs to survive and flourish. This is parallel to the rights that dependent children have on their parents for what they need to flourish, such that, if the parents are not able to provide what is necessary for their child, the state is justified to step in to ensure that the child is placed with someone who is capable of meeting their needs. Or if the parents abandon their responsibilities, they could face criminal charges of child neglect, precisely because the children have a claim on the parents for what they need.

CONCLUSION

In this sometimes-mystifying field of bioethics, the notion of human beings made in the image of God has profound implications for decisions and policies at both the beginning and the end of life. It is critically important to hold that human dignity is an *essential* quality, not dependent on a person's ability or lack of it to perform certain functions deemed foundational to personhood. For if human personhood is dependent on the ability to perform those functions, then it is a *degreed property*, something that a person can have more or less of. But as we discussed with the image of God, human personhood is an *all or nothing property*. This matters because a degreed property cannot be the basis for *equal rights* that are applicable to everyone. Thus, to be biblically faithful to the all-or-nothing aspect of the image of God and to provide a firm foundation for equal rights, human dignity and the sanctity of life must be seen as an essential property that is intrinsic to all human beings because of what they are, not because of how they are able to function.

WHAT IT MEANS TO BE MALE AND FEMALE

Katie J. McCoy

FEW SUBJECTS GENERATE SUCH DISSONANT CULTURAL CLASHES as the relationship between biology and gender and its meaning for human identity. Following the influx of social feminism's influence in the mainstream, evangelicals of various theological convictions sought to delineate theologically their paradigm of gender differentiation and its significance, both through the written word and organizational advocacy. Propelling these efforts was a desire to apply rightly the significance of humans being created male and female.

Two ideologies emerged. To define generally (and avoid belaboring the familiar), the belief that one's biological sex should neither predict nor limit one's relational or ecclesial roles became known as *egalitarianism*, while the belief that one's biological sex indicates and prescribes one's relational or ecclesial roles became known as *complementarianism*.[1] Both views claim male and female are equal; both views claim to interpret accurately the same biblical passages; and both views claim the other is, at least in part, guilty of theological error.

These themes are worthy of our ongoing consideration. Given the tectonic shifts in Western cultural values within the last several decades, we neglect them to the erosion of our public witness as well as to our own ruin. Indeed, every generation must search and apply the enduring precepts of Scripture to their transitory times. Cultural acquiescence threatens the integrity of Christian belief and practice in our day just as it did in the apostle Paul's.

Within evangelicalism, the pervasive questions in these debates are twofold. First and foundationally, how and to what extent does Genesis 1–3 inform and direct our sex-based gender identities and relational roles? For, how one interprets and applies the creation narrative portends all subsequent biblical interpretation related to gender roles and relations. Second, and consequently, in light of our created identities as male or female, how ought men and women express their respective genders socially, relationally, and ecclesiastically? If sexual differentiation is in fact essential to our personhood as God's image bearers, then we must determine why and for what purpose.

However, the digital din of debate over evangelical gender roles has been nearly eclipsed by the clamor of a new rhetoric, with concepts like gender fluidity, gender nonconformity, and transgenderism rapidly transposing cultural mores. Before one can answer the question of what ministries a woman can fulfill in the church, one must now first define what a woman is. Before one can defend marriage as a covenant between male and female, one must be prepared to stipulate that maleness and femaleness are unalterably determined at birth. In short, conversations on *how* one expresses one's gender risk falling on deaf ears apart from a clear defense of *why* gender differentiation matters at all. And in a society that increasingly accepts the idea that one's biology is irrelevant to determine one's gender, answering this *why* seems more urgent than ever.

As the chorus of advocates claiming gender is little more than a social performance continues to grow, much of complementarian discourse has defaulted to amplifying familiar refrains: delineating and debating specific roles, stipulating gender expressions, managing the *how*.[2] However, in view of our present moment, it is all the more urgent that we articulate the *why*. Why did God create sex differentiation? Why did he create male and female? In what follows, I propose that complementarian evangelicals must recover the relational character of mankind as male and female—a characteristic that pervades all of Scripture—and reframe their discourse to emphasize relationality prior to roles. This shift preserves both ontological equality between male and female and the meaning that created sex differentiation gives to manhood and womanhood. I hasten to add that this assertion does not make the idea of specific gender responsibilities mutually exclusive to human relationality; it is an unfortunate and ironic reality in my own theological community that affirming the equality of women leaves one open to suspicion of closeted heterodoxy. Nonetheless, I choose to believe the best of my readers and am confident they will choose not to conclude that which I have not claimed.

Thus, we begin—as all conversations on mankind as male and female must—at the beginning.

RELATIONAL UNDERSTANDING

Scripture's first chapters describe humanity in relational terms.[3] In Genesis 1:26–28, the affiliation between male and female is one of essential equality and distinct personhood in their relationship to God. Both male and female receive undifferentiated commands from the Lord: to rule and reign over creation, and to multiply and fill the earth. They are equal manifestations of the *imago Dei*: concerning activity, they are equal recipients of the divinely given mission; concerning community, they are equal participants in a divinely created relationship; concerning status, they are equal stewards of a divinely delegated authority over his creation.[4]

The very mode of woman's creation portrays her comprehensive equality to the man. The Lord created the woman to mitigate the man's solitude, to provide community in relationship. Rather than create her out of the dust of the earth as he did the man, the Lord fashions her out of the man's side. In Hebrew thought, this signified the man's rational powers; woman shared in man's capacity for comprehension, reason, and agency.[5] She is of the same substance as the man, in every way related and corresponding to him. Even the event of naming the woman confirms this: woman is both of man, yet not man (Gen. 2:18–25). Man could neither disparage her person nor dismiss her intellect or personhood without despising himself—and what man ever despised himself (Eph. 5:29)?

This relational emphasis is consistent with the rest of written revelation. From the first moments of creation to history's culmination, Scripture reveals a relational deity. God created humanity in male and female forms in his image, not out of necessity—the Godhead subsisted in perfect fellowship within himself—but from love, and for his glory. More specifically, he created humanity so that they would know his love and his glory in a relationship unlike any other of his creatures. They were his family (Isa. 43:6–7). As humanity is created in his image, they are likewise relational. The creation mandate of Genesis 1:27–29 instructed the man and the woman to fill the earth and multiply— to increase the family. Thereafter, the Lord continues to reveal himself and his work in relational terms. He calls himself the

Father of Israel, an indissoluble family bond (Exod. 4:22–23). The marital union, a relationship unique among all other familial and social affiliations, was a metaphor portraying Yahweh's covenant faithfulness to Israel and his anguish over Israel's spiritual infidelity (Jer. 3:14; Hos. 2:16). Israel's mediatorial ministry to the surrounding nations was intended to bring pagans into relationship with Israel's God (Isa. 19:16–25; 43:10–12).

This relational prominence continues in the New Testament. The Lord Jesus grounds the motivation for obedience in love for God. The apostle Paul predicates personal holiness upon one's right relationship with God (Rom. 6). The apostle John establishes one's relational union with Christ as the impetus for one's purification (1 John 3:3). The Great Commission entails acting as God's ministers of reconciliation for the expansion of his family. Even the fulfillment of the law—that we would love the Lord our God with the totality of our being and love our neighbor as ourselves— is a fundamentally relational command. And the consummation of the present age is the marital union between the Lord and his people. Within the metanarrative of Scripture, God reveals himself in relational terms.

By allowing this relational theme of Scripture to inform our reading of the creation narrative, we discover the meaning of mankind as male and female with greater insight. The creation story in Genesis 1–2 grounds human identity and personhood in terms of relationship. Although the substance of the *imago Dei* includes various definitions and approaches, humanity's potential for relationship with God constitutes the most unique aspect of being created in his image.[6] John F. Kilner identifies God's purpose for creating humanity as connection and reflection; the Lord intended humanity to know him in a special connection and reflect his attributes such that God receives glory, and his people flourish as he intended.[7] The Lord's relational motivation for creating contrasted with the deities of other ancient Near Eastern cultures. Tom Holland contrasts the creative impulse of Yahweh with the Babylonian god Marduk. The pagan deity created humanity to fulfill the work he was unwilling to do. Yahweh, however, created humanity to know him, to be in relationship with him.

The sexual differentiation between male and female is not merely functional or reproductive. John Paul II in his work *Theology of the Body* describes the significance of the male-female relationship as the "nuptial meaning of the body." The body is a gift, one that subsumes the whole person. To fulfill the body's nuptial meaning, both male and female mutually give themselves to create a "communion of persons."[8] This communion is a dynamic relationship in which both male and female mutually realize the significance of their gendered bodies as embodied gifts to each other.

The character and expression of their respective sexualities (i.e., masculinity and femininity) are inextricably established by their sexual differentiation. The differences between male and female constitute what J. Budziszewski calls "polaric complementarity," a corresponding oppositeness that reflects interdependence and congruence.[9] This polaric complementarity enables both male and female to comprehend themselves through comprehending each other. Within the woman, man recognizes himself. He understands himself through her corresponding similarities and difference. Gerhard Müller describes this as among the reasons God created sexual differentiation: "In sexual difference ... each of the two can only understand himself or herself in light of the other: the male needs the female to be understood, and the same is true for the female."[10] In other words, the man understands himself by understanding what he is not and vice versa. Man cannot comprehend his identity as a man apart from woman and vice versa; both masculinity and femininity find their meaning in contradistinction to one another.[11] One cannot know the meaning of one's gendered self apart from relationship. John Paul II explains, "Femininity is found in relation to masculinity and masculinity is confirmed in femininity. They depend on each other." Ross Hastings asserts that the relationality between male and female is constituted in both unity and "differentiated, complementary, noninterchangeable plurality. . . . *It is otherness and oneness. Otherness in oneness.*"[12]

CREATION AND GENERAL REVELATION

This self-understanding through relational correspondence has been described as an "I-Thou" way of relating.[13] Just as God is not alone in himself, human beings image God by an analogy of relation.[14] This relationship personified the *imago Dei* in a manner that individual man could not in isolation, what Karl Barth called "being in encounter."[15] Dietrich Bonhoeffer explains, "Human beings exist in duality, and it is in this *dependence on the other that their creatureliness exists.*"[16] Thus, human beings cannot image God fully apart from an "in-dependence-upon-one-another" relationship.[17] As humanity images God with their being, and as sexual differentiation is not only functional but also relational, created sexual differentiation itself images the divine.

Likewise, as all creation reveals the existence of a Creator, sex differentiation between male and female comprises general revelation, part of the natural world that proclaims the reality of an intelligent designer and his attributes. Hastings explains, "The fact that humans are sexual beings in a binary way, that they are beings who are not interchangeable with respect to sex, says something particular about who God is."[18] In other words, the sexed body is significant because it images God.[19] The physical creation contains a spiritual meaning.[20] Humanity is like God in its relationality, yet unlike God in interdependence. According to Leslie Cook, a human being's gender, signified by the human body, reinforces the theological belief that humans are distinct from the divine. She claims that "gender, represented through the body, is a symbol of difference. God is undifferentiated unity."[21] As Rabbi Ghatan describes, one gender without the other would bring "destruction to the world."[22] Both male and female qualities are necessary for the benefit of humanity. For Ghatan, the Hebrew concept of sex differentiation obviates competition between male and female: "The question of whether man is superior to woman or vice versa is totally irrelevant. Either sex without the other is incomplete."[23] Again, this pertains not only to reproductive capacity but also to relational completion.

Further, the sexual differentiation between male and female and the unbreakable bond intended by the marital union didactically illustrate God and his own covenant faithfulness. Hastings explains, "Humanity functions as co-humanity in its being male and female together, and by humans being male or female individually. Human relationality structured in this sexual binary manner has correspondence to God and his covenant partner."[24] Human sexuality and its complementarity between male and female also portrays the perfect union God has within the Godhead. Peter Kreeft identifies this as the reason for the power and uniqueness of sexual passion: "*Human* sexuality is that image [of God], and human sexuality is a foretaste of that self-giving, that losing and finding the self, that oneness-in-manyness that is the heart of the life and joy of the Trinity. . . . We love the other sex because God loves God."[25]

This relationality-preceding-functionality—the "communion of persons"—relates to the other as a living "Thou," rather than a static "It." Thus, within the male-female relationship, failure to relate to one another in a communion of persons produces failure to comprehend fully the nature of one's identity as male or female. This "I-Thou" connection—*analogia relationis*—is not mutually exclusive to what may be identified as "roles" in the sense of sex-specific responsibilities and ways of relating; on the contrary, the I-Thou finds its expression in relationships particular to one's personhood as male or female.[26]

Further, equality does not entail indistinguishability. The relational complementarity between male and female is both biological and gendered. The creation account reveals the human body is neither incidental nor accidental to gender identity.[27] Genesis 1 uses the Hebrew terms *zakar* (male) and *neqebah* (female) to depict their sexual differentiation, while Genesis 2 includes the words *ish* (man) and *ishah* (woman) to reflect their gender differentiation. These pairs of terms relate *zakar* to *ish* and *neqebah* to *ishah*. To be a *zakar* makes one an *ish*. To be a *neqebah* makes one an *ishah*. At the risk of inviting the charge of anachronism, this linguistic nuance contradicts the cultural belief that one's biological sex and one's gender are unrelated and confirms the culturally anathema idea that gender is binary. To be sure, biological sex and gender are not *identical* aspects of one's humanity—sex is a primarily reproductive descriptor, while gender is a relational one—but they are indeed *correlative* aspects. From this, we may deduce that one's biological sex indicates and corresponds to one's gender such that both are binary. The sexed body is indivisible from gendered self. On this point, we must elaborate.

EMBODIED

An increasingly accepted yet empirically unestablished belief claims one's sex is unrelated to and divisible from one's gender. According to this ideology, a person who is born male but believes himself to be a woman has a legitimate cause to conform his outer life to his inner "femininized" self and to expect society to do the same. The psychological condition is known as gender dysphoria, in which a person's biology does not coincide with a person's gender identity, causing distress.[28] The gender dysphoric person may attempt to achieve external conformity to his internal self through socialized gender expressions (one's name, personal pronouns, manner of dress and appearance), medical treatments (hormonal therapies), and/or surgical procedures (breast implants, mastectomy, hysterectomy, vaginoplasty, orchiectomy, phallectomy, phalloplasty, and womb transplant).

Transgender advocates substantiate their belief that biological sex and gender identity are divisible by claiming gender is merely a social construct. Males have been socialized into behaving in characteristically masculine ways, females in feminine ways. Remove these social influences and a child is free from the constraints of conforming to external expectations. Hence, the so-called progressive trends like gender-neutral parenting and countries offering a nonbinary option on birth certificates.[29] Validating gender dysphoria is considered a civil right.[30] In some cases, pubescent children are undergoing hormone replacement therapies to alter their natural sexual development.[31]

However, contrary to common parlance, one's sex is not "assigned at birth," but rather identified as that which corresponds to biology. Paul McHugh, University Distinguished Professor of Psychiatry at Johns Hopkins School of Medicine, insists one's sex is biologically unalterable. "People who undergo sex-reassignment surgery do not change from men to women or vice versa. Rather, they become feminized men or masculinized women."[32] To collaborate with one's gender dysphoria is, in McHugh's words, "to collaborate with and promote a mental disorder."[33]

Intrinsic in transgender ideology is the conviction that gender is, at its core, a feeling. In his work *When Harry Became Sally*,

Ryan Anderson notes the epistemological questions transgenderism creates. How does one "know" the embodied experience of the other sex? As Anderson notes, "The claim of a biological male that he is 'a woman stuck in a man's body' presupposes that someone who has a man's body, a man's brain, a man's sexual capacities, and a man's DNA can *know* what it's like to *be* a woman."[34] The remaining "proof" appears to be one's identification with and affinity for stereotyped expressions of gender identity.[35] In other words, the expression of gender is regarded as the essence of gender.

Moreover, that gender identity is socially formed and expressed does not entail that it has nothing to do with the body. In his book *On the Meaning of Sex*, J. Budziszewski notes gender identity "must be disciplined and stewarded; it is not in itself a separate reality of one's being to be followed without critical thought or question."[36] Gender identity is influenced, directed, and formed. Even the gender dysphoric person relies on *some* type of community to validate his or her sense of self.

Consider the research presented by Lisa Littman, assistant professor at the Brown University School of Public Health. Littman endeavored to explain the relative phenomena of an increasing and sudden prevalence of gender dysphoria among adolescents, teenagers who had previously expressed no gender dysphoric symptoms. The condition, known as Rapid Onset Gender Dysphoria, revealed an unexpected—and in certain corners, unwelcome—pattern. Littman discovered the influence of an adolescent's relationships directly affected her gender identity. The phenomenon had a social cause. Among adolescents with Rapid Onset Gender Dysphoria, 87 percent had friends who announced themselves as gender dysphoric, had saturated themselves with material on niche websites discussing gender dysphoria, or both.[37] In other words, a condition believed to find its source and validation in one's intrinsic sense of self has extrinsic factors.[38] Additionally, a majority had also experienced some sort of psychological trauma within the last twelve months, including sexual abuse or assault, serious illness, their parents' divorce, bullying, or moving to a new school.[39] Expressing gender dysphoria became a coping mechanism to distract from the source of distress. When Littman identified Rapid Onset Gender Dysphoria as a peer contagion, she effectively confirmed that it is, at least in part, socially influenced. In other words, the gender dysphoric individual's gender dysphoria may itself be a type of social construction.

As we uphold a biblically sound view of mankind as male and female, we must unwaveringly maintain that our identities are indivisible from our bodies. Biological sex and gender identity are created aspects of our significance as God's image bearers, created aspects that he calls "good." These two aspects of our humanity—sex and gender—were intended to coincide in wholeness. Employing Kilner's twofold purpose for humanity, one's biological sex and one's corresponding gender reflect the image of God in a way that connects us to him and reflects his attributes. In light of this, we must affirm the logically simple yet culturally subversive claim that one cannot choose one's gender. The idea that an *ish* may not be a *zakar* and an *ishah* may not be a *neqebah* reflects the fractured and distorted self-image caused by our sinful world. Even more, it reflects the attempts of God's rebellious image bearers to suppress the truth that nature reveals about God.

We are more than our embodied sex, yet we cannot be separated from our embodied sex.[40] Christianity gives us the framework to affirm that our bodies and reproduction are good yet not ultimate.[41] Andrew Walker clarifies, "Maleness isn't only anatomy, but anatomy shows that there is maleness. And femaleness isn't only anatomy, but anatomy shows that there is femaleness. Men and women are more than just their anatomy, but they are not less. Our anatomy tells us what gender we are. Our bodies do not lie to us."[42] We may also affirm that both one's maleness or femaleness and one's manhood or womanhood are created and bestowed aspects of our identities as God's image bearers. To reject this relationship between sex and gender is but a resurrected form of Gnosticism,[43] a devaluation, and consequently, a denigration of the body.[44] Thus, men and women are neither composites of their biology nor abstractions from their biology. Our sexed bodies are neither accidental nor incidental to our gendered selves. Both are given by God to image himself in holistic relationality.

Transgender persons should elicit our compassion. No social adaptation or surgical procedure will achieve the sense of wholeness they seek. The staggering suicide rate among sex-reassignment recipients is proof. What is inwardly broken has no outward cure. Whether one's psychological distress is symptomatic of another source of pain or the effect of living in a fallen world, the transgender person's hunger for meaning finds its satisfaction only in the satisfaction of Christ on our behalf. Apart from a reconciled relationship with our Creator, we will never comprehend, much less fulfill, the significance of our sexed bodies, our gendered selves, or our relationality with others.

BIBLICAL MANHOOD AND BIBLICAL WOMANHOOD

Evangelical discourse preoccupied with prescribing specific roles may, however unwittingly, neglect the relational emphasis within Christian anthropology. A "role" is an extrinsic property; a relationship is an intrinsic reality. One can adopt or suspend a role like a task or a function. Yet the nature of male or female is not a static position but rather an active relationship, one in which two persons relate to one another as a "Thou" not an "It." One's identity as a man or a woman reflects the intricate wholeness of personhood, one that is neither reduced to one's biological sex nor separate from one's biological sex. To condense the relationship to terms of roles reduces the complexity and comprehensiveness of the maleness and femaleness to a function—to relating to the other as a depersonalized "It." Moreover, emphasizing roles over relationality risks displacing one's relationship with God as the defining factor of one's gender identity and replacing that defining factor with an interpersonal dynamic.

The relational character of sexual differentiation and gendered personhood requires man and woman to know one another primarily as relational persons (Thou), not as static positions (It). This being-in-encounter relationship is distinct from the inhabiting of a role, although the two are not mutually exclusive. This observation is not to dismiss the different ways of relating or relational responsibilities between male and female; Scripture's pattern of male headship in nuclear and spiritual families is clear. Rather, this point considers the idea of male-female roles primarily in terms of personal relationship, not the other way around.

With this in mind, I humbly offer the following definition of biblical manhood and biblical womanhood. Biblical manhood constitutes a biologically born male who submits fully to God and his Word, allowing the precepts of biblical instruction and the implications of that spiritual posture to pervade every aspect of his life and relationships. Likewise, biblical womanhood constitutes a biologically born female who submits fully to God and his Word, allowing the precepts of biblical instruction and the implications of that spiritual posture to pervade every aspect of her life and relationships. The relative ambiguity and correspondence of these definitions stresses a twofold relational emphasis. First, the man or woman who aligns his or her life to biblical instruction will fulfill its gender-specific commands, thus embodying the significance of his or her biological sex and gender identity. One's relationship to the Lord determines one's relationship to the self and to others. Second, as a man or woman submits to and obeys God's commands—both to all Christians and to their respective genders—the Lord accomplishes and fulfills the meaning and significance of one's gender through one's interpersonal relationships. In other words, and at the risk of oversimplifying the issue, when we as men and women worship the Lord in obedience, he is the one who reveals and establishes the meaning of manhood and womanhood. We conform; he confirms.

Undoubtedly, a reader or two will object to such simplicity. Yet consider the perennial efforts to delineate and stipulate gender roles in detail. Preoccupation with prescribing gender roles at the expense of human relationality quickly tends toward conflating culturally gendered activities with the essence and meaning of gender itself. In other words, the gender expression of manhood constitutes the essence of manhood; the gender expression of womanhood constitutes the essence of womanhood. In this way, overzealous complementarian discourse risks committing a similar fallacy as transgenderism: conflating the essence of gender with the expression of gender. Grounding gender differentiation in relationship rather than roles protects sound complementarian theology from devolving into disproportionate concern over gender expression. This is not to denigrate the importance of practicing cultural sensitivity and outwardly behaving in a way that reflects one's acknowledgement of his or her created gender.[45] Rather, it is to demonstrate that complementarian discourse can become so preoccupied with stipulating specific gender roles that it misses the significance of relationality.

Further, in a culture increasingly receptive to the idea that gender is a subjective feeling, expressed exclusively by behaviors (i.e., roles), complementarian discourse jeopardizes its own convictions if it fails to emphasize a relationality that is inseparable from the sexed body and holistic to the gendered self. But to emphasize gender distinctions as respective ways of relating safeguards our theological discourse from devolving into a preoccupation with specific tasks, functions, or cultural expressions. By amplifying the communion of confrontation with a "Thou," we represent the fellowship of Hebrew marriage and the sex differentiation and gender complementarity described in Genesis 1–2.

Grounding gender differences in relationship prior to roles further allows us to maintain that male headship is a relational responsibility by which one bears greater accountability rather than a superior role with which one wields greater control. This permits the possibility of a marriage that both fulfills Scripture's relational pattern and varies in social roles.[46] In contrast, to ascribe approval or disapproval of a marital relationship according to whether it conforms to culturally dominant norms of gender expression reflects a paradigm in which male and female fulfill a role rather than express a relationship. To reiterate, this in no way eschews the biblically established pattern of male headship in the family and the church. Nor does this approach intend to dismiss the relationship of man as spiritual authority and woman as corresponding helper in marriage (Gen. 2:18; Eph. 5:22–33). Rather, this distinction proposes that we present and discuss this pattern to reflect the relational nature of man as male and female prior to stipulating gendered expressions.

Finally, grounding gender differences in relationship prior to roles also frees us from associating certain virtues with gender. A virtuous man will be meek, tenderhearted, and gentle. A virtuous woman will be resolute, bold, and steadfast. While the virtues themselves are not gendered characteristics, the expression of these virtues may correlate to the gender of the person who possesses them.[47] This point also frees us from assessing one's manliness or womanliness by the degree to which they possess specific virtues relative to other persons and, instead, relates all virtue as an expression of one's relationship to God (2 Pet. 1:3–11). This too protects our theological convictions regarding male and female from being reduced to gendered behaviors.

Our created identities as male or female are indispensable to and inseparable from our identities as God's image bearers. If our public witness is to be effective, we must underscore human relationality prior to gender roles. A compelling and cogent defense of the relational intent of male and female provides the platform upon which we may display our relational God, whom we reflect in both our equality and our distinction, our wholeness and our difference. Our world is spiraling into confusion over and celebrating the destruction of our sexed bodies and our gendered selves. May we, as ambassadors of Christ himself, not be entangled in the secondary squabbles over specific roles but be found faithful to proclaim and embody the holistic relationality through which male and female find their meaning.

ARTIFICIAL INTELLIGENCE, TRANSHUMANISM, AND THE QUESTION OF THE PERSON

Jacob Shatzer

TODAY, WE ARE PULLED INTO MANY IDEAS on what it means to be human. On one hand, a radical constructivism rules: *I choose and build my identity, and for you to use any category to describe me that I have not chosen is an offense and affront.* From this perspective, there really is not anything solid that determines what it means to be human, and we can build ourselves into whatever we want. Yet, on the other hand, we construct arguments and movements based on a shared humanity. Furthermore, as we develop more and more sophisticated technology, we cannot help but begin to refer to these technologies as though they bear some marks of what it means to be human. Our digital assistants have names, we use smart robots to provide companionship to the elderly, and we exult at how "intelligent" (a human-oriented trait) our systems are becoming, whether it is the artificial intelligence (AI) built into a thermostat or a robot. When it comes to ourselves, we want to determine our humanity, but when it comes to our machines, we are quick to use static human traits in order to describe the greatness of the works of our hands.

Our technological creations pull in multiple directions at our doctrine of humanity. A robust doctrine of humanity will give us a foundation from which to address these challenges, but these challenges will also affect—or perhaps infect—our understanding of what it means to be human. A basic understanding of AI ("fake humans") and transhumanism ("future humans") will press a variety of challenges onto our theological anthropology, both in what it means to be human and how we might consider and pursue human flourishing in light of these developments.

The history of technology is certainly complex, and there is some debate as to whether technology is neutral or not. However, even if technology on its own is thought of as neutral, it is actually impossible for any of us to ever engage technology "on its own." We always encounter technologies embedded within human cultures, which do carry and cultivate values and ethics.[1] Not only do we always encounter technologies as embedded within cultures, we also struggle to be able to notice the ways that these devices impact our ability to see and desire the good,[2] or in simpler language, to avoid sin and honor Christ.

This issue is particularly important because of the age in which we live. Byron Reese argues in his book *The Fourth Age* that while we think we have seen change in the last one hundred years, we really have not. We're still basically the same as people five thousand years ago. He sees three main ages of humanity so far: fire (one hundred thousand years ago); agriculture, cities, war (ten thousand years ago); wheel and writing (five thousand years ago). We're on the cusp of the fourth: AI and robots.[3] Reese provides a perspective not present in many other treatments: he emphasizes that many proponents of different futures depend on unexamined assumptions about what it means to be human. We have to answer that question before we can understand the way to direct AI and robotics and before we can really decide if these changes will be positive or not.

In other words, the other chapters in this volume on theological anthropology have just as much to do with our response to AI and transhumanism as this chapter does! The questions Reese raises, from a secular perspective, show the fundamentally theological nature of the issue: "The confusion happens when we begin with 'What jobs will robots take from humans?' instead of 'What are humans?' Until we answer that second question, we can't meaningfully address the first."[4] With that in mind, in what follows we will look at AI and transhumanism in order to get a better view of the touchpoints and challenges that they raise for Christian theological anthropology. By going this route, we will begin to see ways that our doctrine of humanity is informed by these challenges and also forms our response to them.

ARTIFICIAL INTELLIGENCE

Artificial intelligence is a large and changing field that also had a broad and varied history, both in reality and in pop-culture expressions. To consider how AI might develop and impact our thinking about what it means to be human, we will have to clear the ground a bit to make sense of what we are talking about.

In his recent book *2084*, John Lennox defines key terms related to AI, and we will rely on his explanation of *robot*, *AI*, and *algorithm*. First, "a robot is a machine designed and programmed by an intelligent human to do, typically, a single task that involves interaction with its physical environment, a task that would normally require an intelligent human to do it."[5] This definition is pretty straightforward and unsurprising. Second, Lennox defines AI in two ways: "The term is now used both for the intelligent machines that are the goal and for the science and technology that are aiming at that goal."[6] Third, Lennox expands on *algo-rithm* using the *OED*: "A precisely defined set of mathematical or logical operations for the performance of a particular task."[7] He points out that such concepts can be found as far back as Babylonia in 1800–1600 BC, though obviously not coded into digital technology. The key feature of the algorithm is that "once you know how it works, you can solve not only one problem but a whole class of problems."[8] Lennox follows up with some mathematical examples, such as instructions for various steps to arrive at, say, the greatest common denominator of two numbers. You can follow the steps for any set of two numbers and it will work. Algorithms, then, are embedded within software that uses them to interact with and evaluate different data inputs.[9] This type of system can take any input that can be digitized (such as sound, text, or images), apply a set of steps to that data, and come up with some sort of conclusion. That conclusion can include or lead to action. Algorithms are vital to understand because they are at the center of how AI works.

There are four main categories of algorithms. First, prioritization algorithms make an ordered list, say, of items you might want to buy or shows you might want to watch. Classification algorithms take data and put it into categories, perhaps automatically labeling photos for you, or isolating and removing inappropriate content from social networks. Association algorithms find links and relationships between things. Filtering algorithms isolate what is important (say, eliminating background noise so a voice-enabled assistant like Siri can "hear" what you're saying).[10]

Let's take a look at a quick example. A smart thermostat can take in pieces of information, such as the current temperature in a room, the time of day, and the weather forecast for the day; run that data through a series of steps; and determine how long and how high to run the furnace to reach a certain temperature.

(Smart thermostats can also take in data on household inhabitants over a period of time to determine what that certain temperature should be.) To incorporate our definitions above, the thermostat would be a type of robot, an example of AI, running an algorithm to achieve climate bliss.

Typically, experts divide AI into "narrow" AI and "general" AI, and our thermostat serves as an example of "narrow." A narrow intelligence can be taught or programmed to do something. A general intelligence can be taught or programmed to do anything.[11] For example, a robot vacuum is able to do one thing: clean up. Now, it certainly relies on various elements, including reading data on mapping a room and even issues like whether its bin is full. But it basically does one thing; no one is worried about their Roomba running away from home and joining the circus.

A general intelligence, on the other hand, is able to adapt and learn a variety of actions. Some thinkers describe artificial general intelligence (AGI) as being able to do anything that humans can do, but that is primarily because humans serve as the standard for the ability to adapt and adopt different ways of doing things and viewing the world. In all likelihood, an AGI would quickly surpass human abilities in many areas, thus rendering this comparison less useful.

We must take one more step in understanding AI to see the complexity and potential growth of this field. My introduction to robotics occurred when I was in second grade. My class went on a field trip to North Idaho College. We worked with some simple robots that could move and pick up items. Our challenge: Program the robots to navigate a course and retrieve an item. How far forward before a right turn? How much more before the next turn? Etcetera. Early advances in AI were made with this same method. Humans were creating algorithms, steps of instructions (vastly more complicated than my second-grade robot example), to allow robots and other smart machines to interact with their environment in desired ways. This is what most of us think about when we think about AI: human programmers teaching robots to do amazing things.

That is the way that it worked for a while. The history of AI provides helpful context in understanding what we should come to expect. Most people are aware of Moore's Law, which relates to the (generally accurate) rule of thumb that computer power doubles every eighteen months (this being related to the construction of microchips). Many assume that AI, since it relies on computing power, has increased at a similar, steady rate, for the last fifty years. That is simply not the case.

Artificial intelligence hit a series of walls—what is referred to as AI winters—for two main reasons. First, creating algorithms is really complicated, and some tasks were just too complex for humans to "crack" with the instructions they could embed in an algorithm. Second, computing power, speed, and storage are not infinite. In other words, we reached the outer limit of our ability to write complex instructions, and we didn't have the computing power to process them quickly and at scale. But this AI winter came to an end in the early 2000s.

Recent advances in AI—its emergence from "winter"—have occurred because of changes in these two areas. The second one is obvious: computers are faster and more powerful, and data storage is exponentially larger now. But the problem of creating algorithms was not as simple as waiting for Moore's Law to catch up. The advent of "machine learning" has led to the great growth in AI in the last ten to fifteen years. The "rule-based algorithms" that humans can create directly are being replaced by "machine-learning algorithms."[12] Basically, AI scientists have gone from creating algorithms for desired outcomes to creating learning algorithms: ways to set up an AI to learn for itself.[13] This occurs by "training" the AI on a set of real-world data. Through machine learning, the AI is able to identify patterns and create algorithms that match those patterns.[14] Once that is done, the AI can be fed pieces of data, and it will use its newly created algorithm to determine the relevant action or outcome. It is predicting what is most likely the proper outcome based on the dataset it used to determine the pattern and algorithm.[15]

Some argue that we should view AI not as intelligence but as prediction: an algorithm takes inputs and, based on patterns recognized within the data, makes a prediction on what the output should be. This could be a prediction about the answer to a question or a prediction about whether to turn or brake or a prediction about consumer behavior. AI will make prediction cheaper, which will mean businesses can do other things better. At some point, cheap prediction might change business models drastically.[16] One example of this is Amazon's work in "anticipatory shipping." There could come a point when Amazon's AI is so good at predicting what consumers want that it is more beneficial for them to simply ship things before people shop. It knows what you want; it sends it. Sure, sometimes it would be wrong, but once its correct predictions cross a certain threshold, it is actually more financially feasible for Amazon to ship and then allow returns on what it gets wrong. Their profit would be so high based on the increased number of items people would buy from them rather than elsewhere that it would be worth eating the costs of returns the times when it gets it wrong.[17]

We will look at some challenges below, but one jumps out here immediately. Machine learning is powerful, but part of its genius is that it works without having human programmers setting it up. In many cases, we're not really sure how these algorithms work. This can lead to biases or other problems. In other words, bad data can lead to bad machine learning, which can then perpetuate the same problems. As one scholar puts it, "When a new technology is as pervasive and game changing as machine learning, it's not wise to let it remain a black box. Opacity opens the door to error and misuse."[18] But the very nature of machine learning makes transparency difficult. Scientists often are not sure exactly how the AI has trained itself on the data set, or whether the data set itself harbors problematic assumptions.

We have not even begun to consider at what point this "artificial intelligence" becomes something meriting a new category. Technologists are already dreaming and planning about creating consciousness. As one puts it, *"techno-optimism about machine consciousness* ... is a position that holds that if and when humans develop highly sophisticated, general purpose AIs, these AIs will be conscious."[19] Schneider uses the "precautionary principle" to argue that if we have any reason to believe an AI to be conscious, we should extend the same rights to it that we would to other sentient beings.[20] In fact, she argues that we should be really careful *not* to create consciousness and should thus limit our development of AI. While some are concerned about AI developing to merit something mirroring human rights, others are looking to technology to change radically what humans are.

TRANSHUMANISM

If we imagine a Venn diagram, AI and transhumanism would be their own circles, but there would certainly be overlap. We need this image, because we do not want to assume that all AI is part of transhumanism, nor do we want to assume that transhumanism is only about merging humans with AI. Both are bigger, but they are related. And, as we will see later, they produce some of the same existential quandaries for us.

At root, transhumanism is about harnessing a broad range of enhancement technologies in order to bootstrap humans to the "next step" in the evolutionary process. Lennox quotes a character in Dan Brown's novel *Origin* who speaks this way about transhumanism: "New technologies . . . will forever change what it means to be *human*. And I realize there are those of you who believe you, as *Homo sapiens*, are God's chosen species. I can understand that this news may feel like the end of the world to you. But I bet you, please believe me . . . the future is actually much *brighter* than you imagine."[21] This quotation captures both the essence of transhumanism—changing what it means to be human—and also the inescapable religious dimension. Transhumanists, by and large, see all religions as opiates of the people distracting from pain and preventing or denigrating the very advances that provide the only "true" hope. (Yet this stance itself is a religious one!)

Even though religion is the *persona non grata* of transhumanism in most cases, more Christians are finding common cause with transhumanism. One group is more theologically progressive, proposing "post-anthropologies" that emphasize "posthuman subjectivity and relationality, multiple embodiments, and hybridity as its key components" and goes so far as to propose a "cyborg Christ" as the center of a posthuman Christology.[22] Most evangelical Christians will not find such proposals alluring due to their radical theological innovation. Theological engagement with such groups will invite further research and thought from evangelical theologians and ethicists, but this response remains mostly peripheral among Christian responses to transhumanism.

However, a growing number of Christians identify with the transhumanist movement and seek to support it theologically without going quite as far in theological innovation.[23] "Christian Transhumanists" have founded an organization and gather in an annual conference. Engaging their thought is more important at this stage because their arguments and thinking are more likely to gain traction in evangelicalism broadly.

A Christian Transhumanist is "someone who advocates using science and technology to transform the human condition—in a way consistent with, and as exemplified by, the discipleship of Christ."[24] They choose to use "transhumanism" intentionally, believing that it provides a touchpoint for conversation with leading-edge thinkers in science and technology. According to their website, "[Transhumanism] originates with Dante in 1320, winds through Christian history, and is picked up in the work of Jesuit priest and paleontologist Pierre Teilhard de Chardin. Teilhard's friend Julien Huxley uses the term in 1957 in attempt to define a philosophy of humanity's ongoing transformation. This leads to secular transhumanism, as it is understood today."

Further, the group thinks that it can "promote positive engagement between Christianity and the leading edges of scientific and technological thought."[25]

The group's statement of faith is fairly short but important: "As members of the Christian Transhumanist Association:

1. **We believe that God's mission involves the transformation and renewal of creation** including humanity, and that we are called by Christ to participate in that mission: working against illness, hunger, oppression, injustice, and death.

2. **We seek growth and progress along every dimension of our humanity:** spiritual, physical, emotional, mental—and at all levels: individual, community, society, world.

3. **We recognize science and technology as tangible expressions of our God-given impulse to explore and discover** and as a natural outgrowth of being created in the image of God.

4. **We are guided by Jesus' greatest commands** to 'Love the Lord your God with all your heart, soul, mind, and strength...and love your neighbor as yourself.'

5. **We believe that the intentional use of technology, coupled with following Christ, will empower us to become more human** across the scope of what it means to be creatures in the image of God. In this way we are Christian Transhumanists."[26]

At the root, "Christians who embrace transhumanism tend to believe that God is not entirely done with the work of creation but is actively creating even now."[27] *Creatio continua* in Silicon Valley.

Christian Transhumanists are interested in gaining a place at the table with technologists and futurists. This is needed because already "Christianity has lost a propaganda war—no matter what we conclude in the dialogue with transhumanism, we currently do not have the power to create any substantial change," because Christians are primarily external to the conversation, much like the "bioethicist" operates separate from and outside the role of the doctor.[28] Instead, Christian Transhumanists hope for an evangelistic impact of sorts, an increased impact of Christian ethics on the development of transhumanism.

Other Christians are more critical of transhumanism because of its dependence on deficient ideas of enhancement. As Jeffrey Bishop puts it, enhancement technology "is the achievement of a rather dark view of the world. It is the achievement of a sinister metaphysics, originating from relatively recent Western cultural ideas about the ambiguity of the body."[29] Furthermore, "Enhancement technologies and the whole transhumanist lifeworld cannot be merely accepted by Christians because at the heart of these transhumanist lifeworlds is a metaphysics and an ontology that is alien to Christianity."[30] Many Christian

Transhumanists identify the work of enhancement with the idea of being "co-creators" with God, who continues to create and work beyond the initial chapters of Genesis. But Bishop argues that the "co-creator" language is just a mask for an instrumental, utilitarian calculus that misrepresents the true nature of the world and is ultimately sub-Christian.[31] It sounds theological because it is rooted in Genesis and supposedly subordinated to God's work, but it, in fact, masks and defends a deficient and non-Christian approach to the world.[32]

Not only does transhumanism (and Christian Transhumanism) depend on a deficient metaphysics and ontology, it also promotes a paradoxical view of human nature. At the same time, "humanity is viewed as a formless work in progress, but also as fundamentally oriented toward desiring specific goods (namely, the goods of control and progress)."[33] Furthermore, there seem to be other paradoxes in play, such as the paradox between the language of artificial "intelligence," which operates based on some level of essentialist definition of "intelligence," but then the completely fluid approach to humanity as evidenced by transhumanism. I introduced this paradox at the start of this chapter, but hopefully now the substance of the paradox is clearer.

FAKE AND FUTURE "HUMANS": THE CHALLENGE TO THEOLOGICAL ANTHROPOLOGY

Now that we have introduced AI and transhumanism, we can explore some ways that these developments will challenge our understanding of what it means to be human and how that relates to the pursuit of human flourishing in our communities and societies. In other words, we will look not only at traditional "doctrinal" issues but also to the ethical problems that are interwoven with our attempt to follow Christ in the face of these particular opportunities and challenges.

1. *Expansion: I define myself.* Transhumanism subtly tempts us to believe that our humanity is infinitely malleable by playing on our hopes for technology-empowered improvement. While we might think that we do not buy into this, we cannot deny that this ethos surrounds us and impacts the way we think about the world. As ethicist Jason Thacker puts it, "Because technology is woven into every aspect of our lives, it will naturally revolutionize how we see ourselves and those around us."[34] If we are not intentional about countering a transhumanist narrative, we will find ourselves and our churches slowly changed by it.[35] AI and transhumanism are poised to influence any self-definition of humanity we might be prepared to create, intentionally or unintentionally.

2. *Reduction: I am data; I am my work.* We will not only see ourselves expanding what it means to be human and thinking we can define it for ourselves, but we also find that as more and more of the world is turned into data (or, perhaps, recorded as data), we risk reducing ourselves and our neighbors to sets of data.[36] As we find data about human behavior increasingly interesting and useful (see comments on commercial interests below), we should see this as a helpful development that can illuminate for us some of the tendencies and consistencies of those around us. However, we must resist the idea that data can represent a person, full stop. A human person will always exceed what can be recorded as data, because humans are more than simply physical bodies with chemical reactions that can be recorded and stored. In short, the coming years are going to present us with a vast increase in the data we can know about ourselves and others. We are going to be sold on these things as though they reveal who we "really are." This data will be enlightening and could be used for great good. But we must not act like or buy into the idea that it fully represents a person.[37]

And while this difficulty is related primarily to the development of machine learning and AI, it also connects with transhumanism. Advocates of "mind uploading" believe that there may be technological pathways to "upgrade" a person from a biological body to a synthetic one. All you need to do is capture all the data that make that person that person (which, according to many, is entirely housed within the brain, without remainder). One perplexing issue among transhumanists is the "reduplication problem": There can only be one you, so what happens when you make a downloaded copy?[38] In other words, even if you grant that a human can be reduced to a certain amount of data, and you can copy all that data out of a biological brain, what do you have when you are done? Two persons? A clone?

The development of AI will also impact our sense of ourselves because it will challenge human beings' sense of work. As erstwhile presidential candidate Andrew Yang argued,

> The lack of mobility and growth has created a breeding ground for political hostility and social ills. High rates of unemployment and underemployment are linked to an array of social problems, including substance abuse, domestic violence, child abuse, and depression.... This is the most pressing economic and social issue of our time; our economy is evolving in ways that will make it more and more difficult for people with lower levels of education to find jobs and support themselves.[39]

As he puts it later, "The challenge we must overcome is that humans need work more than work needs us."[40] These changes will not be isolated to jobs that we can immediately imagine robots doing—say, autonomous trucks replacing truck drivers—but may extend into jobs we had previously considered "safe" because we cannot yet imagine an AI doing them.[41] As one scholar puts it, "The threat to jobs is coming far faster than most experts anticipated, and it will not discriminate by the color of one's collar, instead striking the highly trained and poorly educated alike."[42]

Others argue that this line of thinking falls prey to three myths. These myths assume AI will follow a clear line of "progress" away from human involvement, eventually replacing all human jobs, and leading to a fully autonomous intelligence that can operate on its own. Instead, others believe there will be more creative ways of interacting with and utilizing AI, maintaining human control, jobs, and so on. The future, for these thinkers, is collaboration, not replacement.[43] They explain,

> ... for the vast majority of professions, the new machine will actually enhance and protect employment. We don't think, for example, that a single teacher or nurse will lose their job due to artificial intelligence. Instead, these professions will become more productive, more effective ... and more enjoyable. Workers in such professions will come to view the new machine as their trusted colleague.[44]

Such collaboration will raise a different set of questions for the meaning of human work, and we must be better prepared not to reduce our sense of humanity or our primary identities to our work.

3. *Big business: aligning commercial interests and the common good.* Another economic challenge presented by these developments emerges when we look beyond the impact on jobs to the way economic incentives drive the growth and implementation of AI and the implications these decisions have for society at large. We also must consider the impact that AI will have on the development of human economies and societies. In *The Big Nine*, Amy

Webb draws out how nine major corporations have a large impact on the direction of this field, and there are a variety of ways that it could turn out.[45] Christians must consider these elements, not only to hope for the ideal direction, but also to consider how best to minister to people in the midst of some of the less-optimistic future scenarios. Webb's basic argument is that the development of AI is currently controlled by nine main companies that could take it in three different directions depending on a variety of factors. She wants especially Western countries to invest more in AI so that it does not have to simply be about being quick to market and therefore making a profit for investors and shareholders.

As Webb lays out the nine companies, they fall into two main groups or tribes. G-MAFIA is the Western group (Google, Microsoft, Amazon, Facebook, IBM, and Apple), and it is primarily dependent upon the profit motive. They are well intended, but they have to focus on products that are quick to market and fit the consumeristic desires that would make them attractive. Meanwhile, the coding and so on that is going on right now will be incredibly important for the way AI continues to develop. Webb hopes that Western countries can help the G-MAFIA collaborate and be motivated and guided by the common good, not just profit.

The other group, BAT (Baidu, Alibaba, Tencent) are the Chinese companies controlled by that government. According to Webb, China is considering the long-term in a way the West is not. But their long-term goals are bent on world domination. They have more data to build on, so they are ahead in many ways.

Webb's three futures are interesting and well-developed. There is an ideal scenario, in which we learn to collaborate and align the development to a common-good future. There is a pragmatist scenario, in which Webb describes many "paper cuts" that lead to an adequate but still difficult future. The worst-case scenario is one in which China comes to dominate and ultimately eliminate the West. While only time will tell the outcome, this angle should encourage Christians to consider how to align technology with neighbor love, not only on the individual level, but also in how we hope and work to see technology deployed in our societies. The common good must be a human good and one rooted in a true sense of human flourishing.

4. *Surveillance and privacy; policing and justice.* Another way that the technology of algorithms becomes more problematic in societies is when combined with machine learning. As noted above, machine learning takes a known data set and then teaches itself how to create an algorithm that can work with future data points for accurate predictions. So, for instance, you could "give the computer" a dataset on criminal statistics that pull in all sorts of factors, including verdicts. Once it teaches itself by interpreting patterns, you can plug in other data, let it work, and it'll give you results that fit the pattern of the original data set. Such systems are used in policing (to determine which areas of a city to patrol more carefully) and in sentencing (to determine how likely a particular person is to re-offend). The problem is that no one knows how it works. For instance, an algorithm built via machine learning for criminal justice could be racist, relying overtly on race or racial signifiers in sentencing. If no one knows how it works because it is too complex, there is no way to evaluate the ethics of the way it is making decisions.

One of the most profound questions for AI, I think, is how to make machine learning ethical, if we can. One of Hannah Fry's most helpful ideas is the notion of "algorithmic regulation":

> Should we insist on only accepting algorithms that we can understand or look inside, knowing that taking them out of the hands of their proprietors might mean they're less effective (and crime rates rise)? . . . In part, this comes

down to deciding, as a society, what we think success looks like. What is our priority? Is it keeping crime as low as possible? Or preserving the freedom of the innocent above all else? How much one would you sacrifice for the sake of the other?[46]

Or would such regulation grind development and profit to a halt?

These issues weigh heavily in the actual pursuit and prosecution of justice, but they also impact our overall understanding and expectations of privacy. In her book *The Age of Surveillance Capitalism*, Shoshana Zuboff reveals how companies are built on collecting, analyzing, selling, and utilizing data.[47] This issue of surveillance ties in with the issues related to how AI can be turned more toward the common good rather than merely short-term financial interests. Easy answers aren't options here, but we must be ready to consider how viewing humans primarily as data, building companies to turn that data into profit, and the ubiquitous surveillance it relies on impacts our understanding of what it means to be human.

5. *Warfare and world domination.* Of course, ad companies using surveillance and AI might end up being the least of our worries. As Vladimir Putin said in 2017, the country that takes the lead in AI will rule the world.[48] But why?

To understand the current developments in this, we need to rewind to the ways AI has developed. Kai-Fu Lee explains the new era in AI by tying it to AI's history and then putting all of that in a political context. Basically, there were two camps: rule-based approaches (which sought to program algorithms) and neural-network approaches (machine learning and, ultimately, deep learning). As noted earlier, AI research has gone through "winters," when development is slow. Deep learning is narrow AI, which draws from data in one field for use to achieve a specific outcome. Basically, in the mid-2000s neural networks research made a leap forward and then proved better in competition in 2012.[49] This leap puts us into the age of implementation.

Neural networks need three things: data, computer power, and the work of strong engineers.[50] Computing power and engineers are easier to get. What is going to make the difference going forward is access to data. China is way ahead on this front because their internet has developed differently and has gobbled up so much more data on so many more people. All of this data can be fed into innovative algorithms for implementation. We have shifted from the discovery phase (figuring out how it works) to the implementation phase (applying it in a variety of ways); from the age of expertise (when we need experts to develop the theory) to the age of data (the neural networks work; they just need more data). While the West had advantages in the early stages of development, now China has the clear edge.[51]

But how might this tie into, not only economic advantage, but ruling the world? Paul Scharre served in the military and has been involved with policymaking regarding autonomous weapons. His book *Army of None* wrestles with "lethal autonomy" and how nations should approach that, given that AI is getting faster and faster, but warfare requires an understanding of context that seems to require a human "in the loop." He is not against using AI, but he warns against a rush to autonomous robot killers. These are questions we must face now because the technology is already available to make many of these things happen. What policy can limit this on an international scale? More than ninety nations have drones patrolling the skies, and more than thirty already have defensive supervised autonomous weapons.[52] The Israeli Harpy drone has already crossed the line to full autonomy: It "can search a wide area for enemy radars and, once it finds one, destroy it without asking permission. It's been sold to a handful of countries and China has reverse engineered its own variant."[53] As Scharre puts it, "AI is emerging as a powerful technology. Used the right way, intelligent machines could save lives by making war more precise and humane. Used the wrong way, autonomous weapons could lead to more killing and even greater civilian casualties."[54] We should not underestimate the significance AI will play in future global conflicts and balances of power.

6. *The limitations*. We should certainly be wary of the many ways that technology could go wrong. At the same time, we should be wary of too much hype. A robust doctrine of humanity reminds us that humans are the crown of God's creation. This does indeed mean we can do great things, but we should not expect our own creations to do everything. One realm to consider, even from a secular perspective, comes down to meaning and value. As Scharre explains, "Machines can do many things, but they cannot create meaning. They cannot answer these questions for us. Machines cannot tell us what we value, what choices we should make. The world we are creating is one that will have intelligent machines in it, but it is not for them. It is a world for us."[55] We might want to situate that sentiment a little more theologically, but at its root we are reminded of the limitations of our technology and our responsibility to orient not only the tools but the culture around the tools in a way that honors the kingdom of God rather than building the idolatrous kingdom of man.

CONCLUDING WITH PERSONHOOD

Where do we go from here? There are many possible routes to address AI, transhumanism, and the challenges and opportunities they raise from a Christian perspective. We could talk about the *imago Dei* in Genesis, the prohibition of idolatry throughout the Bible, the prophetic call for justice, Jesus' teachings on caring for the marginalized, or the Great Commission's charge to make disciples. In *2084*, John Lennox turns to the book of Revelation for insight.

But what about considering personhood, seeking a better understanding of how we can know a person when we "see" one? This idea can help us notice the difference between humans and artificial intelligences, as well as the false promises of transhumanism. While we're used to the language of personhood in a theological context, its use in a secular context is already growing in significance in relation to these challenges. Susan Schneider asks the question, "What is a person?" in her book *Artificial You: AI and the Future of Your Mind*. She goes on to highlight four main theories before roughly combining two of them to argue for ways that personal existence could persist outside the physical brain. Going into her argument would take us too far afield at this point,[56] but this shows that the question of personal existence is tied into these questions of what exactly a person is and how that relates to the material world and the "digitizable" world. Here we are, back at the doctrine of humanity.

Secular approaches to AI and transhumanism have to make a call on what it means to be a person because they must explain whether AIs should be considered persons, and they must also explain how some of these radical extensions of "life" would still be the same "person." But they actually lack the ability to provide a solid definition. They lack this because they refuse to allow God to speak, and they also lack it because they are pulled in opposite directions. Techno-utopians insist on essential definitions of things like "intelligence," but they resist any essential definition of "human" or "person," because the whole transhumanist project is built on exceeding and improving everything, which resists the idea of preserving any "essence."

As Christians, we must develop a strong doctrine of humanity not only to guide our use of particular technologies for ourselves (the temptations associated with transhumanism) but also in how we consider, evaluate, and "treat" emerging technologies (AI).

One chapter of a book cannot provide a robust enough treatment of the doctrine of humanity. But we can start, and we can point in directions of further development. I would like to propose one quick litmus-test question for evaluating whether or not something is or is not a person. Can it make or break a covenant with God? To be a person is to be one who can enter covenant with God. Or, perhaps we might say, to be a person means to be able to exist in obedience or disobedience to the triune God. As Michael Horton puts it, "Can there be any doubt that human beings are uniquely suited among the creation to be covenant partners with God?"[57] If we develop our understanding of the image of God into a series of capabilities, we might very well see that AI can replicate many of them. Some sort of transhumanist intelligence built off a copy of a biological brain might also be able to replicate some. But does that make either of those *things* into *persons*? I do not think so, because personhood is ultimately given by God, the Creator, to those he calls into relationship with himself for his glory. We can only acknowledge that we have received this gift; we cannot create it ourselves.

We could also recast this litmus test with the question the Gospel writers put before us, reminding us that Jesus asked, "But who do you say that I am?" While an AI might be able to answer with facts or even repeat statements that sound like praise, only a person can give and live by Thomas's later exclamation: "My Lord and my God."

PART 3

FOR OUR CULTURAL CONFUSION

FAITHFUL LIVING IN A CULTURE OF CONFUSION

John Stonestreet

IN 2018, EVEN BEFORE THE COVID-19 PANDEMIC BEGAN, Americans witnessed a troubling trend arising: it was the third year in a row that the average life expectancy for an American male went down.[1] The last time in American history where life expectancy declined three years in a row was in 1915 to 1918, years that included World War I and the outbreak of the Spanish influenza. This means that throughout the rest of the tumultuous twentieth century, which includes the Great Depression, World War II, the Korean War, the Vietnam War, and the Cold War as only the most notable crises among many others, life expectancy continued to rise. Then in 2015 it dropped, and it just kept dropping.

Since 1915, of course, our ability to treat disease and to extend life through medical intervention has advanced in ways that people a hundred years ago would find unbelievable. Recalling that COVID-19 was not a factor in 2015 through 2018, we must ask, "What exactly contributed to the decline in life expectancy at a time of technological miracles?"

The two statistics that account for the change in life expectancy in the mid-2010s are increases in deaths by drug overdose and increases in suicide.[2] These are known as "deaths from despair," deaths from opioid addiction, mental illness, and depression—conditions that have become even more common in the wake of COVID-19-induced lockdowns. These deaths, which often claim the lives of the young, have become a regular feature of our culture of death.

Despair is not confined to opioid addiction and suicide. As of the time of this writing, Americans have suffered forty-nine shootings in public schools this year alone.[3] In 2021 and the first half of 2022, three grocery stores were the scenes of mass shootings. All too often, these tragedies become political footballs, with people scrambling to offer analyses that support some ideological cause or other. But looking at these trends, we can see, at the broadest level, a deep-seated desperation manifesting itself sometimes in opioid addiction, sometimes in suicide, and sometimes in violence, but always driven by a profound existential despair.

That despair manifests in another way too, one that may be harder to recognize because it receives massive social support. Think of it this way: would a healthy culture grounded in love of reality, life, and human dignity encourage its young people to mutilate their bodies, sterilize themselves, and become lifelong dependents on a cocktail of little-tested medications—all as part of their "search for their true selves?" The answer is obviously no, but that is what we are seeing happen all around us, and people who refuse to go along with the charade face social stigmas and even professional and personal consequences. This desperation that drives healthy young people to ruin their bodies is a feature of the culture of death.

When I received an invitation to share my thoughts on "faithful living in a culture of death" for this book, the immediate context was the *Dobbs* case at the Supreme Court. That case was the impetus for the Supreme Court to overturn *Roe v. Wade* in June 2022. *Roe* had alleged to find a right to abortion in the Constitution. In *Dobbs*, the justices returned the question of abortion to the states.

Suddenly, with this historic decision, the albatross that had been hanging around the neck of our nation, this legal decision that basically granted death on demand for the preborn, had a chance of being lifted off of us. *Roe* had been interpreted in a way that prevented states from placing limits on abortion; then all at once, in June 2022, there was a real possibility for state legislatures to protect the lives of the unborn.

That does not mean, of course, that the culture of death is suddenly over. Far from it. The message of *Roe* was that certain lives do not matter; it is a message that has now permeated every corner of our culture. Overturning *Roe* does not end the lie that is destroying our nation, for that lie is not merely a legal one. It is a spiritual one, and it will require spiritual means to overcome it, to truly combat the culture of death, and to restore a love of all life as a gift from God.

LAW FIRST OR CULTURE FIRST?

The relationship between law and culture is a compelling question, and different answers lead to different strategies for influencing society. Does law shape culture, or does culture inspire legal change? Chuck Colson often repeated and popularized a line first coined by Bill Wichterman that politics and law are downstream from the culture. This tends to be true, but not always.

For example, in the case of civil rights legislation, the law was upstream from much of the culture. Large swathes of American culture were not open to ending segregation, but the law advanced side by side with a handful of committed civil rights activists, and eventually the culture shifted. There can be a symbiotic relationship between law and culture, but sometimes it does not work out that way. The classic example of this is prohibition. Legally, prohibition went forward, but the culture did not support it. The compelling and winsome activists who carried civil rights legislation from law to culture, the dedicated behind-the-scenes citizens who prayed and labored for racial justice—prohibition had no such cultural champions. If a law is passed and the culture will not sustain it, then that law will not survive. Prohibition lasted only thirteen years in America.

Christians who have poured their energy into the struggle to secure legal protections for the unborn should attend to this historical lesson. Though *Roe* is at the root of much of our culture of death, overturning it will not end that culture. *Roe v. Wade* bears responsibility for the seeping poison of dehumanization. Our nationwide fascination with protecting abortion rights is, at its core, a fascination with having the right to choose who is human and who is not, who deserves to live and who does not. That is the same poison we see infecting those who shoot innocents in schools or grocery stores; it is the same poison that infects the person who condemns himself to death through opioids or suicide.

Even if states continue to pass legal protections for the unborn, that is not sufficient to create a true culture of life (though those state-level protections are crucial, and we should pray and work towards them). Even if states restrict gun access or pour money into the opioid crisis or do every number of the myriad policy things that politicians promise in every election season, it will not be sufficient. Legal protections are only secure if there are corresponding cultural protections, and that is where all Christians, in any walk of life, can serve God.

Now let me be clear: I do not intend to join the conversation about what it means to be "pro-life" versus "whole life." Much of that conversation is unhelpful and is an excuse for people to avoid admitting that abortion is never morally permissible. In a real sense, though, we cannot be pro-life unless we are whole life. The conversation we need to have as Christians is not whether we should attempt to protect the lives of the unborn now or whether we should focus our energy on other social issues. The conversation we need to have is how individual Christians can work for a culture of life in their day-to-day lives. This is not about a legal or a political victory; this is about the future of civilization.

Recently I heard Os Guinness describe our time as a "civilizational moment." He compared our days to a tsunami wave; a person out on the ocean in the midst of the wave may not realize just how catastrophic and consequential it is because the wave moves along somewhat stealthily underneath him. But the person on the shore can see it: a massive, destructive wall crashing down and bringing catastrophe with it. Guinness said that when we look back at the rise and fall of great civilizations, we—standing here on the shore—can see the gathering tsunami that led to their downfall. We see the economic or cultural or political or geographic or moral factors that crashed down finally and destroyed the civilization; but at the time, living in the midst of it, people did not always recognize the wave that threatened them with destruction.

The events we are seeing around us—from mass shootings to declining life expectancies to rising suicide rates—are not themselves the pivotal moments. These are not themselves the cause of our social unrest and misery. They are symptoms of a tidal wave that has been moving for a long time, under the surface, and is beginning to break on our nation, a tidal wave that we can call the "culture of death."

The danger is that we come to think that the signs and symptoms of this death-culture are normal. Abortions, shootings, opioid deaths, general despair—this has all become such a regular part of our culture that we do not feel the sense of shock and violation that we should feel. Instead, we tend to simply step into our ideological corners and tout some kind of policy response, like gun control or banning violent video games or restricting abortion. Those policy responses are not in themselves necessarily bad; when our laws do not cultivate a culture of life, we need to work to change that. But changing the law does not get to the heart of the issue.

THE SOURCE OF OUR DIGNITY

The core of the problem is that, for decades, our culture has undermined human dignity. It has detached the idea of human dignity from its true source in the *imago Dei*, the image of God. Cut off from its root, the whole concept has withered and is in danger of dying altogether.

Truly understood, the belief that every human being has inherent dignity because we are all created in the image of God has the capacity to create a culture of respect for *all* life. This respect can overcome class differences, sex differences, age and race and education differences, because if we are created in God's image, then every single human person bears a unique mark of God, and every person merits the respect and dignity due to that mark. But when we deny that our dignity has its origins in God's nature revealed through us, we must scramble to find some other source of dignity—and any source but God will prove divisive and corrosive. For example, if our human dignity comes from our pursuit of self-expression and self-fulfillment, then any form of self-expression must be celebrated—even if that expression defies reality. If our dignity comes from our identity as members of a certain group, we will instinctively see members of any other group as less digni- fied—and therefore less valuable—than ourselves. If dignity is something that we must earn, we descend into vicious power struggles like the ones we see unfolding in our culture today, where groups battle it out for the "dignity"—and the cultural pull—that comes with being considered "victims." Only when we trace our human dignity to our shared identity as bearers of the image of God do we find that this dignity brings unity and respect.

The cultural and legal tsunami threatening to break over us started with a spiritual earthquake deep beneath the surface of our culture. When we sundered our beliefs about our own nature from any understanding of God's nature, we started an earth-shattering reaction the scale of which we are just beginning to understand. But when did the earthquake start—and what can we do today to mend what has been broken?

Before we begin to answer these questions, we must take a step back and remember that no culture is perfect. In the biblical story of creation, fall, redemption, and restoration, the marks of the fall spread through all human institutions and structures— including cultures and nations. Even as Christ's death and resur- rection defeated sin and redeemed the world, he has not yet brought his kingdom to earth. We live in a strange in-between time, where we know that sin and death are defeated but we still live elbow-to-elbow with them.

So when we talk about restoring our culture, we are not trying to bring about God's perfect kingdom on earth through political, legal, social, or cultural means. We know from Christ's own words that his kingdom is not of this world, so no culture on earth will ever fully or perfectly express God's nature. Our goal cannot be a perfect culture.

That does not mean, however, that we sit back and do nothing. Far from it! Throughout Christian history, men and women of God have worked to bring justice, charity, and truth into their cultures, and God has blessed many of those efforts. The trick is this: our intention must be to serve and honor God, which may well include working for cultural restoration. If we pin our hopes on our cultures, we will be disappointed; if we labor to restore culture because we love God, we will be filled with joy and hope.

With all that in mind, what can we as individual Christians do?

BEING THE CHURCH

The first thing Christians must do is commit to being involved in the church. Christianity is not a one-on-one faith. Obviously, each Christian has a unique and personal relationship with God, and that relationship grows and deepens through individual prayer and contemplation of Scripture. But from the very beginning, Christianity has been a community-based religion. From the first chapter of Acts, we see the apostles gathering together, then going out into the world, then coming back together. Everywhere the apostles went, they formed communities; they encouraged new Christians to worship together. That gives us a model for the Christian life as one that is lived in Christian community—a community we call the church.

I know that this may irritate some Christians, because far too many of us have bought into the notion that we don't "need" church. That notion is, however, part of the overall dissolution of our culture. Church is the most important of the institutions Edmund Burke called "mediating structures." It is an institution that exists in between the individual and the state; it is not a political institution, but it is communal. It brings people into relationship with each other and gives them a clear sense of meaning and significance for their day-to-day lives and activities.

In America today, however, we no longer believe that we need these kinds of mediating institutions. We believe that as long as we have absolute freedom to do what *we* want to do as individuals, and a government that is constantly solving more and more of our problems for us, we will be fine.

Let me offer an example of what I mean. During the COVID-19 pandemic, government officials across the nation ordered churches to shut down. They called churches and spiritual centers "nonessential services." That itself is not the core of the problem. The problem is that everyday Christians agreed with them that the church is not essential. Not only did Christians consent to their churches being closed for several months, but once the bans were lifted and churches reopened, many Christians chose not to return right away. And now, years later, huge numbers of churches across the country report 30 percent to 40 percent decreases in attendance since before the pandemic. This indicates that many Christians secretly thought that church was not all that important; the pandemic merely gave them an excuse to let church fall out of their lives.

When we stop attending church—when we stop gathering in a community of God's people to hear God's story—something else will fill the void. Some other story will creep in. And slowly, or not so slowly, our thinking will shift from looking at our culture through God's eyes, through the lens of God's story that we experience at church, to looking at God through our culture's eyes.

That leads us to the second thing Christians must do in order to begin cultural restoration. We must acknowledge sin. This is the part of God's story that our culture struggles with the most: the reality that sin is a part of the world, and that each and every one of us feels a pull deep inside—call it total depravity, call it original sin, call it concupiscence—away from God. Every person must choose whether to follow his own inclinations or to submit to God's will. But our culture rejects that truth; our culture says that only by following our own inclinations can we be happy. That is a fundamental disagreement between the story of our culture and the story of our God, and Christians have a responsibility to work unceasingly to bring their own lives into accordance with God's story—even if that means going against the culture.

Cornelius Plantinga, longtime professor at Calvin Seminary, wrote a book called *Not the Way It's Supposed to Be: A Breviary of Sin*, in which he reminds Christians that we need to think about sin as a real and active enemy. In his book *The Road to Character*,[4] columnist David Brooks observed that the only time we use the word *sin* anymore is when we are talking about desserts. Dr. Plantinga reminds Christians that sin is a real foe, one that threatens to keep souls from God. Of course, he also says that sin is a defeated foe because Christ stripped sin of its victory by his death on the cross. But that foe, despite its defeat, still kicks and struggles, and we cannot become casual about it.

This is the framework in which we must consider the cultural moment we find ourselves in and the cultural realities that surround us. Our culture of death is not accidental or incidental context in which Christians live out our calling. Restoring that culture and redeeming the particular sin-pocked corners of it becomes a calling itself.

This is what we see in Paul's wonderful apology for the existence and nature of God on Mars Hill, recorded in Acts 17. In that apology, Paul takes his setting—classical Athens—and transforms it into his calling, which is to send out the gospel to the Gentiles. The particular Gentiles he is speaking to are Epicurean and Stoic philosophers. Epicureans and Stoics have very different understandings of reality, and specifically of the gods. In an Epicurean framework, the gods have lost interest in human affairs. They have no engagement with human history. This is

FAITHFUL LIVING IN A CULTURE OF CONFUSION • *195*

why Epicureanism looked so much like hedonism; in the words of Solomon (or centuries later, Dave Matthews Band), "Eat, drink, and be merry, for tomorrow we die." Stoics had an exact opposite view, in which the gods controlled every detail of life. Free will itself was an illusion. In both of these settings, the Christian story of creation, fall, redemption, and restoration was radical.

The philosophers asked Paul to speak about Christ and the resurrection. But Paul actually began with creation, telling them that the God who created everything determines the exact times that people live in "the boundaries of their dwellings" (Acts 17:26 NKJV; see also 17:22–31). In other words, it is no accident that we find ourselves in this time and in this place. Our setting is our calling.

All this makes it clear why Christians must be connected to the church—because unless we find our meaning and our grounding in something besides the culture, we will lose our footing. We will begin to think of the culture as merely our setting, merely the water in which we swim and the air through which we breathe, when the truth is that our culture is the realm we are called to restore. But in order to restore something, we have to have a vision of what we are restoring it *to*.

THE STORY AND OUR MOMENT

If we want to equip Christians to live faithfully in our current cultural moment, we must begin by grounding Christians in what is beyond our current moment: the story God has written, the story we are all living. That story transforms the way we approach our culture. When we find our meaning in God's story and not the culture's, we just live differently.

Let me share an example. Each summer I speak for Summit Ministries, a wonderful organization based in Manitou Springs, Colorado. Summit provides worldview training for high school and college students from across the country. I met a group of freshmen and sophomores from Oklahoma Christian University, many of whom were studying nursing and pre-med. One of the topics that came up during the week was how people going into the medical profession right now are going to be spending tens of thousands, maybe hundreds of thousands, of dollars for their education, and Christians going into the medical field will very likely face some ethical dilemma in the course of their career, where they run the risk of being fired or being stripped of their certifications.

Recently I had the honor of meeting Jack Phillips and Barronelle Stutzman, both of whom have poured their lives into becoming excellent at what they do: baking cakes and designing flowers, respectively. But despite everything they did to become good at their crafts, eventually they faced the choice: whether to live from God's story or to acquiesce to another story.

Not everyone will face that choice. But more and more Christians in the days ahead certainly will. When we think about our cultural moment as not merely an incidental context in which we do our jobs but as a calling where we can "work out our salvation in fear and trembling" (see Phil. 2:12), we begin to understand our jobs differently. Career is not a source of meaning in itself; it only makes sense in relation to God.

So how do we become people who can face something as grueling as job or career loss with joy and hope? It is only possible if we live in a framework of restoration. I want to explore that framework in terms of four questions.

The first question is this: "What is good that we can celebrate and promote?" This is a chance for Christians to correct a widespread misunderstanding: Christians do not believe that the world is bad. Christians believe that the world is a fallen good. That is a fundamental difference. Do we believe that the biblical account of reality starts in Genesis 3 or in Genesis 1? If God's story of humanity truly starts in Genesis 1, we know that there are good things in the world. Some of these good things come out of creation itself: the beauty, the innovation, the cleverness. Just as all truth finds its source in God, it is also the case that all goodness finds its ultimate source in God who is good. Whenever we see something good and beautiful and praiseworthy, Paul tells us to think on those things. Christians have a responsibility to seek out the good in the world, to celebrate it, protect it, and promote it. Simply acknowledging that life is good, that the world is full of goodness, is a strong tonic against the culture of despair.

The first question, "What is good in the world that we can acknowledge and uphold?" The second question is, "What is evil in the world that we can confront and resist?" God in his grace sometimes allows his people to overcome a certain evil more or less completely. Consider how race-based slavery, once a worldwide and almost universally accepted norm, is now unthinkable in the West. This was the result of tireless effort from many people of faith across generations, and God blessed that work. It is our prayer that God sees fit to deal this way with abortion, and with such practices as cross-sex hormones for children and mutilative transgender surgeries. Christians do not seek merely a society where these destructive practices are illegal; we seek to build a culture where they are unthinkable.

Speaking out against evil is difficult and often discouraging. In the fight against race-based slavery, generations of abolitionists worked for their whole lives and died without seeing the horrible practice ended. When we resist evil, we must not do it because we assume we will win. We must do it because it is the right thing to do. This is where it is key to recall that *sin has already been defeated*; no matter how bleak things may look in our lifetimes, the battle is already won.

The third question is an exciting one. Once we have proclaimed good and spoken out against evil, we get to ask, "What is missing that we can innovate?" Think of artists and entrepreneurs who look at the world and see what's not there and then work to bring that thing into existence. That is what Christians can do.

In fact, this is what Christians have done since the beginning. Very early in the history of the church, Christians like St. Augustine, Tertullian, and others began gathering together the best of human thought and innovating with it, incorporating it into the story God revealed to us through his Son, and offering it back to a culture that desperately needed it.

Here is just one example of how this looked for the church in its early centuries. In recent years, there has been a remarkable shift in scholarship about the early church's relationship with the pagan world. The progressive secular narrative is that the pagan world was sexually free and expressive, and the early church ruined all that by imposing hard-and-fast rules like marriage. That narrative is simply false. A number of scholars, most recently Tom Holland, have argued persuasively that the real narrative goes like this: Rather than pagan culture being a place of freedom and fulfillment, pagan societies had become so sexually brutal, so abusive, especially for women and children, that people were desperate for a new approach to sexuality. When Christianity appeared with its ideas of marriage and virtue and chastity, which set up safeguards for women and children and curbed rapacious sexual appetites, pagan cultures came to see those ideas as life-giving, powerful, holistic, and freeing in their own right.

This opens a fascinating train of thought: What are the notions of twenty-first century America that are as brutal, as abusive, as reckless as pagan sexuality was? And how can Christianity offer a truly edifying, dignifying response to those notions? This flips the narrative on its head; rather than being prudish and stuffy, Christians who resist trends like abortion and gender identity theory position themselves to offer hope and meaning.

And then finally, the fourth question, "What is broken that we can restore?" The New Testament is full of *re-* words: *renew, restore, redeem, repent, reconcile*. That prefix *re-* means "to go back; to return to an original place; to go home, in a sense." Thus, the Christian mandate is one of bringing wholeness to what has been broken.

One very practical way Christians can do this is by defending the body. Since the beginning, the church has had to resist Gnosticism, or the idea that the body is inherently evil and the "real essence" of a person is separate from his or her body. That idea has reared its head in different forms all throughout Christian history. Today, it manifests as disembodied pietism. Many believers think that the "real essence" of our Christian faith and practice is disembodied; they believe that they can love Jesus with their hearts but remain completely disconnected from living out that love in the world. All around us, Gnosticism shows through in our culture's rejection of the good of the human body and the created order. This is where Christians must take their stand and declare to the culture our bodies are a gift from God, a unique and essential part of who we are, and that they are a good thing.

Dietrich Bonhoeffer encouraged his former seminary students every Christmas, even when he was in prison, exhorting them to have the courage to come out into the tempest of the living. In another letter, he made the statement that since he had been imprisoned, he had learned to recognize the "this-worldliness of Christianity."

Christianity is a very worldly religion. It alone among the great world religions is not actually an other-worldly religion. It is a this-worldly religion. Now, that might strike a lot of Christians as unbiblical, so let me explain what I mean. The story of Christianity begins with this world, with God creating humans and placing them into history and into physical reality, which he declares is good. In the High Priestly Prayer of John 17, Jesus prays, "Father, don't take them out of the world. Protect them from the evil one." To follow God and to glorify him requires us to see our existence in this time in this place as a calling, not merely an accident.

CONCLUSION

Faithful living in a culture of death will not be easy. Looking back over the four questions, it is clear that this whole effort must begin with a widespread commitment to reinstitute the cultivation of virtue among Christian young people. We cannot know what is good; we cannot resist what is evil; we cannot innovate; we cannot restore if we do not have a vision of a reality beyond what our culture offers. We cannot hope to return our culture to its home in God if we do not know that home ourselves.

But that home is a way of living. It is a way of living that sees our own personal good as intrinsically bound up with the good of those around us. It calls us to be accountable for our decisions, to uphold our vows, to lay down our lives for others. It is, quite simply, virtue. And virtue must be intentionally and actively formed.

This brings us back to where we started: forming communities that celebrate and honor life in a culture of death and despair. The church must do this. Christian communities and schools must do this. Christian families must do this. Every single individual Christian must do this. By giving ourselves this task of truly forming virtue—no matter how anti-cultural or unpopular this may make us—out of a spirit of joy and obedience, Christians have the opportunity to cast a vision of a life that is meaningful and fruitful. And this is a vision desperately needed in this time of cultural confusion.

APOLOGETIC APPROACHES FOR OUR CULTURAL CONFUSION

THE CHRISTIAN WORLDVIEW AND THE *IMAGO DEI*

Robert B. Stewart

THE TWENTY-FIRST CENTURY SHARES a number of similar features with the first century. Pluralism is prominent in both. In the first century, there were Jews, Greeks, Romans, and other Gentiles. There were Platonists (of many stripes), Stoics, Epicureans, and other adherents to philosophies. Worldviews were clashing in the first century, and they still are today. Today, there are metaphysical naturalists (especially the New Atheists), agnostics, and adherents of other world religions, to say nothing of theological liberals who deny central tenets of the Christian faith. The two centuries are alike in other ways. We see this in the New Testament.

In Acts 17, the gospel was well received in Thessalonica until some unbelieving Jews stirred up the populace to the point of violence. Paul and his company then went on to Berea where the Berean Jews carefully investigated Paul's message, and as a result, they believed the good news of the gospel. Unfortunately, the troublemakers in Thessalonica then came to Berea, stirred up the people, and Paul and his party once again had to depart.

In Athens, the gospel also received a hearing, but before a different audience. Paul was conversing with philosophers, specifically Stoic and Epicurean philosophers, in the agora, and though they initially believed him to be mistaken,[1] they brought him to the Areopagus to receive a fair hearing. As is usually the case in such situations, when Paul was finished, some mocked his message, some were undecided, and some believed (Acts 17:32–34). This was a remarkable success given the fact that the council of Areopagus had been founded on these words of Aeschylus: "When a man dies, the earth drinks up his blood. There is no resurrection."[2] In other words, the Athenians were predisposed to reject his message, yet they listened respectfully, and some, after hearing him, changed their minds. I wish twenty-first century North America were more like first-century Athens in this respect.

In both Berea and Athens Paul was received charitably yet critically, yet we should note one important difference between the two cities. In Berea he spoke primarily to Jews, along with some Gentiles who were sympathetic to Judaism, by appealing to the Scriptures (the Hebrew Bible). His audience then searched the Scriptures to see if what they heard was so. At the Areopagus Paul was speaking to Gentile philosophers who did not accept the Jewish Scriptures, so instead of appealing to special revelation, God's word contained in Scripture, he appealed to general revelation, God's word expressed through nature and reason.[3] In Acts 13, Paul and Barnabas were called as the first Christian missionaries; in Acts 17, Paul became the first Christian natural theologian. As any good missionary would do, Paul spoke to the Athenians in ways they could understand about things they cared about, and he quoted authorities that they respected.[4] Paul was wise in taking this approach. Though on occasion I have heard lay preachers criticize Paul for not beginning with Scripture when he addressed the Athenians, Paul's method was not only respectful but also effective: "But some men joined him and believed, among whom also were Dionysius the Areopagite and a woman named Damaris, and others with them" (Acts 17:34 NASB).

Christian apologists today should do the same. In other words, Christian apologists, like missionaries, must contextualize their message to ensure that their audiences understand and appreciate their message. Like first-century Athenians, many today, whose views on the human person are at odds with the Christian worldview, do not recognize the authority of Scripture.[5] So how should we seek to find connecting points with them? We must initially explore natural theology; and to that end we should appeal to science, especially to the hard sciences (for example, biology, genetics, chemistry, biophysics) to point to the work of God in nature.

THE IMAGE OF GOD AND OUR PRESENT CULTURAL MOMENT

The image of God factors into apologetics in important ways in relation to the cultural debates we are presently involved in concerning abortion, gender, and marriage. The obvious truth is that the cultural ground has shifted under the feet of the Christian apologist. This is nothing new. Christian apologetics has always been a missionary endeavor, and missions should always be a contextual discipline. When I was a recent convert and budding apologist in college in the late 1970s, the primary question for apologists was, "Are the central truth claims of Christianity true?" As a husband and a father to young children in the 1990s, however, the primary question was, "Isn't it arrogant to claim that your faith is the only true religion?" The focus had shifted from asking *if Christianity was true* to asking *if Christianity was the only truth*. Typically, my interlocutors happily conceded that Christianity was *true for me*, but insisted that there were many different truths. Today, the front-burner questions for the Christian apologist revolve around the *goodness* of Christianity. Many today view traditional Christians as bigots for claiming that marriage is what the Bible teaches, one man and one woman for life, rather than a flexible romantic relationship between two or more consenting adults. The claim that biology, not psychology, determines who is a man and who is a woman is seen as narrow-minded and mean-spirited. The crucial questions now are not at all about the truthfulness or uniqueness of Christianity, but rather the goodness of Christianity, or the character of the apologist.

The greatest cultural issues of our day—abortion, gender, and marriage—all revolve around the issue of what it means to be a human person. Such issues are not only about persons, they are also personal issues. They concern all of us; they impact your life and mine. They are not abstract or theoretical. In other words, they engage the heart as well as the head—they involve our emotions as well as our minds. Importantly, they go to the very heart of who each one of us is and who we are corporately. Changing the understanding of a person, of male and female, or of marriage is like manipulating DNA; one is radically restructuring one's culture.

Today, ours is a secular culture in a bad sense. In the sense that a variety of religions are worthy of respect and worthy of a religious-liberty defense, secularism can be a good thing. That sort of pluralism should be applauded. I am not speaking of that sort of secularism. The kind of secularization our culture currently embraces is the kind that requires the silencing of religious voices, or at least declaring that such voices are irrelevant.

In other words, we are governing as though God does not exist. We have gone from being neutral about religion in the public square to banishing religion from the public square. The result of this sort of secularization is that if God does not exist, then none of us bears his image. In this way, we have gleefully stripped ourselves of our own dignity. In our efforts to free ourselves from the constraints of a creator, we have made ourselves a little higher than the other beasts. Tragically, in seeking autonomy we have forgotten a lesson of the Holocaust. Before the Nazis began to experiment surgically on Jews, or to burn them in ovens, or gas them in the concentration camps, they first had to see them as less than fully human. Ironically, we have adopted this dehumanizing agenda with regard to ourselves.

We are presently at an odd point in history where information is more readily available than at any previous time—my phone contains more data than the first five computers that I owned combined—yet we lack the wisdom to productively use the information that we have. Simply put, knowledge is not wisdom, and information is neither knowledge nor wisdom. Yet we seem to be intent on living as if we all knew it all. Social media has made the world more connected than ever before, but social media has also made the world more immature—and aggressive—than at any time in history. All over the World Wide Web people regularly say things to one another that they would never say to each other in person. Opinions on important matters are expressed through memes. In an odd way, it is as though we have all gone back to high school, and the mean girls rule.

Romans 1, particularly verses 21–23, teaches us that when God is banished something else takes his place; when we reject God, we don't become atheists, we become idolators (atheism is simply a mental idol through which we worship ourselves). Human beings seem to be cursed with an almost infinite ability to create idols. The idol of our age is technology. We are creating ever more human-like machines. In making machines more and more like us, we also make ourselves more and more like machines. We should remember the lesson of James Cameron's movie *The Terminator* and tread carefully lest we invent a "Skynet" of our own.

We also seem to be incarnating the story of *Frankenstein*. The lesson of *Frankenstein* is that scientific technology cut loose from faith and ethics creates monsters. To be clear, I am not suggesting that those who have undergone gender reassignment surgery or those living in same-sex "marriages" or women who have had elective abortions are monsters—they are victims. The monster in *Frankenstein* is not the creature Frankenstein created, but rather Frankenstein himself, a scientist intoxicated with his discoveries, who believes that he can bring the inanimate to life yet never pauses to ask whether he should. The creature was one of Frankenstein's victims. Nothing can stand in the way of the idol of technology progressively taking over our lives. That is the problem with idols—idolators must serve them. One would think that we in the first quarter of the twenty-first century would remember the lessons of the twentieth century (in which most of us were born), yet it seems that the lessons of the Holocaust, Hiroshima, and chemical warfare, to name but a few examples of science and technology going wrong, have too soon been forgotten.

I may have been overly optimistic in saying that we are having a cultural debate. Perhaps a cultural food fight would be a more appropriate term for what we see taking place in Western culture today. Too many people refuse to reason; they simply accuse, condemn, and cancel (or "unfriend") those with whom they disagree. Many today refuse to debate these issues; instead they insist that they are settled—especially if the Supreme Court rules in a particular direction. They shout down disagreement and seek to have those who disagree with them silenced in the court of public opinion. This is neither intellectually legitimate nor mature. I fear for Western culture as a whole.

As Gregg Allison points out in his book *Embodied: Living as Whole People in a Fractured World*,[6] Gnosticism is alive and well in contemporary culture. I agree, and surprisingly, I think Rudolf Bultmann would too. Bultmann's article on *ginōskō* (knowing) is one of the most important entries in Gerhard Kittel's *Theological Dictionary of the New Testament*. In his article Bultmann described three ideas that characterize Gnosticism: (1) Metaphysical dualism, (2) Anti-Rationalism, and (3) Classification.[7] *Metaphysical dualism* privileges the mind or spirit over the material, and in particular the mind over the body and knowledge gained through the senses. *Anti-rationalism*, which must be sharply distinguished from non-rationalism, is the denial of knowledge gained through the senses or the physical sciences. *Classification* is the idea that there is an elite class whose members have deeper knowledge (*epignosis*) than the general population, and that the less insightful must learn from the enlightened class to benefit from their special knowledge.

Two of these Gnostic characteristics seem especially apparent in contemporary discussions of gender: metaphysical dualism (mind over body) and anti-rationalism (denial of biological knowledge). The privileging of mind over body seems apparent when one accepts that a person with an XY chromosome pair can actually be female simply because that person says that they feel like their gender has been misassigned. Anti-rationalism seems to be operative when one makes biology and genetics subservient to psychology. This seems to me to be nothing less than making science subservient to our individual feelings.

I recognize that many people feel conflicted when it comes to their bodies. I want to help them, but I believe that choosing to accept their first-person reports, when these reports conflict with genetics, is neither rational nor helpful.[8] One measure of a scientific hypothesis is the principle of parsimony, or Ockham's razor, which simply stated is, "All things being equal, the simpler solution is to be preferred." I am not denying that many people experience gender dysphoria, the sense of not being comfortable in their own bodies or with their own sex, but it seems to me that experience has taught us that our psychology is more likely to become confused than is our biology. This is particularly so when the hard science of genetics tells us A and the only support for $not\text{-}A$ is the first-person testimony of an individual's perception of himself or herself. Not only does accepting that a person is the victim of gender misassignment seem unscientific and irrational on such insubstantial evidential basis, it also seems very unloving to me.

Several years ago, a family member had a severe eating disorder. Her parents didn't say, "Of course you're fat if you think you are. We will support you in starving yourself, vomiting up most of what you eat, and abusing diuretics." Even though she swore to them that she "knew her own body," so they should leave her alone,[9] they didn't accept her first-person testimony based on her perception of herself because the relevant scientific measurements said differently—and because they loved her. They certainly did not suggest that she get weight loss surgery. They believed that science was right because a scale revealed her weight in a way that was measurable, testable, public, and objective, i.e., not susceptible to any individual's perception. After examining the evidence, their reasoned judgment was that she had a perception problem rather than a weight problem. Thankfully, after counseling, prayer, and time, she recovered and returned to a healthy weight.

Sadly, our culture seems intent on taking the anti-rational, and in my view, unloving approach to the issue of gender dysphoria.

Sadder still, it seems as though those who trumpet diversity will brook no disagreement on this point. The last word has not yet been spoken on this topic. But if the present trend continues, it's not difficult to imagine a time when speaking a contrary word will make one not only a pariah but also a criminal. We are not the first Christians to face this prospect.

CHRISTIAN PERSECUTION

First Peter was written to Christian converts who either were suffering persecution under the emperor Nero or were about to experience persecution for their faith. The Roman historian Tacitus claims that Nero made scapegoats out of Christians because it served his political purposes.

> Neither human resources, nor imperial munificence, nor appeasement of the gods eliminated sinister suspicions that the fire had been instigated. To suppress this rumor, Nero fabricated scapegoats and punished with every refinement the notoriously depraved Christians (as they were popularly called)....First, Nero had self-acknowledged Christians arrested. Then, on their information, large numbers of others were condemned—not so much for incendiarism as for their anti-social tendencies. Their deaths were made farcical. Dressed in wild animals' skins, they were torn to pieces by dogs, or crucified, or made into torches to be ignited after dark as substitutes for daylight. Nero provided his Gardens for the spectacle, and exhibited displays in the circus, at which he mingled in the crowd—or stood in a chariot, dressed as a charioteer. Despite their guilt as Christians, and the ruthless punishment it deserved, the victims were pitied. For it was felt that they were being sacrificed to one man's brutality rather than to the national interest.[10]

Few if any in Peter's audience had a Christian parent when they were born because the Jesus movement was less than forty years old—it was a fledgling position with very shallow historical roots.[11] The vast majority of his readers (and listeners, who would have been the majority of his audience because the New Testament epistles were meant to be read aloud to the congregation) were converts. Each of them had already paid a price for converting, whether they were Jews who believed that in their day YHWH had fulfilled his promise to Israel to send Messiah, or Gentiles who were leaving their religion or religions for another, which they believed to be the only true faith.

The important thing to grasp, with regard to Gentile converts, is that everybody in the Greco-Roman world was religious; in fact, most people worshiped multiple gods. Religious addition—worshiping one more god than you had before—was no big deal in the Greco-Roman world. But when those to whom Peter was writing became Christians, they did not merely add on another god, they rejected all previous gods in order to follow the one true God who had revealed himself through Jesus of Nazareth, a crucified Jew whom some said had been raised from the dead. By doing so, they made themselves outcasts primarily for one reason: *they were inflexible*.

Conversion was also a radical path for Jewish believers to take because in following Jesus they were saying that the long-awaited Messiah had finally come. But how many Messiahs could there be? Exactly one. In following Jesus, they were making a statement to all their Jewish friends and family who did not view Jesus as the Messiah. Family, that is, lineage was a very important thing in Jewish culture. So important, in fact, that the phrase "Lineage, Law, and Land" along with "Temple and Covenant" is a fair shorthand summary of first-century Judaism. Note how historical figures in the Hebrew Bible, what we call the Old Testament, were identified according to their family or tribe. For instance, in Philippians 3, Paul identifies himself as being of the tribe of Benjamin. One did not lightly walk away from one's family. By following Jesus as the Messiah, Peter's Jewish readers had in effect said to their family members who did not convert that they were not only mistaken but also unfaithful. If Jesus fulfilled the covenant, then those Jews who did not follow him were living under a false covenant.

In fact, Jesus himself demanded this. He was the one who gave them their regularly repeated ritual of the Lord's Supper. Every time they took the Lord's Supper, they affirmed that the shed blood of Jesus was *the cup of the new covenant*! This was a most serious assertion to make. Even baptism in Jesus' name marked them out as converts just as the Jewish baptism of Gentile converts to Judaism identified those converts as belonging to a new community, which walked a different path and followed a different God.[12] In these two ways, Jesus took two widely known Jewish rituals and reshaped them around himself. The Lord's Supper was a reshaping of the Passover meal, one of Israel's most sacred rituals. Baptism, which was around before Christianity, was a reshaping of the *mikva'ot*, Jewish ritual cleansing, which by the time of Jesus was one of the identity markers that converts to Judaism underwent, the other being circumcision. Have you ever wondered why the Bible says nothing about how to baptize or that nobody asked what John was doing when he came baptizing? The answer is that they already knew what baptism was. They did not understand, however, exactly what John's baptism or Christian baptism meant. Needless to say, to monkey around with the Passover and the *mikva'ot* was no small matter.

Through the ministry, death, and resurrection of Jesus, God had done a new thing in history. This new thing, which God had done through Jesus, called for an existential commitment on the part of all who heard of it. *Follow Jesus or not*. There was no comfortable middle path. Jesus himself had declared as much when he said that no man could be his disciple unless he was willing to take up his cross, leave everything behind (even to hate his own family members) and follow him (Luke 14:26–27, 33). Those who followed Jesus left everything behind to join a small fledgling community opposed by the majority religions of their day, religions that had power, prestige, and privilege. The majority religions also had the power to persecute Jesus' disciples. This was the position that Jesus' disciples found themselves in when Peter wrote to them. Simply put, they were following Jesus in a *pre-Christian* culture.

Disciples of Jesus are still challenged to live radical lives, to deny what the world clamors for, and to pay a price for their inflexibility. One difference, however, between twenty-first century believers and first-century believers is that we no longer live in a predominantly pre-Christian culture; we now live in a *post-Christian culture* that is rapidly becoming an *anti-Christian culture*. Disciples of Jesus still face the same challenge: count the cost of discipleship, and choose to follow Jesus or not.

THE IMAGE OF GOD AND THE CENTRALITY OF RELATIONSHIPS

Before Christian apologists can argue for the existence of God, the resurrection of Jesus, the deity and uniqueness of Christ, or the historicity of the Gospels, they must convince the culture that Christians have their best interests at heart. In other words, Christian apologists must be seen as people of good will. Apologists frequently give apologetics a bad name because too many of them resemble doctors with a bad bedside manner. Often, sound arguments are derailed by a lack of concern for relationships. All truly effective apologetic encounters depend upon relationships.

Apologists must always be aware that God's plan for them is that they not be "children, tossed here and there by waves and carried about by every wind of doctrine, by the trickery of people, by craftiness in deceitful scheming; but speaking the truth in love, we are to grow up in all aspects into Him who is the head, that is, Christ" (Eph. 4:14–15 NASB). Relationships do matter!

All truly significant human relationships depend in some sense upon the image of God. God is one and yet exists eternally as Father, Son, and Spirit. God is love—but love is not love if it is not expressed relationally. He is not simply a being who can have relationships; he is a being who is inherently relational, and who has eternally been in a relationship of love and mutual self-giving.

The image of God is what enables Christians to engage effectively in apologetics. In practice, apologetics is always a relational discipline. This is not always evident at first glance. Sometimes arguments are what one sees first. Other times one notices defeaters, i.e., an idea or evidence that either rebuts the beliefs of skeptics or adherents of other religions, or that undermines those beliefs and leads those who hold them to doubt the legitimacy of their beliefs. But apologetics *in practice*, as opposed to apologetics *in theory*,[13] always takes place within the context of a relationship of some sort. This is because, in practice, apologetics takes place between two or more human beings. We must never forget that every human being is made in the image of God.

MADE IN THE IMAGE OF GOD

The French philosopher Blaise Pascal, who was well aware of both humanity's greatness and disgrace, proclaimed, "What sort of freak then is man! How novel, how monstrous, how chaotic, how paradoxical, how prodigious! Judge of all things, feeble earthworm, repository of truth, sink of doubt and error, glory and refuse of the universe!"[14] Much earlier the psalmist asked, "What is man that You are mindful of him?" (Ps. 8:4 NKJV). One is struck by the grandeur of humanity's original state and the grotesqueness of his current condition in comparison. There is still, however, a qualitative difference between human beings and the rest of God's creation because only humans are made in the image of God. But of what does the image of God consist? Or what does it mean to say that humanity is made in the image of God?

While Christian theologians differ over what it means to be made in the image of God (Gen. 1:26–28), it has been pointed out in earlier chapters that the dominant position throughout Christian history has been that the image of God is to be identified with an ontological property or characteristic possessed by humans. This is sometimes referred to as the substantive view, though the relational and functional views must also be considered in our overall understanding.[15]

God does endow us with certain inherent characteristics and abilities because he made us in his image. Yet I also believe that an understanding of the image of God is complex rather than monistic in nature. Simply put, to some degree we do all these things because we bear God's image. We have the capacity to reason because we are made in the image of a rational God. We can have relationships with God and others because we bear the image of a God who is inherently relational. We can represent God because we bear his stamp. We are creative because we are made in the image of our Creator God. Despite the fact that we do not do any of these things in the same way as God does, we can do them, nonetheless. Human beings are inherently different than animals; we don't simply *function* differently than animals. The source of human uniqueness is our being made substantively in the image of our Creator.

Understanding the relational basis for Christian apologetics allows our apologetic efforts to be effective, when God's Spirit is working in his mysterious way. To paraphrase Augustine, this is because God has made us for himself, and our hearts are restless until they find their rest in him.[16] Christianity is unique among the world's religions in that Christianity teaches that humanity's key problem is not a lack of knowledge or a lack of ritual obedience, but rather a broken relationship with the Creator. Christianity also declares that though God was the wronged party, he took it upon himself to repair the relationship, and in so doing to set fallen creation right, including fallen humans made in his image.

ADVICE FOR CHRISTIAN APOLOGISTS

Knowing that all human beings are made in the image of God should condition how apologists engage with others in apologetic encounters. Yet many apologists behave as though apologetics is simply knowing answers to hard questions, but it is far more than that. At its heart apologetics is relating to nonbelievers—and believers struggling with their faith[17]—in such a way that you clearly and winsomely make a case for Christ that hears and addresses their objections or concerns and helps them to see the gospel for what it is—good news—so that their lives are transformed, or their faith is strengthened.

According to 1 Peter 3:15, the keystone New Testament verse for apologists, the most important thing in Christian apologetics is to "sanctify Christ as Lord in your hearts" (NASB; the only command in 1 Peter 3:15). In my experience, however, the stress is typically laid on what follows the command to sanctify Christ as Lord, "always *being* ready to make a defense to everyone who asks you to give an account for the hope that is in you." Peter knows that if Christ is Lord in the hearts of Peter's audience, then they will be prepared to defend their faith because we all defend what we value. The important thing to note is that the latter clause is the logical consequent of the former. The implied logic works thus:

1. If Christ is Lord in your hearts, then you will be prepared to defend and commend your faith.[18]
2. Christ is Lord in your hearts.
3. Therefore, you will be prepared to defend and commend your faith.

This is simply the classical syllogism known as *modus ponens* (the way of positing). But every syllogism whose major premise is based on a conditional, as *modus ponens* is, could also work out negatively, in a classical syllogism known as *modus tollens* (the way of removing). In this case, *modus tollens* would run thus:

1. If Christ is Lord in your hearts, then you will be prepared to defend and commend your faith.
2. You are not prepared to defend and commend your faith.
3. Therefore, Christ is not Lord in your heart.

It is fallacious to think that the consequent guarantees the antecedent. After all, an atheist actor could be prepared to defend the Christian faith for a role in a movie, but that would not guarantee that Christ was Lord in his or her heart. Simply put, apologists must never divorce the task of apologetics from discipleship and obedience to Christ.

Crucially, 1 Peter 3:15 concludes with this: "But with gentleness and respect." This often-neglected clause cries out for our attention. We must never forget that even those who attack the faith are God's image bearers. Have you ever thought seriously about the fact that Adolf Hitler was made in the image of God? Or that Stalin was made in the image of God? We dare not treat disrespectfully those who question, or even attack, the faith. We don't even have the right to treat our enemies as our enemies. Jesus put it this way in his Sermon on the Mount:

> You have heard that it was said, "YOU SHALL LOVE YOUR NEIGHBOR and hate your enemy." But I say to you, love your enemies and pray for those who persecute you, so that you may prove yourselves to be sons of your Father who is in heaven; for He causes His sun to rise on the evil and the good, and sends rain on the righteous and the unrighteous. For if you love those who love you, what reward do you have? Even the tax collectors, do they not do the same? And if you greet only your brothers and sisters, what more are you doing than others? Even the Gentiles, do they not do the same? (Matt. 5:43–47 NASB)

Notice that our behavior toward our enemies is to be like that of the one in whose image we—and they—are made, and that by loving them we show ourselves to be sons and daughters of God. How we treat others shows how well we understand what it means to be made in the image of God, but even more how much we love God. What better apologetic than this can there be?

In my experience, skeptics are often bad theologians, which should not surprise us. But surprisingly, I also find that some apologists are bad theologians, which is truly a shame. I often tell my apologetics students that the single best skill they can develop to be an effective apologist is to be a good theologian, whose beliefs are based on a knowledge of Scripture, sound reason, and a proper awareness of and appreciation for Christian tradition.[19]

One reason that unbelievers sometimes reject our efforts to commend the gospel is that what they reject is not the biblical gospel or the Christian worldview. It may not have been contrary to the biblical gospel, but it was too thin. They were presented with a short list of truths that left out important components of the biblical worldview and focused on others in such a way that consequents were seen as primary and peripheral parts were seen as central, while all along studiously avoiding the heart of the matter, which is loving and knowing God and living a life directed and empowered by the Holy Spirit. It is no wonder that many react to a bare plan of salvation as though they are uninterested. What is there in it, other than the eternal nature of the policy, that is different from any other life insurance pitch?

Jesus said that the greatest commandment in all the law is to love God (*love* God—not serve him, not understand him, not teach his Word—love him!) with all that you are. The Great Commission is not the main thing. It is certainly important, but it's not the main thing. Loving God is. The second is like it: Love your neighbor as yourself. Have you ever wondered why Jesus added a second command to the first? Jesus mentioned the second because the two are inseparable. We show how much we love God by how much we love others. Loving God entails loving others. One thing that we must remember is that love does not mean giving people everything they desire—that's bribery; true love is doing what is genuinely in the best interest of the other person.

My advice to apologists is to love: love God above all else, then love your neighbor as yourself because you recognize that you both bear the image of God. Then, because you love God and neighbor, respectfully challenge your unbelieving neighbors with the truth, and give them reasons to believe. By doing so you will show yourself to truly be an adopted child of your heavenly Father. I also suggest that you allow those two loves to guide all that you do for the glory of God and the good of others who have been created in the image of God.

CONCLUSION

THE IMAGE OF GOD AND
THE DIGNITY OF HUMANS

Daniel Darling and Lauren McAfee

WHO AM I? WHY AM I HERE? What is my responsibility to my neighbor? These questions are at the heart of our cultural confusion in the West. Technological advancement, the sexual revolution, and the flood of atrocities that cross our social media timelines every day provoke us to return once again to the ethic that has transformed countries and communities: the image of God.

The book of beginnings, the book of Genesis, in the Bible is filled with significant teachings that lay the groundwork for the rest of Scripture. Genesis is a book that stands out with its importance for proclaiming God's will and the role of humans in God's creation.[1] In the first chapter of the first book of the biblical canon, the significant concept of *imago Dei* is initially made known as the first man and first woman are created in God's image and likeness (Gen. 1:26–27). It's not an exaggeration to say that the idea of human dignity, so ubiquitous in our common cultural language and expressed by people possessing a variety of philosophical and religious commitments, has its origin in the Christian story.

Historian Timothy Shah writes that "apart from the Christian Scriptures, classical civilization lacked the concept of human dignity."[2] Most recently, historian Tom Holland has made the persuasive case that Christianity lives unconsciously at the root of most modern notions of the value of human life.[3] Apologist Glen Scrivener, among others, has made a similarly persuasive case.[4] There are, of course, elements of the *imago Dei* in other philosophies and religions, but the most robust vision of what it means to be human originated and is contained in the story the Bible tells.

In his book *Neither God nor Beast*, ethicist Gilbert Meilaender writes that when the landmark Universal Declaration on Human Rights was created, the drafters understood their need for such language, but struggled to understand its basis:

> While these philosophers were able to agree on many particular claims, they were perhaps, unsurprisingly, unable to agree on "why" these claims were true—unable that is, to develop any shared vision of human nature or the human person on which such claims could be based.[5]

Meilaender goes on to declare that there is no basis for human rights without Christianity:

> I doubt that there is any way to derive a commitment to equal respect for every human being from the ordinary distinctions in merit and excellence that we all use in some spheres of life; it is grounded, rather, not in our relation to each other, but in our relation to God.[6]

Oliver O'Donovan states that "the equality of individual human beings . . . is only and ever a theological assertion."[7]

This reality is why, in a secularizing West, ideas of what it means to be human are increasingly confused and in need of an increased focus by the people of God. Human dignity is among the best gifts that Christianity gives to the world. This is not to say, of course, that everywhere Christians have always lived up to the Scripture's rich vision for humanity in the cultures in which they are located. While the creation of man and woman in the image of God has vast and beautiful implications, those implications, if misunderstood or misapplied, can be detrimental. On the other hand, the beauty of such a theological concept brings powerful liberation and purpose.[8] Where the church has attempted to value the *imago Dei* as the Bible does, it has had a transformative impact. The world today needs a full recovery of the doctrine of human dignity to meet the manifold challenges of a confused world.

BEING HUMAN IN THE CONTEXT OF SALVATION HISTORY

One of the most important reasons evangelicals need to do this work is because without the gospel story, contemporary concepts of human dignity are either incomplete, impartial, or incongruent. If "humans are valuable" is the extent of our understanding of the image of God, we will be ill-equipped to meet the challenges of the moment.

The Bible not only tells us that human beings are valuable, but it also tells us why humans are prone to commit violence against each other and how God, in the incarnate Son, has visited us and has restored humanity to its God-glorifying purposes. Human dignity, as explained by the Scriptures, is one of beauty, fallenness, and redemption.

In this concluding chapter, our intent is to offer a summary of what has been previously written in the various chapters in this volume, offering a fitting conclusion by examining the gift of the *imago Dei* within the metanarrative of Scripture. The exploration of the story of humanity through the arc of creation, fall, redemption, and restoration provides needed clarity to the gift of human dignity in a complex and broken world, as well as our place in that narrative as we live out such a beautiful doctrine.

1. *Creation*. It is important to note that the story of humanity as told by Christian Scripture begins not with humans, but with God: "In the beginning God . . ." (Gen. 1:1). Moses opens his narrative by describing the formation of the world as an act that begins with the one who had no beginning, who is always there. Jesus Christ, the Son of God, would later testify to religious leaders that "before Abraham was, *I am*" (John 8:58 KJV; emphasis added). Derek Kidner notes, "It's no accident that God is the subject of the first sentence of the Bible, for this word dominates the whole chapter and catches the eye at every point of the page."[9]

"I make known the end from the beginning, from ancient times, what is still to come. . . . I am the first and I am the last," God whispers to the prophet Isaiah (Isa. 46:10; 48:12 NIV). John reminds us that God was "in the beginning" (John 1:1). The psalmist declares, "Before the mountains were born, before you gave birth to the earth and the world, from eternity to eternity, you are God" (Ps. 90:2 CSB).

Everything in our lives had a beginning and has a fixed end point, but God is eternal and transcendent. He is outside of and above time. Theologian John Frame insightfully observes, "It is significant that the world has a beginning, and that God exists before that beginning . . . the Creator precedes the creation."[10] To understand what it means to be human, we must understand that God is no mere character, but he is the story, the author, the beginning of creation. God stands *outside* of his creation; he is *other* than his creation; he is *above* his creation.[11]

To be human is first to understand that we are not God but created by God. But what a glorious creation it is. When it comes to the creation of humanity, the biblical narrative slows down as if to emphasize that above everything else in God's good world, humans are God's prized creation. In the creation of humankind, God is no longer simply commanding creation into existence, he is consulting among himself as he creates man and woman.[12]

Herman Bavinck says that this feature of the text of Genesis is not accidental:

> The account of the origin of heaven and earth converges in the first chapter of Genesis upon the creation of man. The creation of the other creatures, of heaven and earth, of sun and moon and stars, of plants and animals, is reported in brief words, and there is no mention made at all of the creation of the angels. But when Scripture comes to the creation of man it lingers long over him, describes not only the fact but also the manner of his creation, and returns to the subject for further broad consideration in the second chapter. This particular attention devoted to the origin of man serves already as evidence of the fact that man is the purpose and end, the head and crown of the whole work of creation. And there are various material details which also illuminate the superior rank and worth of man among the creatures.

In the first place, there is the special counsel of God, which precedes the creation of man. At the calling into being of the other creatures, we read simply that God spoke and by His speaking brought them into existence. But when God is about to create man, he first confers with himself and rouses himself to make men in his image and likeness. This goes to indicate that especially the creation of man rests on deliberation, on divine wisdom and goodness and omnipotence. Nothing, of course, came into existence by chance. But the counsel and decision of God is far more clearly manifest in the making of man than in the creation of the other creatures.[13]

God reached down to the dirt with his hands and sculped Adam from "the dust of the ground" (Gen. 2:7) and breathed into Adam "the breath of life" (Gen. 2:7), and upon Adam was stamped the image of God (Gen. 1:26–27). As Bavinck noted above, the Trinitarian echo of "let us make man in our image" implies a certain deliberation among the Trinity. No such care is given toward any other part of God's creation. King David would later write of his own conception that God "knit me together in my mother's womb" (Ps. 139:13–14 CSB). Of all God's creative acts—a breathtaking waterfall, the majesty of an eagle in flight, the soaring mountain peaks—nothing is as magnificent as the creation of humans.

2. *Fall*. Something happened, however, that marred God's good creation. Something sinister and malevolent. One doesn't have to be particularly religious to look around and understand this reality. All it takes is the ability to scroll a social media timeline to witness the breadth of human suffering in the world, often perpetrated by image bearers themselves. There is something fundamentally broken about the human experience.

The origin of human brokenness happened in the same garden where God crafted human life from the dust and breathed into Adam and Eve the breath of life. The temptation to the first humans was that they could be more than mere image bearers of the Almighty. The serpent whispered a false promise that humans could "be like God" (Gen. 3:5). Ironically, in their attempt to be more than human, Adam and Eve took orders from an animal, subverting their own humanity. Self-worship is always an assault on our own dignity.

This act would drive a wedge between image bearers and the image-giver, and it would fracture the relationship between humans as the cycle of guilt and blame-shifting, so common to the human condition, began. The penalty for sin entered the world, affecting relationships, and bringing death to innocence and intimacy with God. Human bodies began the slow process of decay. Eden's reality reminds us of the truth of the apostle James's words: "Sin, when it conceives, brings forth death" (James 1:15; author paraphrase). Sin is now embedded as a deep and pervasive corruption in every human heart (Ps. 51). In Romans, Paul would point back to the garden as the source of our deepest sorrow: "Just as sin came into the world through one man, and death through sin, and so death spread to all men because all sinned" (Rom. 5:12 ESV).

Sin is what dehumanizes us. To be fully human is to enjoy bearing God's image in the joy of relationship with our Creator. But sinful humanity flees the relationship for which it was made; Adam and Eve used the garden God had given them to hide from him (Gen. 3:8). And sin causes us to dehumanize others.[14] It would only take one generation for Adam's choice to bear its ugly fruit, resulting in violence between his two sons (Gen. 4). Yet even in this fallen state, the value of human life was not diminished in the eyes of God. "Your brother's blood cries out to me from the ground," said God rebuking Cain (Gen. 4:10 CSB). Every drop of innocent blood shed is seen by the Creator. Humanity's fallen state means that humans no longer live up to their image-bearing responsibilities even while they retain their image-bearing value.

Considering how sin does not change a human being's status as an image bearer, theologian Wolfhart Pannenberg writes, "A feature of the dignity that accrues to us by virtue of our being destined for fellowship with God is that no actual humiliation that might befall us can extinguish it."[15] Through the gift of the image of God, despite our own sin, our dignity remains intact even as we experience the consequences of sin in and around us. Because sin damaged our ability to reflect God perfectly in our own lives, many of today's cultural ills are directly related to the lack of image-bearer perspective applied in our world. Examine the current cultural ills in society that are a direct reflection of the lack of understanding of our own dignity and identity as God's image bearers, and the list will be long. Whether its human trafficking, pornography, racism, abortion, sexism, or sexual identity issues and more, all of these have roots in the broken understanding of our own identity and the dignity of all. This is why, in the metanarrative of Scripture, the fall has such a significant impact on our understanding of the *imago Dei*.

3. *Redemption*. Yet even amidst the bad news of the fall, embedded in God's pronouncement of the curse in Genesis 3 is the promise of redemption. God prophesied a violent clash between the offspring of the woman and the offspring of the serpent. This thread is the storyline that plays out in the rest of Scripture. There would come another Adam, who unlike the first Adam, would not yield to the temptation of Satan and who would defeat sin, death, and the grave.

The apostle Paul points to Jesus as this second Adam, "For as in Adam all die, so also in Christ shall all be made alive" (1 Cor. 15:22 ESV). Jesus, fully human, fully divine, is the exact and perfect image of God (Col. 1; Heb. 1). Jesus fulfilled what Adam could not; those who have been redeemed by the second Adam are being made into the likeness of Christ (Col. 3:10). Because of Christ's work, whoever is in him is restored to our image-bearing purposes (Eph. 2:10). Believers are now also called into a new identity—an identity of Christ and his righteousness applied to our lives, that we might be transformed into a greater reflection of him who has created and saved us (2 Cor. 3:18).

Christ, who is the perfect reflection of God, who is the full image bearer of the Father, is our example of what it means to live in our purpose of glorifying God by reflecting him as he is formed in us through sanctification.[16] It is because of Christ's perfect reflection of God that he was able to be the perfect sacrifice, taking on our penalty for sin. It is because of the gospel that we can not only understand the diagnoses of the human condition, but we can also find, in Jesus, the cure for our broken humanity.

4. *Restoration*. Through redemption made available to image bearers by the perfect image bearer, Jesus Christ, those who are in him have the promise of a future restoration where all dehumanization will be made right. The anguish brought into the world by the fall will someday be erased. Tears will be wiped away, death will be no more, and that which threatens the dignity of image bearers will be made new (Rev. 21:4).

God, the Creator of all things, the Beginning and the End, will make all social ills right. Sin, which has cast a wedge between image bearer and image Creator, will be fully and finally stamped out. As with the beginning of creation, God himself will dwell amid his people. "Behold, the dwelling place of God is with man. He will dwell with them, and they will be his people, and God himself will be with them as their God" (Rev. 21:3 ESV). Unity with God, as it was in Eden, will be restored. This is the hope given to believers.

5. *Response*. With what Scripture teaches us about our identity as image bearers, the reality of sin's effects on human dignity issues, and the hope we now have from our own redemption and future restoration through Christ, believers are given a vision for response. Those who have been reconciled to Christ are to

now walk in their understanding that they "are God's handiwork, created . . . to do good works, which God prepared in advance for us to do" (Eph. 2:10 NIV).

Christ followers ought to be the ones who step out into the darkness of a broken world and bring renewed hope and identity to all image bearers. As those who have been reconciled, we are now to be about the ministry of reconciliation to bring more beauty and God's glory in the world by pointing others to their need for Christ, the perfect image of God (2 Cor. 5:18).

Stepping into the darkness of the world's distortions on human dignity certainly brings with it the scars and sorrows from stepping face-to-face with dehumanization and all of the evils it entails. Yet, Orlando Saer claims that "those nails may have disfigured his flesh, but at the same time they have made him more beautiful, more celebrated, more glorious—for all eternity."[17] As we go about Christ's work, we may bear the scars, but in those scars, and their healing, we bring about more of our Creator's glory.

Christ set this example when he walked on earth among his creation. He went about his Father's work of showing truth and love. Christ pointed people toward the Father and cared for the vulnerable. He went to the cross so that broken image bearers like us might have a path forward to be constantly reshaped into more of the likeness of Christ. As we reflect Christ, we reflect more fully our own image-bearer identity, and we point others toward their own identity as well.

6. *Our Path Forward.* The picture offered in Scripture of creation, fall, redemption, and restoration provides a framework for engaging in human dignity challenges of our culture today. Everyone is searching for a metanarrative, a story to place ourselves within our context that will illuminate the path forward. All of us want a narrative to guide our journey through

life, giving us purpose and meaning. The Bible and its narrative unlock that purpose.[18]

Through the Bible, we find ourselves, as created in God's image, and we find our meaning, to glorify our Creator God. The path forward is pointing others to that truth through our words and actions. Understanding what it means to be created in the image of God not only helps us to see that all human life is valuable, but it also informs *how* we engage in our work of bringing that truth into the world. Equipped with an understanding of the *imago Dei*, we approach our mission with conviction and compassion.

Believers must maintain this deep theological rootedness regarding our understanding of human dignity joined with a perspective shaped by our knowledge of the whole of Scripture so that it might play out practically in our church body and communities for the glory of God as imitators of Christ. Kilner summed up this motivation for Christians saying, "Both this perspective of needy people as created in God's image and that of Christian service as conforming to the image of Christ became powerful motivators for helping people."[19]

Wholistic application of this scriptural understanding of human dignity will be required. This application must be applied equally to all peoples. Throughout church history, there have been significant consequences when believers did not apply their understanding of the *imago Dei* to every person, choosing instead to apply it selectively, excluding various groups.

In this cultural moment, where we see so many human dignity challenges, the church has an opportunity to provide loving, compassionate engagement as well as genuine hope and authentic care. This is how believers must continue forward in their desire to be light in the darkness by reflecting God in our world and bringing his glory to bear on a broken and dying culture. We hope the chapters of this book have informed your mind and encouraged your heart for the path forward into each of these complex human dignity issues in our world as we seek to stand for life and the fullness of its value at every stage.

ACKNOWLEDGMENTS

Wɪᴛʜ ʜᴇᴀʀᴛꜰᴇʟᴛ ɢʀᴀᴛɪᴛᴜᴅᴇ, we offer our thanks to God for the privilege to work on this important volume. We are truly thankful for the outstanding Christian scholars and leaders who have joined us in this project. For the support provided by Jonathan Merkh, Lauren Ward, Jennifer Gingerich, Kate Etue, Landon Dickerson, and the Forefront Books team, we are exceedingly grateful. We express our appreciation for the helpful assistance provided by Wang Yong Lee as well. Everyone involved in the project has helped to create a joyful process for each aspect of this publication.

This volume grew out of a conference held on the campus of Southwestern Baptist Theological Seminary in May of 2022, which focused on understanding the importance of the Christian teaching regarding the image of God (*imago Dei*) and its implications for service in church and culture in our twenty-first century context. Lauren McAfee and Elizabeth Graham initiated the idea for the conference. The organization, Stand for Life, offered generous support for the conference and the book. Daniel Darling and the Land Center for Cultural Engagement at Southwestern Seminary were involved in the conference planning. The coordination of the conference and the overall oversight for the project was provided by the International Alliance for Christian

Education. We are also thankful for the support of the YHWH Foundation. The collaborative efforts of all these people have resulted in this fine volume, which we trust will serve the people of God well for years to come. We pray that the volume will bring glory to our great and majestic Triune God.

Soli Deo Gloria

The Editors

CONTRIBUTORS

Gregg R. Allison (Ph.D., Trinity Evangelical Divinity School) serves as Professor of Theology, The Southern Baptist Theological Seminary.

Daniel Darling (M.A., The Southern Baptist Theological Seminary) serves as Director of the Land Center for Cultural Engagement and Assistant Professor of Faith and Culture, Southwestern Baptist Theological Seminary.

David S. Dockery (Ph.D., University of Texas System) serves as President of the International Alliance for Christian Education and as Distinguished Professor of Theology and Editor of the *Southwestern Journal of Theology*, Southwestern Baptist Theological Seminary.

J. Scott Horrell (Ph.D., Dallas Theological Seminary) serves as Senior Professor of Theology at Dallas Theological Seminary.

John F. Kilner (Ph.D., Harvard University) is Emeritus Professor of Bioethics, Trinity Evangelical Divinity School.

Lauren McAfee (Ph.D. [in progress], The Southern Baptist Theological Seminary) serves as Founder and Visionary of Stand for Life.

Katie J. McCoy (Ph.D., Southwestern Baptist Theological Seminary) serves as Director of Women's Ministry, Baptist General Convention of Texas.

C. Ben Mitchell (Ph.D., University of Tennessee) is the Emeritus Graves Professor of Moral Philosophy, Union University.

Jennifer Marshall Patterson (Ph.D. [in progress], Catholic University of America) serves as Director of the Center for Theology and Public Life, Reformed Theological Seminary.

Scott Rae (Ph.D., University of Southern California) serves as Special Assistant to the President and Professor of Philosophy and Ethics, Biola University.

Jacob Shatzer (Ph.D., Marquette University) serves as Associate Professor of Theological Studies and Assistant Provost at Union University.

Robert B. Stewart (Ph.D., Southwestern Baptist Theological Seminary) holds the Greer-Heard Chair of Faith and Culture and serves as Professor of Philosophy and Theology, New Orleans Baptist Theological Seminary.

John Stonestreet (M.A., Trinity Evangelical Divinity School) serves as President of the Colson Center for Christian Worldview.

NOTES

INTRODUCTION, by David Dockery

1 The summary thoughts in this introduction have been drawn from and adapted from the following sources: David L. Smith, "Humankind and Sin," in *New Dimensions in Evangelical Thought: Essays in Honor of Millard J. Erickson*, ed. David S. Dockery (Downers Grove: IVP, 1998), 287–98; David L. Smith, *With Willful Intent: A Theology of Sin* (Wheaton: BridgePoint, 1994); Robert L. Reymond, *A New Systematic Theology of the Christian Faith* (Nashville: Thomas Nelson, 1998), 415–60; G. C. Berkouwer, *Man: The Image of God*, trans. Dirk Jellema (Grand Rapids: Eerdmans, 1962); William Kynes and Greg Strand, *Evangelical Convictions* (Minneapolis: Free Church Publications, 2011), 69–89; Donald G. Bloesch, *Essentials of Evangelical Theology* (2 vols.; San Francisco: Harper & Row, 1978), 1:88–119; Donald Guthrie, *New Testament Theology* (Downers Grove: IVP, 1981), 116–218; James Leo Garrett Jr., *Systematic Theology: Biblical, Historical, and Evangelical* (2 vols.; Grand Rapids: Eerdmans, 1990), 389–523; Michael Horton, *Pilgrim Theology: Core Doctrines for Christian Disciples* (Grand Rapids: Zondervan, 2011); 107–57; John Hammett, "Human Nature," in *Theology for the People of God*, ed. Daniel L. Akin (Nashville: B&H, 2014), 285–335; Anthony Hoekema, *Created in God's Image* (Grand Rapids: Eerdmans, 1986); C. John Collins, *Did Adam and Eve Really Exist? Who They Were and Why You Should Care* (Wheaton: Crossway, 2011); Kenneth A. Mathews, *Genesis 1:1—11:26*, New American Commentary (Nashville: B&H, 1996); Millard J. Erickson, *Christian Theology*, 3rd ed. (Grand Rapids: Baker, 2013); John F. Kilner, *Dignity and Destiny: Humanity in the Image of God* (Grand Rapids: Eerdmans, 2015); Mark Cortez, *Resourcing Christian Anthropology* (Grand Rapids: Zondervan, 2018); Gregg R. Allison, *Embodied: Living as Whole People in a Fractured World* (Grand Rapids: Baker, 2021); Scott Rae, *Moral Choices: An Introduction to Ethics*, 4th ed. (Grand Rapids: Zondervan, 2018); Jacob Shatzer, *Transhumanism and the Image of God: Today's Technology and the Future of Christian Discipleship* (Downers Grove: IVP, 2019); Joshua R. Farris, *An Introduction to Christian Anthropology: Humans, Both Creaturely and Divine* (Grand Rapids: Baker, 2020); Kelly Kapic, *You're Only Human: How Your Limits Reflect God's Design and Why That's Good News* (Grand Rapids: Brazos, 2022); John Paul II, *Man and Woman He Created Them: A Theology of the Body* (Alexandria, VA: Pauline Books, 2006); Daniel Darling, *The Dignity Revolution* (Epsom, UK: The Good Book Company, 2018); John Hammett and Katie McCoy, *The Doctrine of Humankind* (Nashville: B&H, 2023).

The Image of God and Human Dignity:
Recovering a Biblical Treasure, by John F. Kilner

1 This conviction is elaborated and further documented in John F. Kilner, *Dignity and Destiny: Humanity in the Image of God* (Grand Rapids: Eerdmans, 2015) and John F. Kilner, ed., *Why People Matter: A Christian Engagement with Rival Views of Human Significance* (Grand Rapids: Baker, 2017), from which the present chapter is adapted and updated.

2 For more on this observation, see G. C. Berkouwer, *Man: The Image of God* (Grand Rapids: Eerdmans, 1975), 67.

3 Thomas A. Smail, *Like Father, Like Son* (Grand Rapids: Eerdmans, 2006), 43–44, develops this theme.

4 For over a thousand examples, see the "Resources Cited" section at the end of Kilner, *Dignity and Destiny*.

5 For further documentation and many more examples, see Kilner, *Dignity and Destiny*, 4–17.

6 Gary B. Ferngren, "The *Imago Dei* and the Sanctity of Life: The Origins of an Idea," in *Euthanasia and the Newborn: Conflicts Regarding Saving Lives*, eds. Richard C. McMillan, H. Tristram Engelhardt, and Stuart F. Spicker (Dordrecht: D. Reidel, 1987), 32–33; Gary B. Ferngren, *Medicine & Health Care in Early Christianity* (Baltimore: Johns Hopkins University Press, 2009), 103.

7 Martin Luther King Jr., *Where Do We Go from Here: Chaos or Community?* (Boston: Beacon Hill, 1968), 180.

8 Ferngren, *Medicine & Health Care*, 145.

9 Darrel W. Amundsen, *Medicine, Society, and Faith in the Ancient and Medieval Worlds* (Baltimore: Johns Hopkins University Press, 1996), 50–69.

10 Goran Collste, *Is Human Life Special?* (Bern: Peter Lang, 2002), 45.

11 A good example of the former is the multicampus Harvest Bible Chapel in Chicago, Illinois, where the name of the fellowship of people with disabilities is "In His Image." For the latter, see World Council of Churches, *Christian Perspectives on Theological Anthropology* (Geneva: WCC, 2005), par. 119.

12 These categories are used to identify various peoples who have been oppressed and do not indicate that all native peoples in the Americas are in the same people group, nor that all people from Africa enslaved elsewhere are the same people group.

13 Richard Mouw, "The *Imago Dei* and Philosophical Anthropology," *Christian Scholar's Review* 43 (2012): 264.

14 As Lincoln observed: in opposition to "the doctrine that none but rich men, or none but white men, were entitled to life, liberty and the pursuit of happiness," the authors of the Declaration of Independence insist that "nothing stamped with the Divine image and likeness was sent into the world to be trodden on, and degraded, and imbruted by its fellows." See Lincoln's "'Speech at Lewistown, Illinois' (August 17, 1858)," in *The Collected Works of Abraham Lincoln*, ed. Roy Basler, vol. 2 (New Brunswick, NJ: Rutgers University Press, 1953), 546.

15 Richard W. Wills Sr., *Martin Luther King Jr. and the Image of God* (New York, Oxford University Press, 2009), 13, 15.

16 Mercy Amba Oduyoye, "Spirituality of Resistance and Reconstruction," in *Women Resisting Violence: Spirituality for Life*, eds. Mary John Mananzan et al. (Maryknoll, NY: Orbis, 1996), 170.

17 Hope S. Antone, "Reminiscing 25 years of IGI, 20 Years of AWRC," *In God's Image* 26 (2007), 1, https://awrc4ct.org/publications/in-gods-image/

18 For further documentation and many more examples, see Kilner, *Dignity and Destiny*, 17–36.

19 For further discussion see Douglas J. Hall, *Imaging God: Dominion as Stewardship*

(Grand Rapids: Eerdmans, 1986), 108–9.

20 Thomas Aquinas, *Summa Theologica*, trans. Fathers of the English Dominican Province (New York: Benziger, 1947), 1.93.8. This misunderstanding flows from seeing the image of God as being "in people" rather than—to use the Bible's language—people as being "in the image of God." See Eleonore Stump, *The Image of God* (New York: Oxford University Press, 2022), 140–41. And see further discussion in Anthony A. Hoekema, *Created in God's Image* (Grand Rapids: Eerdmans, 1994), 37. For Emil Brunner (*The Christian Doctrine of Creation and Redemption*, trans. Olive Wyon [Philadelphia: Westminster, 1952], 57), the protection of being in the image of God "ceases where true human living ceases—on the borderline of imbecility or madness." Robert N. Wennberg (*Life in the Balance* [Grand Rapids: Eerdmans, 1985], 131), reflecting on whether all people are fully in God's image and so have full moral standing, concludes: "the grossly retarded . . . need not be assumed to possess a moral standing as full as that of a normal human adult."

21 As developed in Mary Catherine Hilkert, "Imago Dei: Does the Symbol Have a Future?" *The Santa Clara Lectures* 8, no. 3 (2002): 7–8.

22 Adolf Hitler, *Mein Kampf* (New York: Reynal and Hitchcock, 1939), 606.

23 See Richard H. Cracroft, "The American West of Karl May," *American Quarterly* 19 (1967): 249–58; and discussion in Robert F. Berkhofer, Jr., *The White Man's Indian* (New York: Alfred A. Knopf, 1978), 101.

24 Oliver W. Holmes, "Oration, 1855," in *The New England Society Orations*, eds. Cephas Brainerd and Eveline Warner Brainerd (New York: The Century Co., 1901), 298. See discussion in Thomas F. Gossett, *Race: The History of an Idea of America* (New York: Oxford University Press, 1997), 243.

25 Karen Teel, *Racism and the Image of God* (New York: Palgrave Macmillan, 2010), 166.

26 Kyle D. Fedler, *Exploring Christian Ethics* (Louisville: Westminster John Knox, 2006), 82.

27 Charles Carroll, *"The Negro a Beast" or "In the Image of God"* (Reprint; Miami: Mnemosyne, 1969), 90, 311.

28 See David Pilgrim, "The Brute Caricature," http://www.ferris.edu/jimcrow/brute.

29 Leonard Zeskind, *The "Christian Identity" Movement* (New York: National Council of Churches, 1986), 7.

30 The Covenant, the Sword, and the Arm of the Lord, "What We Believe," in *Extremism in America: A Reader*, ed. Lyman T. Sargent (New York: New York University Press, 1995), 329–330. Also, see discussion in Zeskind, *The "Christian Identity" Movement*, 45.

31 Richard Abanes, *America's Militias: Rebellion, Racism & Religion* (Downers Grove: IVP, 1996), 166–68, describes an Aryan Nations's publication that celebrates members involved in "murderous exploits" as "Aryan Heroes" in the footsteps of "Heroes of the Confederate States" and "Heroes of the Third Reich."

32 See Michelle A. Gonzalez, *Created in God's Image: An Introduction to Feminist Theological Anthropology* (Maryknoll, NY: Orbis, 2007), 161.

33 Margaret A. Farley, "New Patterns of Relationship: Beginnings of a Moral Revolution," *Theological Studies* 36 (1975): 629.

34 As documented in Kilner, *Dignity and Destiny*, 29–36.

35 Julia O'Faolain and Lauro Martines, *Not in God's Image: Women in History from the Greeks to the Victorians* (New York: Harper & Row, 1973).

36 Max L. Stackhouse, "Why Human Rights Need God: A Christian Perspective," in *Does Human Rights Need God?* eds. Elizabeth Bucar and Barbara Barnett (Grand Rapids: Eerdmans, 2005), 27, attributes this expression to George Williams.

37 Hans Wildberger, "Tselem/Image," in *Theological Lexicon of the Old Testament*, eds. Ernst Jenni and Claus Westermann, trans. Mark Biddle, vol. 3 (Peabody, MA:

Hendrickson, 1997); Wildberger there notes the "remarkable flexibility" of this term (1081).

38 David J. A. Clines, "The Image of God in Man," *Tyndale Bulletin* 19 (1968): 87–88.

39 J. Richard Middleton, *The Liberating Image: The* Imago Dei *in Genesis 1* (Grand Rapids: Brazos, 2005), 104–7.

40 Hans Walter Wolff, *Anthropology of the Old Testament* (London: SCM, 1974), 160–61.

41 G. K. Beale, *The Temple and the Church's Mission: A Biblical Theology of the Dwelling Place of God* (Downers Grove: IVP, 2004), 88–90.

42 I. Howard Marshall, "Being Human: Made in the Image of God," *Stone-Campbell Journal* 4, no. 1 (2001): 50–51.

43 W. Randall Garr, *In His Own Image and Likeness* (Leiden: Brill, 2003), 134–35.

44 Hermann Kleinknecht, "The Greek Use of *Eikon*," in *Theological Dictionary of the New Testament*, ed. Gerhard Kittel, vol. 2 (Grand Rapids: Eerdmans, 1964), 389.

45 David H. Kelsey, *Eccentric Existence: A Theological Anthropology*, vol. 2 (Louisville: Westminster John Knox, 2009), 966.

46 These are the attributes of God that Christ reflects in his perfect humanity. See Marc Cortez, *ReSourcing Theological Anthropology* (Grand Rapids: Zondervan, 2017), 129, 169–72.

47 On the connection of Heb. 2 here with Christ as God's image, see Michael S. Horton, "Image and Office: Human Personhood and the Covenant," in *Personal Identity in Theological Perspective*, eds. Richard Lints, Michael Horton, and Mark Talbot (Grand Rapids: Eerdmans, 2006), 190.

48 On the importance of paying careful attention to the ways that the authors of the Bible adjust ideas they employ from their contemporary cultural context, see Paul Niskanen, "The Poetics of Adam: The Creation of *Adam* in the Image of *Elohim*," *Journal of Biblical Literature* 128, no. 3 (2009): 420.

49 On prepositions in the Bible as basically signifying relationships between things, see Murray J. Harris, *Prepositions and Theology in the Greek New Testament* (Grand Rapids: Zondervan, 2012), 27. On the distinction between Christ as God's image and people as "according to" God's image, see John S. Hammett, "A Whole-Bible Approach to Interpreting Creation in God's Image," *Southwestern Journal of Theology* 63 (Spring 2021): 33.

50 For further explanation, see Philip E. Hughes, *The True Image: Christ as the Origin and Destiny of Man* (Grand Rapids: Eerdmans, 1989), 21.

51 The standard *Hebrew and Aramaic Lexicon of the Old Testament* by Ludwig Koehler and Walter Baumgartner (rev. Walter Baumgartner and Johann Stamm, trans. M. E. J. Richardson [Leiden: Brill, 2001], 104) specifies that "according to" is the best rendering of both prepositions, *be* and *ke*, in image-of-God passages in Gen. 1 and 5.

52 On the importance of this distinction see Sean M. McDonough, *Christ as Creator: Origins of a New Testament Doctrine* (Oxford: Oxford University Press, 2009), 91.

53 The parallel passage Eph. 4:24 similarly includes the preposition *kata*, suggesting that it is central to the concept. In support of translating *kata* in Col. 3:10 as "according to" the model/pattern of Christ—and for the renewal here as parallel to the original creation "according to" the image of God in Gen. 1:27—see Peter T. O'Brien, *Colossians, Philemon* (Nashville: Nelson, 1987), 191; Murray J. Harris, *Colossians and Philemon* (Nashville: B&H, 2010), 133; McDonough, *Christ as Creator*, 90–91.

54 Just as Paul can envision some people as justified, glorified, and conformed to God's image in Rom. 8:29, he can also refer to some as being the glory and image of God in 1 Cor. 11:7. However, he is not affirming in Rom. 8 that people are already image-conformed or glorified, or in 1 Cor. that they are already God's glory or image. Rather, Paul is recognizing the present dignity connected with their ultimate destiny. Paul knows all too well, for instance, that "all have sinned and fall short of the glory of

God" (Rom. 3:23 NKJV)—in fact, they have given up the glory of God (Rom. 1:23). In 2 Cor. 3:18 he reminds the Corinthians that glory must increase before their transformation into God's image can be accomplished. See Kilner, "Humanity's Creation in God's Image," in *Dignity and Destiny*, 85–133, for more detailed biblical and scholarly support. Others such as Hughes (*True Image*, 22) agree that 1 Cor. 11:7 does not affirm that anyone is already God's image, offering additional exegetical rationales.

55 Although Jesus was only addressing implications for the community of believers, James applies the expansive principle to the wider human context that both he and the author of Gen. 9:6 had in view. For more on the James passage, see Andrea L. Robinson, "Reflecting the Image of God through Speech: Genesis 1–3 in James 3:1–12," *Evangelical Review of Theology* 44 (November 2020): 313–23.

56 For numerous examples, see Kilner, *Dignity and Destiny*, 17–36≥

57 On the image of Christ and the image of God as essentially the same thing, see Victor P. Furnish, *II Corinthians* (Garden City, NY: Doubleday, 1984), 215; Kelsey, *Eccentric Existence*, 2:999.

58 Stanley J. Grenz, *The Social God and the Relational Self: A Trinitarian Theology of the Imago Dei* (Louisville: Westminster John Knox, 2001), 193–94.

59 Regarding this logic, see Marc Cortez, *Theological Anthropology: A Guide for the Perplexed* (London: T&T Clark, 2010), 20. See also Roger Ruston, *Human Rights and the Image of God* (London: SCM, 2004), 282–83.

60 For a discussion of both the biblical inadequacy of each of these attributes as the definition of what it means to be in God's image and the historical figures who have championed them, see \Kilner, "Misunderstandings about God's Image," in *Dignity and Destiny*, 177–230.

61 Martin Luther King Jr., "The American Dream," in *A Knock at Midnight*, eds. Clayborne Carson and Peter Holloran (New York: Warner, 2000), 88.

62 Although this passage refers to God's "likeness," it is addressing the same "image" concept in view here.

63 For elaboration see Clines, "Image," 92; Hughes, *True Image*, 7–8; Grenz, *Social God*, 202.

64 Theologians ranging from Karl Barth to various Eastern Orthodox leaders recognize the central place of "intention" here, though their theologies differ in many other ways. See Barth, "The Doctrine of Creation," in *Church Dogmatics*, eds. Geoffrey Bromiley and Thomas Torrance (Edinburgh: T&T Clark, 1958), III/I:200. For Eastern Orthodox views, see Linda Woodhead, "Apophatic Anthropology," in *God and Human Dignity*, eds. R. Kendall Soulen and Linda Woodhead (Grand Rapids: Eerdmans, 2006), 237–38.

65 Christ, as the one who has the power to destroy death itself, is imperishable (1 Cor. 15:25–26), and Christ now has a spiritual body (1 Cor. 15:44–47). "Just as we have borne the image of the man of dust, we will also bear the image of the man of heaven" (1 Cor. 15:49 NRSV)—including an imperishable spiritual body.

66 For a discussion of various ways to categorize such attributes, see Oladotun Paul Kolawole, "God's Image in Man: A Biblical Perspective," *Journal of Biblical Theology* 2 (July–September 2019): 45–47.

67 For elaboration see Bernd Oberdorfer, "Human Dignity and 'Image of God,'" *Scriptura* 204 (2010): 238.

68 Christoph Schwöbel, "Recovering Human Dignity," in *God and Human Dignity*. eds. R. Kendall Soulen and Linda Woodhead (Grand Rapids: Eerdmans, 2006), 53. See also Vorster, *Created*, 16, 22.

69 Joan Lockwood O'Donovan, "Human Dignity and Human Justice: Thinking with Calvin about the *Imago Dei*," *Tyndale Bulletin* 66, no. 1 (2015): 136. Needless to say, the concept of human dignity is easier to invoke in secular settings without explicitly in-

voking this theological grounding. See Andrew Lustig, "The Image of God and Human Dignity: A Complex Conversation," *Christian Bioethics* 23 (December 2017): 328–31.

70 On human life as a loan as well as a gift, see John F. Kilner, *Life on the Line* (Grand Rapids: Eerdmans, 1992), 67.

71 For elaboration of these implications, along with relevant sources, see Kilner, *Dignity and Destiny*, 316–30.

72 For further discussion, see Jason D. Whitt, "In the Image of God: Receiving Children with Special Needs," *Review and Expositor* 113, no. 2 (2016): 209–13.

73 For more detailed applications for the classroom, see John F. Kilner, "Made in the Image of God: Implications for Teaching and Learning," in *Christian Higher Education: Faith, Teaching, and Learning in the Evangelical Tradition*, eds. David S. Dockery and Christopher W. Morgan (Wheaton: Crossway, 2018), 101–119.

74 For elaboration and support, see John F. Kilner, "Bioethics and a Better Birth," in *Why the Church Needs Bioethics: A Guide to Wise Engagement with Life's Challenges*, ed. John F. Kilner (Grand Rapids: Zondervan, 2011), 82–83.

"Persons" Divine and Human: The Concept of Person in and beyond Nicaea for Today, by J. Scott Horrell

1 Behind the immediate question of why do I exist, of course, stands the greater cosmological question of why there is anything at all—why is there something instead of nothing?

2 The theme is not new and certainly echoes down from Augustine's *Confessions* and Chalcedon's *prosopon* to J. R. Illingworth, *Personality, Human and Divine*, 2nd ed. (Bampton Lectures, London, 1894; Macmillan, 1904); Vladimir Lossky, *In the Image and Likeness of God*, eds. John H. Erickson and Thomas E. Bird (London: Mowbrays, 1975); John D. Zizioulas, *Being as Communion: Studies in Personhood and the Church* (Crestwood, NY: St. Vladimir's Seminary Press, 1985); Christoph Schwöbel and Colin Gunton, eds., *Persons, Divine and Human: King's College Essays in Theological Anthropology* (Edinburgh: T&T Clark, 1991); Stanley J. Grenz, *The Social God and the Relational Self: A Trinitarian Theology of the Imago Dei* (Louisville: Westminster John Knox, 2001).

3 Yuval Noah Harari, *Sapiens: A Brief History of Humankind* (Heb. 2011; Eng. ed., London: Vintage/Penguin, 2014), 445. Elsewhere he writes, "We don't need to wait for the Second Coming in order to overcome death. A couple geeks in a lab can do it." Harari, *Homo Deus: A Brief History of Tomorrow* (Heb. 2015; Eng. ed., London: Vintage/Penguin, 2017), 26.

4 Lev Grossman, "Singularity: n. The moment when technological change becomes so rapid and profound, it represents a rupture in the fabric of human history," *TIME* (Feb. 21, 2011), 43, cf. 42–49.

5 Vern S. Poythress, *Knowing and the Trinity: How Perspectives in Human Knowledge Imitate the Trinity* (Phillipsburg, NJ: P&R, 2018), 3–23.

6 See Veli-Matti Kärkkäinen, *The Trinity: Global Perspectives* (Louisville: Westminster John Knox, 2007).

7 Vladimir Lossky, *Orthodox Theology: An Introduction* (trans. Ian and Ihita Kesarcodi-Watson; Crestwood, NY: St. Vladimir's Seminary Press, 1978), 83.

8 Recent Christian works include: Marc Cortez, *Resourcing Theological Anthropology: A Constructive Account of Humanity in the Light of Christ* (Grand Rapids: Zondervan, 2017); Oliver D. Crisp and Fred Sanders, eds., *The Christian Doctrine of Humanity: Explorations in Constructive Dogmatics* (Grand Rapids: Zondervan, 2018); Nonna Verna Harrison, *God's Many-Splendored Image: Theological Anthropology for Christian Formation* (Grand Rapids: Baker, 2010); John F. Kilner, *Dignity and Destiny: Humanity in the Image of God* (Grand Rapids: Eerdmans, 2015); Brian S. Rosner, *Known by*

God: A Biblical Theology of Personal Identity (Grand Rapids: Zondervan, 2017); Hans Schwarz, *The Human Being: A Theological Anthropology* (Grand Rapids: Eerdmans, 2013); Klyne R. Snodgrass, *Who God Says You Are: A Christian Understanding of Identity* (Grand Rapids: Eerdmans, 2018); and Rowan Williams, *Being Human: Bodies, Minds, Persons* (Grand Rapids: Eerdmans, 2018).

9   Hans Urs von Balthasar, "On the Concept of Person," *Communio* 13:1 (Spring 1986), 18–26.

10 Walter Taylor, "Humanity, NT View of," *ABD* 3:321.

11 Moisés Silva, *"prosōpon," NIDNITTE* 2nd ed., ed. M. Silva, 5 vols. (Grand Rapids: Zondervan, 2014), 4:155–56; Eduard Lohse, *"prosōpon," TDNT* ed. G. Kittel, et al., 10 vols. (Grand Rapids: Eerdmans, 1964), 6:769–74.

12 Scripture quotations in this essay are taken from the NIV unless otherwise noted.

13 Balthasar, "On the Concept of Person," 20.

14 Richard A. Muller, "Persona," *Dictionary of Latin and Greek Theological Terms: Drawn Principally from Protestant Scholastic Theology* (Grand Rapids: Baker, 1985), 223.

15 Basil Studer, "Prosopon," *Encyclopedia of Ancient Christianity* [EAC], gen. ed. A. Di Bernardino, 3 vols. Eng. trans. (Downers Grove: IVP, 2006–2008), 3.326.

16 In Greek natural science *hypostasis* described "sediment in a liquid" carrying a two-fold sense of solidification and visibility, thus in the New Testament as *fundamental reality* (Heb. 1:3; 3:14; 11:1). Already in Origen, *hypostasis* was employed to emphasize "three divine realities" against Sabellian modalism.

17 Cited from the *ICET* version of the Creed (1975) but omitting the later *filioque* ("and the Son"), in Thomas C. Oden, ed., *Ancient Christian Doctrine*, 5 vols. (Downers Grove: IVP, 2009), front page in each volume.

18 Khaled Anatolios, "Personhood, Communion, and the Trinity in Some Patristic Texts," in *The Holy Trinity in the Life of the Church*, ed. Khaled Anatolios (Grand Rapids: Baker/Brookline, MA/Holy Cross Orthodox Press, 2014), 151 (italics and enumeration his); see 151–68.

19 *De Trinitate* 7.4.7–6,11. Augustine observes that Greeks explain Trinity as one "being" (*ousia*) and three "substances" (*hypostases*), whereas Latins deem "being" and "substance" as synonymous. He adds, Scripture neither directly speaks of three persons nor disallows our doing so (7.3.7).

20 Consonant with the dominant philosophic worldview of the Greco-Roman world that began with the transcendent, unknowable One—as in Plotinus, Porphyry, and the Christian convert Marius Victorinus—Augustine considered Neoplatonist philosophy, rightly considered, "the truest philosophy and the pinnacle of all human thought.... His enthusiasm for Plotinian philosophy accompanied Augustine throughout the entirety of his life." Salvatore Lilla, "Platonism and the Fathers," *EAC*, 3:225.

21 Lewis Ayres, "Augustine on the Trinity," in *The Oxford Handbook of the* Trinity, eds. Gilles Emery and Matthew Levering (Oxford: Oxford University Press, 2011), 125.

22 John Peter Kenney, "Augustine and the Platonists," in *Augustine and Tradition: Influences, Contexts, Legacy*, eds. David G. Hunter and Jonathan P. Yates (Grand Rapids: Eerdmans, 2021), 152.

23 Lilla, "Platonism" *EAC*, 3:200–226. Debate continues as to the relationship between Platonism and patristic thought: Tertullian and Hippolytus saw Platonic integration as a fall from truth, whereas Justin Martyr, Athenagoras, Clement of Alexandria, Origen, and others affirmed Platonic idealism (201).

24 John Locke, *An Essay Concerning Human Understanding* (Reprint, Oxford: Oxford University Press, 1975), 2:xxvvii.

25 The evolution from objective standards of reason to individual subjectivism is best described in Charles Taylor, *Sources of the Self: The Making of the Modern Identity*

(Cambridge, MA: Harvard University Press, 1992).

26 John Macmurray, *The Self as Agent* 2nd ed. (Atlantic Highlands, NY: Humanities Press, 1991), 31.

27 Judith Butler, *Giving an Account of Oneself* (New York: Fordham University Press, 2005), 40.

28 Ronald Dworkin, *Religion without God* (Cambridge, MA: Harvard University Press, 2013), 1.

29 Jordan B. Peterson, *12 Rules for Life: An Antidote to Chaos* (New York: Penguin/Random House, 2018). A more Christian approach is that of Roger Scruton, *The Face of God* (London: Bloomsbury, 2012), 177–78; and *On Human Nature* (Princeton, NJ: Princeton University Press, 2017), 142–44.

30 Peter Singer, *Animal Liberation: A New Ethics for Our Treatment of Animals*, rev. ed. (London: Random House, 2015).

31 Harari, *Homo Deus*, 119.

32 An incisive Christian historical overview is Carl R. Trueman's *The Rise and Triumph of the Modern Self: Cultural Amnesia, Expressive Individualism, and the Road to Sexual Revolution* (Wheaton: Crossway, 2020).

33 A multitude of works seek to define *imago Dei* typically dividing into (or combining) three categories: ontological/substantive (personhood, nature), relational, and functional (dominion, reproduction). Others center the *imago Dei* in Jesus Christ and believers being conformed to his image.

34 See the helpful exploration of Marc Cortez, *Christological Anthropology in Historical Perspective: Ancient and Contemporary Approaches to Theological Anthropology* (Grand Rapids: Zondervan, 2016).

35 These similarities between the Trinity and humanity are developed also in Horrell, "The Marriage Bed: The Fullness of God's Design," in *Sanctified Sexuality: Valuing Sex in an Oversexed* Culture, eds. Sandra L. Glahn and C. Gary Barnes (Grand Rapids: Kregel, 2020), esp. 182–87.

36 See Vern S. Poythress, *The Mystery of the Trinity: A Trinitarian Approach to the Attributes of God* (Philipsburg NJ: P&R, 2020), 81–135, 540–1.

37 Michael Denton, *The Miracle of Man: The Fine Tuning of Nature for Human Existence* (Seattle, WA: Discovery Institute, 2022), 29. "It is as if, in an act of extraordinary prescience, there was built into nature from the beginning a suite of properties finely calibrated for beings of our physiological and anatomical design . . ."

38 Nancy R. Pearcey, *Love Thy Body: Answering Hard Questions about Life and Sexuality* (Grand Rapids: Baker, 2018), confronts the modern division between *person* (given moral and legal standing) and *body* (an expendable biological organism); cf. p. 19.

39 Multiple interrelated factors form our self-identities. Klyne Snodgrass, *Who God Says You Are*, 49–222, reminds readers, "You are your . . ." body, history, relations, mind, commitments, actions, boundaries, ongoing changes, and future.

40 One recognizes a certain asymmetry with the Holy Spirit: Rev. 22 presents the Lamb's coregency with God on the throne, the coequal deity of Jesus Christ, yet the Spirit seems likened to the crystal river flowing forth from the throne giving life to the tree of life, hence to the nations. Nonetheless, tellingly, it is the Spirit and the bride who announce the final invitation of Scripture: "Come!"

41 Hence, many in the West have preferred to define the three persons with muted phrases such as "subsistent relations" (Augustine), "subsisting relation" (Thomas Aquinas), "modes of being" (Karl Barth), "distinct manners of subsisting" (Karl Rahner), and so forth.

42 Anatolios, "Personhood, Communion, and the Trinity," 156; Also, see Basil, *On the Holy Spirit*, 16.38. Likewise, as noted earlier, Lossky, *Orthodox Theology*, 43; and Lossky, "The Theological Notion of the Human Person," in *In the Image and Likeness*

of God, eds. John H. Erickson and Thomas E. Bird (Crestwood, NY: St. Vladimir's Seminary Press, 1974), 120. Rowan Williams concurs, *Being Human*, 29–31.

43 Robert Miner, *Thomas Aquinas on the Passions* (Cambridge, UK: Cambridge University Press, 2009), 134.

44 Basil Studer, "Perichoresis" *EAC*, 3:143.

45 Michael O'Carroll, "Circumincession," in *Trinitas: A Theological Encyclopedia of the Holy Trinity*, ed. Michael O'Carroll (Wilmington, DE: Michael Glazier, 1987), 68–69.

46 Gregory of Nyssa, *Commentary on the Song of Songs*, 15, parallels the inner unity of the Trinity with the eschatological indwelling and fullness of the Spirit in the age to come.

What It Means to be Human, by C. Ben Mitchell

1 John Locke, *An Essay Concerning Human Understanding* (Indianapolis: Hackett, 1996), 40.

2 Immanuel Kant, *Groundwork of the Metaphysics of Morals*, trans. H. J. Paton (New York: Harper Torchbooks, 1964), 100.

3 From a "Pragmatic Point of View (1798)" in Robert Louden and Gunter Zoller, eds. and trans., *Anthropology, History and Education* (Cambridge: Cambridge University Press), 227.

4 Paul Ramsey, *Ethics at the Edges of Life: Medical and Legal Intersections* (New Haven: Yale University Press, 1980).

5 John Swinton, *Dementia: Living in the Memories of God* (Grand Rapids: Eerdmans, 2012), 5.

6 Swinton, *Dementia*, 63

7 Swinton, *Dementia*, 65.

8 Swinton, *Dementia*, 72.

9 Swinton, *Dementia*, 81. The brain in a vat is an allusion to a now-famous thought experiment in the philosophy of mind, first advanced by Princeton philosopher Gilbert Harman in *Thought* (Princeton: Princeton University Press, 1973) and further developed by Hilary Putnam, *Reason, Truth, and History* (Cambridge: Cambridge University Press, 1981).

10 James K. A. Smith, *You Are What You Love: The Spiritual Power of Habit* (Grand Rapids: Brazos, 2016), 3.

11 James Leo Garrett, *Systematic Theology: Biblical, Historical, and Evangelical*, 2 vols. (Grand Rapids: Eerdmans, 1990), 1:394–403.

12 This is among several reasons I think of the *imago Dei* as an ontological status conferred by God on humanity (who humans are), rather than a description of what functions humans perform (what humans do).

13 See Mark Cortez, *Christological Anthropology in Historical Perspective: Ancient and Contemporary Approaches to Theological Anthropology* (Grand Rapids: Zondervan, 2016); and *Embodied Souls, Ensouled Bodies: An Exercise in Christological Anthropology and Its Significance for the Mind/Body Debate* (Edinburgh: T&T Clark, 2011). For a biblical theological treatment of theological anthropology see Graham Cole, *The God Who Became Human: A Biblical Theology of Incarnation* (Downers Grove: IVP, 2013).

14 Gilbert Meilaender, *Neither Beast Nor God: The Dignity of the Human Person* (New York: Encounter, 2009).

15 The Nicene Creed

16 Cited in Kelly M. Kapic, *You're Only Human: How Your Limits Reflect God's Design and Why That's Good News* (Grand Rapids: Brazos, 2022), 41–42.

17 Kapic, *You're Only Human*, 5.

18 Kapic, *You're Only Human*, 10.

19 Kapic, *You're Only Human*, 43

20 Kapic, *You're Only Human*, 70.
21 Kapic, *You're Only Human*, 74. See Stanley Hauerwas and William H. Willimon, *The Truth about God: The Ten Commandments in Christian Life* (Nashville: Abingdon, 1999), 68.
22 Kapic, *You're Only Human*, 77.

Human Beings Created in and for Relationship, by Jennifer Marshall Patterson
1 "Rebalancing: Children First," AEI/Brookings Working Group on Childhood in the United States (Washington, D.C.: AEI/Brookings, 2022), 45–46.
2 Wendy Wang, "More Than One-third of Prime-age Americans Have Never Married," Institute for Family Studies, Sept. 2020, https://ifstudies.org/ifs-admin/resources/final2-ifs-single-americansbrief2020.pdf; Paul Hemez and Chanell Washington, "Percentage and Number of Children Living With Two Parents Has Dropped Since 1968," U.S. Census Bureau, April 12, 2021, https://www.census.gov/library/stories/2021/04/number-of-children-living-only-with-their-mothers-has-doubled-in-past-50-years.html.
3 Daniel A. Cox, "The State of American Friendship: Change, Challenges, and Loss," American Enterprise Institute, June 8, 2021, https://www.aei.org/research-products/report/the-state-of-american-friendship-change-challenges-and-loss; Jacob Ausubel, "Older People Are More Likely to Live Alone in the U.S. than Elsewhere in the World," Pew Research Center, March 10, 2020, https://www.pewresearch.org/fact-tank/2020/03/10/older-people-are-more-likely-to-live-alone-in-the-u-s-than-elsewhere-in-the-world.
4 Robert Spaemann, *Persons: The Difference between "Someone" and "Something,"* trans. Oliver O'Donovan (Oxford: Oxford University Press, 2017), 27.
5 Herman Bavinck, *The Christian Family*, trans. Nelson D. Kloosterman (Grand Rapids: Christian's Library, 2012), 3.
6 Bavinck, *The Christian Family*, 7.
7 Bavinck, *The Christian Family*, 111.
8 See for example, Robert N. Bellah et al, *Habits of the Heart: Individualism and Commitment in American Life* (Los Angeles: University of California, 1996), 333–34; Charles Taylor, *A Secular Age* (Cambridge, MA: Harvard University Press, 2007), 299, 473–75; and Carl Trueman, *The Rise and Triumph of the Modern Self: Cultural Amnesia, Expressive Individualism, and the Road to Sexual Revolution* (Wheaton: Crossway, 2020), 46–50.
9 O. Carter Snead, *What It Means to Be Human: The Case for the Body in Public Bioethics* (Cambridge, MA: Harvard University Press, 2020), 5–7.
10 Snead, *What It Means to Be Human*, 6–8.
11 Snead, *What It Means to Be Human*, 267.
12 Autumn Alcott Ridenour's discussion of the role of active and passive virtues as we approach the end of life, considered more fully below (see note 27), has shaped my thinking on these points. Ridenour's observations provide insights not only for the conclusion of life, but also across the life cycle as we experience seasons of weakness and strength.
13 Spaemann, *Persons*, 32, 68.
14 Spaemann, *Persons*, 68.
15 Spaemann, *Persons*, 185.
16 Spaemann, *Persons*, 185.
17 Herman Bavinck, *Reformed Dogmatics*, Vol. 2, ed. John Bolt, and trans. John Vriend (Grand Rapids: Baker Academic, 2008), 577.
18 Spaemann, *Persons*, 17.
19 O. Carter Snead, "Inhuman Nature," *National Review*, Nov. 29, 2021, https://www.

nationalreview.com/magazine/2021/11/29/inhuman-nature.

20 Snead, *What It Means to Be Human*, 173.

21 Robert L. Woodson Sr., *Lessons from the Least of These: The Woodson Principles* (New York: Post Hill Press, 2020), 1.

22 Chris Sicks, *Tangible: Making God Known Through Deeds of Mercy and Words of Truth* (Colorado Springs: NavPress, 2013), 18.

23 "Physician-Assisted Suicide Disregards the Dignity Of Human Life," Americans United for Life, accessed August 8, 2022, https://aul.org/physician-assisted-suicide.

24 Brittany Maynard, "My Right to Death with Dignity at 29," CNN.com, November 2, 2014, https://www.cnn.com/2014/10/07/opinion/maynard-assisted-suicide-cancer-dignity.

25 Maggie Karner, "An Open Letter to Brittany Maynard," *National Right to Life News*, September 28, 2015, https://www.nationalrighttolifenews.org/2015/09/a-genuine-profile-in-courage-maggie-karner-rip.

26 Maggie Karner, "An Open Letter."

27 Autumn Alcott Ridenour, *Sabbath Rest as Vocation: Aging Toward Death* (London: T&T Clark, 2018), 12.

28 Ridenour, *Sabbath Rest*, 15.

29 Ridenour, *Sabbath Rest*, 77.

30 Ridenour, *Sabbath Rest*, 15.

31 Ridenour, *Sabbath Rest*, 13.

32 Her Pregnancy and Life Assistance Network, https://herplan.org.

A Theology of Human Embodiment, by Gregg R. Allison

1 Other passages affirm that no one sees God: Exod. 33:20; John 5:37, 6:46; Col. 1:15; 1 Tim. 6:16; 1 John 4:20.

2 Vern S. Poythress, *A Biblical Theology of God's Appearing* (Wheaton: Crossway, 2018). For a counterargument to Christophanies, see Andrew S. Malone, *Knowing Jesus in the Old Testament?: A Fresh Look at Christophanies* (London: IVP UK, 2015).

3 For further discussion, see Graham A. Cole, *Against the Darkness: The Doctrine of Angels, Satan, and Demons*, Foundations of Evangelical Theology (Wheaton: Crossway, 2019), 76–78.

4 The following discussion is taken from Gregg R. Allison, "Four Theses concerning Human Embodiment," *SBJT* 23, no. 2 (2019): 157.

5 Justin E. H. Smith, "Introduction," in *Embodiment: A History*, ed. Justin E. H. Smith, Oxford Philosophical Concepts (Oxford: Oxford University Press, 2017), 1.

6 Thomas J. Csordas, "Somatic Modes of Attention," *Cultural Anthropology* 8, no. 2 (May 1993): 135.

7 Csordas, "Somatic Modes," 135.

8 I am cheered by the growing literature on human embodiment from a biblical and theological perspective, the most recent of which is Timothy Tennent, *For the Body: Recovering a Theology of Gender, Sexuality, and the Human Body* (Grand Rapids: Zondervan, 2020). As a discipline of study, embodiment began with John Paul II, *Man and Woman He Created Them: A Theology of the Body* (Boston: Pauline, 1986, 2006). Others have continued to develop this field: Mary T. Prokes, *Toward a Theology of the Body* (Grand Rapids: Eerdmans, 1996); John B. Nelson, *Body Theology* (Louisville: Westminster John Knox, 1992); idem, *Embodiment: An Approach to Sexuality and Christian Theology* (Minneapolis: Augsburg, 1978); Benedict Ashley, *Theologies of the Body: Humanist and Christian* (Braintree, MA: The Pope John Center, 1985); Carlo Maria Martini, *On the Body: A Contemporary Theology of the Body*, trans. R. M. Giammanco Frongia (New York: Crossroad, 2001); Elisabeth Moltmann-Wendel, *I Am My Body: A Theology of Embodiment*, trans. John Bowden (New York: Continuum,

1995); Nancy R. Pearcey, *Love Thy Body: Answering Hard Questions about Life and Sexuality* (Grand Rapids: Baker, 2018); Ola Sigurdson, *Heavenly Bodies: Incarnation, the Gaze, and Embodiment in Christian Theology*, trans. Carl Olsen (Grand Rapids: Eerdmans, 2016); Luke Timothy Johnson, *The Revelatory Body: Theology as Inductive Art* (Grand Rapids: Eerdmans, 2015); Samuel M. Powell and Michael E. Lodahl, eds., *Embodied Holiness: Toward a Corporate Theology of Spiritual Growth* (Downers Grove: IVP, 1999). From a nontheological perspective, contributions include Smith, ed., *Embodiment: A History*; Bessel Van der Kolk, *The Body Keeps the Score: Brain, Mind, and Body in the Healing of Trauma* (New York: Penguin, 2014).

9   Allison, "Four Theses concerning Human Embodiment," 157–58.

10 Luke Timothy Johnson emphasizes that "humans bear God's image in the world somatically." Johnson, *Revelatory Body*, 55.

11 For the notion of Edenizing the world, see William J. Dumbrell, *The Search for Order: Eschatology in Focus* (Eugene, OR: Wipf & Stock, 2001), 11.

12 Dichotomy was first articulated by Tertullian in his *Treatise on the Soul*. Trichotomy, against which Tertullian argued, had been proposed earlier by Irenaeus in his *Against Heresies*. For further discussion of the development of these two views, see Gregg R. Allison, *Historical Theology: An Introduction to Christian Doctrine* (Grand Rapids: Zondervan, 2011), 322–27.

13 The statement by Vladimir Iljine is quoted without bibliographic detail in Moltmann-Wendel, *I Am My Body*, 2.

14 Smith, "Introduction," 2.

15 Brooke Holmes, "The Body of Western Embodiment: Classical Antiquity and the Early History of a Problem," in *Embodiment: A History*, 41–42.

16 Helen Lang, "Embodied or Ensouled: Aristotle on the Relation of Soul and Body," in *Embodiment: A History*, 55.

17 Lang, "Embodied or Ensouled," 54.

18 Lang, "Embodied or Ensouled," 55, 58. The citation is from Aristotle, *On the Soul* II.1,412a21.

19 Lang, "Embodied or Ensouled," 66–67.

20 Tertullian, *Treatise on the Soul*, 38, in *ANF*, 3:219.

21 Justin Martyr, *First Apology*, 1.28, in *ANF*, 1:172.

22 *Letter to Diognetus*, 6, in *ANF*, 1:27.

23 Lactanius, *The Divine Institutes*, 4.25 and 7.5, in *ANF*, 7:127 and 202.

24 Patrick Lee and Robert P. George, *Body-Self Dualism in Contemporary Ethics and Politics* (New York: Cambridge University Press, 2008), 4.

25 Lee and George, *Body-Self Dualism*, 17.

26 George MacDonald, *Annals of a Quiet Neighborhood* (London: Hurst and Blackett, 1867), ch. 28.

27 C. S. Lewis, *The Four Loves* (New York: Harcourt Brace, 1960), 101.

28 Johnson, *Revelatory Body*, 80.

29 For further discussion, see Moltmann-Wendel, *I Am My Body*, 1. She further illustrates this point: "'I've a fever,' 'my stomach's on strike,' 'my back's out of action'—that's how we first perceive our illnesses. We keep them from us, see them as an isolated defect which can be remedied in isolation, until one day we have to say, 'I'm sick.' Then we are saying something that we do not normally say of ourselves: that our destiny is to be bound up with our bodies. In a variety of situations, we can distance ourselves from our bodies, but at some point, they get hold of us and will not let go. 'I am my body.'. . . It is not only my body that is sick; I am sick. I am in my body. I have no other identity" (21-22).

30 Time and space constraints do not permit me to discuss the differences between sex and gender, so I will use the two words interchangeably.

31 Scott B. Rae, *Moral Choices: An Introduction to Ethics*, 4th ed. (Grand Rapids: Zondervan, 2018), 339.
32 Allison, *Embodied*, 40.
33 Megan DeFranza, *Sex Difference in Christian Theology: Male, Female, and Intersex in the Image of God* (Grand Rapids: Eerdmans, 2015).
34 Estimates vary, but the number of different genders claimed by people runs between fifty and eighty.
35 Frederica Mathewes-Green, "The Subject Was Noses: What Happens When Academics Discover That We Have Bodies," *Books and Culture* (January/February 1997): 14–16. Her reference is to Dave Barry, *Babies and Other Hazards of Sex* (New York: Rodale Books, 2000).
36 For further discussion, see Aimee Byrd, *Why Can't We Be Friends? Avoidance is Not Purity* (Phillipsburg, NJ: P&R, 2018).
37 Mathewes-Green, "Subject Was Noses," 14–16.
*Aspects of this chapter previously appeared in Gregg R. Allison, "A Theology of Embodiment," *Southwestern Journal of Theology* 63:2 (Spring 2021): 65–80, as well as Gregg R. Allison, *Embodied: Living as Whole People in a Fractured World* (Grand Rapids: Baker, 2021).

The Sanctity of Human Life, by Scott B. Rae

1   Roe v. Wade, 410 U.S. 113 (1973).
2   Dobbs vs. Jackson Women's Health Organization
3   *Washington v. Glucksberg*, 521 U.S. 702 (1997).
4   Ryan Burge, *Twenty Myths About Religion and Politics in America* (Louisville: Fortress, 2022), 31–40.
5   Peter Singer and Helga Kuhse, *Should the Baby Live? The Problem of Handicapped Infants* (New York: Oxford University Press, 1985).
6   Alberto Giubillini and Francesca Minerva, "After-birth Abortion: Why Should the Baby Live?" *Journal of Medical Ethics* 39 (1993): 261–63. The entire issue is devoted to this paper and the various responses it generated.
7   Conor Friedersdorf, "Why Dr. Kermit Gosnell's Trial Should Be a Front Page Story," *The Atlantic* (April 12, 2013).
8   Mara Hivstendahl, *Unnatural Selection: Choosing Boys Over Girls and the Consequences of a World Full of Men* (New York: Public Affairs Books, 2011).
9   "Gendercide: The Worldwide War on Baby Girls," *The Economist*, March 4, 2010, https://www.economist.com/international/2010/03/04/the-worldwide-war-on-baby-girls.
10 See for example, Derek Humphry, *Final Exit: The Practicalities of Self-Deliverance and Assisted Suicide for the Dying*, 3rd ed. (New York: Dell, 2002).
11 In my view, the U.S. Supreme Court ruling in *Cruzan* was exactly right. There the Court ruled that medically provided nutrition and hydration was indeed legitimate medical treatment, which could be refused by a competent adult patient or could be refused by a surrogate decision maker if there was clear and convincing evidence that such was the wish of the patient. See Cruzan v. Director, Missouri Department of Health, 497 U.S. 261 (1990).
12 Spriggs M., "Lesbian couple create a child who is deaf like them," *Journal of Medical Ethics* 28 (2002): 283. See also Jonathan Glover, *Choosing Children: Genes, Disability, and Design* (New York: Oxford University Press, 2008).
13 See the classic articulation of this in Mary Ann Warren, "On the Moral and Legal Status of Abortion," *The Monist*, 57, no. 4 (1973): 43–61. See also Joseph Fletcher, "Indicators of Humanhood," *Hastings Center Report* 2, no. 5 (1972): 1–4.

What It Means to be Male And Female, by Katie J. McCoy

1 Complementarianism is the view to which I hold. See "The Danvers Statement," *The Council for Biblical Manhood and Womanhood*, accessed September 1, 2020, https://cbmw.org/about/danvers-statement/.

2 Judith Butler, "Performative Acts and Gender Constitution: An Essay in Phenomenology and Feminist Theory," *Theatre Journal* 40, no. 4 (1988): 519–31.

3 Portions of this article appeared in "Recovering the Communion of Persons: How Hebrew Anthropology Counters Aristotelian Thought Concerning Male and Female Roles," *Eikon: A Journal for Biblical Anthropology* 1, no. 2 (Fall 2019): 44–59.

4 The manner in which male and female express their authority over creation is intrinsic to their relationship to each other. While the man and the woman had equal authority over creation in Genesis 1–2, they did not necessarily have identical authority over each other.

5 Earle Bennett Cross, *The Hebrew Family: A Study in Historical Sociology* (Chicago: University of Chicago Press, 1927), 42. Within Hebrew thought, emotional affections were located in the bowels.

6 Other understandings of the *imago Dei* contain a relational underpinning: the functional view reflects humanity's positional relationship to the Lord in comparison to all other creation (Gen. 1:27); conscience or moral law presumes humanity's instinctive knowledge of right and wrong and consequently accountability to a personal God (Rom. 1:18–23).

7 John F. Kilner, *Dignity and Destiny: Humanity in the Image of God* (Grand Rapids: Eerdmans, 2015), 228.

8 John Paul II, *Theology of the Body in Simple Language* (Internet Archive, Philokalia Books, 2008), 19. John Paul II discusses at length how the celibate person also fulfills the nuptial meaning of the body by being "married" to God (168, 173).

9 J. Budziszewski, *On the Meaning of Sex* (Wilmington: ISI Books, 2012), 38–40. Not merely do biologically quantifiable brain differences between male and female exist, but they exist in corresponding ways, the differences of one balancing what the other lacks (41).

10 Gerhard Müller, "An Opening to the Mystery of God," in *Not Just Good, But Beautiful: The Complementarity Relationship Between Man and Woman*, ed. Steven Lopes and Helen Alvaré (Walden, NY: Plough, 2015), 12.

11 John Paul II, *Theology of the Body*, 16.

12 Ross Hastings, "The Trinity and Human Sexuality: Made in the Image of God," *Crux* 53, no. 3 (Fall 2017): 15.

13 Karl Barth, *Church Dogmatics*, trans. G. W. Bromiley (Edinburgh: T&T Clark, 1975), 185. "The analogy between God and man [*imago Dei*] is simply the existence of the I and the Thou in confrontation." The I-Thou motif originates with Martin Buber, *I and Thou* (New York: Scribner, 1970).

14 Dietrich Bonhoeffer, *Creation and Fall: A Theological Exposition of Genesis 1–3*, ed. John W. deGruchy, trans. Douglas Stephen Bax (Minneapolis: Fortress, 1997), 65. Bonhoeffer contrasts this with an *analogia entis* (analogy of being). "The creature is free in that one creature exists in relation to another creature, in that one being is free for another human being" (66).

15 "The analogy between God and man [*imago Dei*] is simply the existence of the I and the Thou in confrontation." Barth, *Church Dogmatics* 1/1:185. "Hence humanity is the determination of our being as a being in encounter with the other man." Barth, *Church Dogmatics* III/2:248. "The only real differentiation and relationship is that of man to man, and in its original and most concrete form of man to woman and woman to man. Man is no more solitary than God. But as God is One, and He alone is God, so man as man is one and alone, and two only in the duality of his kind, i.e., in the

duality of man and woman. In this way he is a copy and imitation of God. In this way he repeats in his confrontation of God and himself the confrontation in God." Barth, *Church Dogmatics* I/1:186. This is not to say that individual humanity does not fully image God. The image of God is not contingent upon relationship, but it is manifested in relationship.

16 Bonhoeffer, *Creation and Fall*, 64. Italics original.
17 Bonhoeffer, *Creation and Fall*, 64.
18 Hastings, "Trinity and Human Sexuality," 13.
19 Hastings, "Trinity and Human Sexuality," 13.
20 Lisa Aiken, *To Be a Jewish Woman* (Northvale, NJ: J. Aronson, 1992), 27.
21 Leslie Cook, "Body Language: Woman's Rituals of Purification in the Bible and Mishnah," in *Women and Water: Menstruation in Jewish Life*, ed. Rahel R. Wasserfall (Hanover, NH: Brandeis University Press, 1999), 42.
22 Yedidiah H. E. Ghatan, *The Invaluable Pearl: The Unique Status of Women in Judaism* (New York: Bloch, 1986), 42.
23 Ghatan, *Invaluable Pearl*, 43; cf. 1 Cor. 11:11–12.
24 Hastings, "Trinity and Human Sexuality," 14.
25 Peter Kreeft, "Is There Sex in Heaven?" in *Everything You Ever Wanted to Know about Heaven but Never Dreamed of Asking* (San Francisco: Ignatius, 1990), 132.
26 Barth, *Church Dogmatics* III/2:297,310–11. Within this mutuality, Barth explains the analogical relationship between God and Israel and Christ and the Church. "This basic order of the human established by God's creation is not accidental or contingent."
27 By "gender identity," I do not mean the idea that one may determine the gender with which one subjectively identifies. Rather, I mean the gender that one's biology empirically signifies.
28 "What Is Gender Dysphoria?" *American Psychiatric Association*, accessed August 31, 2020, https://www.psychiatry.org/patients-families/gender-dysphoria/what-is-gender-dysphoria.
29 Ariel Jao, "Gender 'X': Ontario Issues Its First 'NonBinary' Birth Certificate," *NBC News*, May 9, 2018, https://www.nbcnews.com/feature/nbc-out/gender-x-ontario-issues-its-first-ever-non-binary-birth-n872676.
30 Adam Liptak, "Civil Rights Law Protects Gay and Transgender Workers, Supreme Court Rules," *New York Times*, updated June 16, 2020, https://www.nytimes.com/2020/06/15/us/gay-transgender-workers-supreme-court.html.
31 Jason Rafferty, "Ensuring Comprehensive Care and Support for Transgender and Gender-Diverse Children and Adolescents," *Pediatrics* 142, no. 4 (2018); "Pubertal Blockers for Transgender and Gender Diverse Youth," *Mayo Clinic*, August 16, 2019, https://www.mayoclinic.org/diseases-conditions/gender-dysphoria/in-depth/pubertal-blockers/art-20459075; Michelle Cretella, "I'm a Pediatrician. How Transgender Ideology Has Infiltrated My Field and Produced Large-Scale Child Abuse," *The Daily Signal*, July 3, 2017, https://www.dailysignal.com/2017/07/03/im-pediatrician-transgender-ideology-infiltrated-field-produced-large-scale-child-abuse/.
32 Ryan T. Anderson, "*The New York Times* Reveals Painful Truths about Transgender Lives," *Public Discourse*, November 25, 2018, https://www.thepublicdiscourse.com/2018/11/47220.
33 Anderson, "*Times* Reveals."
34 Ryan T. Anderson, *When Harry Became Sally: Responding to the Transgender Movement* (New York: Encounter, 2018), 104.
35 Anderson, *When Harry Became Sally*, 104.
36 Budziszewski, *On the Meaning of Sex*, 41.
37 Lisa Littman, "Parent Reports of Adolescents and Young Adults Perceived to Show Signs of a Rapid Onset of Gender Dysphoria," *PLOS ONE 3*, no 8, August 16, 2018.

https://journals.plos.org/plosone/article?id=10.1371/journal.pone.0202330.

38 Katie McCoy, "Gender, Sexuality, and Family in the Context of Baptist Witness in Society," paper presented at Research Institute for the Ethics and Religious Liberty Commission, Dallas, TX, 2018.

39 Littman, "Parent Reports."

40 Hastings, "Trinity and Human Sexuality," 10.

41 Angela Franks, "Andrea Long Chu Says You Are a Female, and He's Only Partly Wrong," *Public Discourse*, December 10, 2019, https://www.thepublicdiscourse.com/2019/12/58719.

42 Andrew Walker, *God and the Transgender Debate* (The Good Book Company, 2017), 54; cf. 50–51.

43 Craig Carter, "The New Gender Gnostics," *Eikon* 2, no. 1 (Spring 2020): 28–39.

44 Nancy R. Pearcey, *Love Thy Body: Answering Hard Questions about Life and Sexuality* (Grand Rapids: Baker, 2018).

45 1 Cor. 11:2–16 addresses this point.

46 For instance, consider a couple who chooses to invest in their children's education through homeschooling. Both parents are vocationally capable of earning the income the family needs. But the father, a professional educator, is more qualified to direct his children's education. So both parents agree that the mother will work full time so the father can invest in their children's future academic success. Is the father abdicating his role to provide and lead, or is the mother failing to make her family a priority by working outside the home? Perhaps the answer will depend on whether one understands headship as a relationship or a function.

47 A woman is no less feminine because she is brave, yet she does not suspend her femininity in displaying bravery. In the same way, a man does not suspend his masculinity by displaying kindness or nurture. We look forward to seeing more research on the difference between complementarity and gender essentialism.

*Aspects of this chapter have been adapted from Katie J. McCoy, "God Created Them, Male and Female," *Southwestern Journal of Theology* 63:2 (Spring 2021): 49–64, as well as John Hammett and Katie J. McCoy, *The Doctrine of Humankind* (Nashville: B&H, 2023).

Artificial Intelligence, Transhumanism, and the Question of the Person, by Jacob Shatzer

1 For more on the history of technology and understanding the connection between technology and ethics, see Eric Schatzberg, *Technology: Critical History of a Concept* (Chicago: University of Chicago Press, 2018).

2 For an interesting take on this from a secular philosophical angle, see Shannon Vallor, *Technology and the Virtues: A Philosophical Guide to a Future Worth Wanting* (Oxford: Oxford University Press, 2016).

3 Byron Reese, *The Fourth Age: Smart Robots, Conscious Computers, and the Future of Humanity* (New York: Simon & Schuster, 2018).

4 Reese, *The Fourth Age*, xi.

5 John C. Lennox, *2084: Artificial Intelligence and the Future of Humanity* (Grand Rapids: Zondervan, 2020), 16.

6 Lennox, *2084*, 17.

7 Lennox, *2084*, 19.

8 Lennox, *2084*, 19.

9 For a deeper explanation of algorithms, see Kartik Hosanagar, *A Human's Guide to Machine Intelligence: How Algorithms Are Shaping Our Lives and How We Can Stay in Control* (New York: Viking, 2019).

10 Hannah Fry, *Hello World: Being Human in the Age of Algorithms* (New York: Norton,

2018), 8–10.

11 Lennox, *2084*, 13.

12 Fry, *Hello World*, 10.

13 I am of course simplifying here. To get a better grasp of the different types of algorithms and approaches to this aspect of AI, see Pedro Domingos, *The Master Algorithm: How the Quest for the Ultimate Learning Machine Will Remake Our World* (New York: Basic, 2015).

14 Darrell M. West, *The Future of Work: Robots, AI, and Automation* (Washington, D.C.: Brookings Institution Press, 2018), 24.

15 See Ajay Agrawal, Joshua Gans, and Ayi Goldfarb, *Prediction Machines: The Simple Economics of Artificial Intelligence* (Boston: Harvard Business Review Books, 2018).

16 See Agrawal, Gans, and Goldfarb, *Prediction Machines*.

17 Agrawal, Gans, and Goldfarb, *Prediction Machines*, 16.

18 Domingos, *Master Algorithm*, xvi.

19 Susan Schneider, *Artificial You: AI and the Future of Your Mind* (Princeton, NJ: Princeton University Press, 2019), 23.

20 Schneider, *Artificial You*, 67.

21 Lennox, *2084*, 45–46.

22 Jeanine Thweatt-Bates, *Cyborg Selves: A Theological Anthropology of the Posthuman* (New York: Routledge, 2012), 13.

23 For a recent edited volume that covers a variety of perspectives on the issue, see Steve Donaldson and Ron Cole-Turner, eds., *Christian Perspectives on Transhumanism and the Church: Chips in the Brain, Immortality, and the World of Tomorrow* (New York: Palgrave McMillan, 2018).

24 "Frequently Asked Questions," *Christian Transhumanism*, accessed June 8, 2020, https://www.christiantranshumanism.org/faq.

25 "Frequently Asked Questions," *Christian Transhumanism*.

26 "The Christian Transhumanist Affirmation," *Christian Transhumanism*, accessed June 8, 2020, https://www.christiantranshumanism.org/affirmation.

27 Ronald Cole-Turner, "Introduction: Why the Church Should Pay Attention to Transhumanism," in *Christian Perspectives on Transhumanism and the Church*, eds. Steve Donaldson and Ronald Cole-Turner (Switzerland: Palgrave MacMillan, 2018), 9.

28 Boaz Goss, "Christianity's Rigged Debate with Transhumanism," in *Christian Perspectives on Transhumanism*, 84.

29 Jeffrey P. Bishop, "Nietzsche's Power Ontology and Transhumanism: Or Why Christians Cannot Be Transhumanists," in *Christian Perspectives on Transhumanism*, 118.

30 Bishop, "Nietzsche's Power Ontology," 119.

31 Bishop, "Nietzsche's Power Ontology," 131.

32 Further, instead of buying into the promises of transhumanism, Christians should cling to the doctrines of creation and resurrection. At root, "The Christian message of resurrection is that bodies matter, they have significance, and they are not just clay to be molded to our wills." See Bishop, "Nietzsche's Power Ontology," 133.

33 Ysabel Johnson, "Rivalry, Control, and Transhumanist Desire," in *Christian Perspectives on Transhumanism*, 230.

34 Jason Thacker, *The Age of AI: Artificial Intelligence and the Future of Humanity* (Grand Rapids: Zondervan, 2020), 44.

35 For more on this line of argument, see my (Jacob Shatzer) *Transhumanism and the Image of God: Today's Technology and the Future of Christian Discipleship* (Downers Grove: IVP, 2019).

36 Thacker, *Age of AI*, 66–67.

37 The more we accept these ideas and interact with them uncritically, the more like machines we actually become. Some argue that mindless technology use actually

turns people into simple machines, programmable and controllable by powerful interests. In *Re-Engineering Humanity*, Brett Frischmann and Evan Selinger worry about "techno-social engineering," which "refers to processes where technologies and social forces align and impact how we think, perceive, and act. That's the 'techno' and 'social' components of the term. 'Engineer' is quite close in meaning to 'construct,' 'influence,' 'shape,' 'manipulate,' and 'make,' and we might have selected any of those terms" (4). They argue that we need the freedom to be "off" and freedom from an engineered determinism that many tech companies are after, whether in relation to AI or transhumanism. In other words, our resistance to the idea that we are merely lumps of data can help keep us from patterns of life that do in fact reduce us to almost that. See Frischmann and Selinger, *Re-engineering Humanity* (Cambridge: Cambridge University Press, 2018), 4.

38 Schneider, *Artificial You*, 84.

39 Andrew Yang, *The War on Normal People: The Truth about America's Disappearing Jobs and Why Universal Basic Income Is Our Future* (New York: Hachette, 2018), xiv.

40 Yang, *The War on Normal People*, 68.

41 See, for instance, the work of West, *The Future of Work*.

42 Kai-Fu Lee, *AI Superpowers: China, Silicon Valley, and the New World Order* (New York: Houghton Mifflin Harcourt, 2018), 5.

43 See, for instance, David Mindell, *Our Robots, Ourselves: Robotics and the Myths of Autonomy* (New York: Viking, 2015), 8–9.

44 Malcolm Frank, Paul Roehrig, and Ben Pring, *What to Do When Machines Do Everything: How to Get Ahead in a World of AI, Algorithms, Bots, and Big Data* (Hoboken, NJ: Wiley, 2017), 8–9. See also Paul R. Daugherty and H. James Wilson, *Human + Machine: Reimagining Work in the Age of AI* (Boston: Harvard Business Review Press, 2018); Andrew McAfee and Erik Brynjolfsson, *Machine, Platform, Crowd: Harnessing Our Digital Future* (New York: Norton, 2017); Thomas H. Davenport and Julia Kirby, *Only Humans Need Apply: Winners & Losers in the Age of Smart Machines* (New York: Harper, 2016); Nick Polson and James Scott, *AIQ: How People and Machines Are Smarter Together* (New York: St. Martin's, 2018).

45 See Amy Webb, *The Big Nine: How the Tech Titans and Their Thinking Machines Could Warp Humanity* (New York: Public Affairs, 2019).

46 Fry, *Hello World*, 173.

47 Shoshana Zuboff, *The Age of Surveillance Capitalism: The Fight for a Human Future at the New Frontier of Power* (New York: Public Affairs, 2019). See my review, "On Being Watched, and Remembered," *Front Porch Republic*, May 15, 2019, https://www.frontporchrepublic.com/2019/05/on-being-watched-and-remembered.

48 Radina Gigova, "Who Vladimir Putin Thinks Will Rule the World," accessed June 10, 2020, https://www.cnn.com/2017/09/01/world/putin-artificial-intelligence-will-rule-world/index.html.

49 Lee, *AI Superpowers*, 9.

50 Lee, *AI Superpowers*, 14.

51 Lee, *AI Superpowers*, 15.

52 Paul Scharre, *Army of None: Autonomous Weapons and the Future of War* (New York: Norton, 2018), 4.

53 Scharre, *Army of None*, 5.

54 Scharre, *Army of None*, 8.

55 Scharre, *Army of None*, 362.

56 See Schneider, *Artificial You*, 74–81.

57 Michael Horton, "Image and Office: Human Personhood and the Covenant," in *Personal Identity in Theological Perspective*, ed. Richard Lints, Michael S. Horton, and Mark R. Talbot (Grand Rapids: Eerdmans, 2006), 184.

*Aspects of the chapter previously appeared in Jacob Shatzer, "Fake and Future 'Humans': Artificial Intelligence, Transhumanism, and the Question of the Person," *Southwestern Journal of Theology* 63:2 (Spring 2021): 127–46; as well as Jacob Shatzer, *Transhumanism and the Image of God: Today's Technology and the Future of Christian Discipleship* (Downers Grove: IVP, 2019).

Faithful Living in a Culture Of Confusion, by John Stonestreet

1 Meilan Solly, "U.S. Life Expectancy Drops for Third Year in a Row, Reflecting Rising Drug Overdoses, Suicide," *Smithsonian Magazine*, December 3, 2018, https://www.smithsonianmag.com/smart-news/us-life-expectancy-drops-third-year-row-reflecting-fising-drug-overdoxe-suicide-rates-180970942.
2 Solly, "U.S. Life Expectancy."
3 Jaclyn Diaz, "27 School Shootings Have Taken Place So Far This Year," NPR, May 25, 2022, https://www.npr.org/2022/05/24/1101050970/2022-school-shootings-so-far; "School Shootings This Year: How Many and Where," *EdWeek*, https://www.edweek.org/leadership/school-shootings-this-year-how-many-and-where/2022/01.
4 David Brooks, *The Road to Character* (New York: Random House, 2016).

Apologetic Approaches for Our Cultural Confusion, by Robert B. Stewart

1 The word in Acts 17:18 translated "idle babbler" (*spermologos*) was a term of derision that meant something like "seed-picker." In fact, at least some were mistaken as to what Paul was saying because they seem to have thought that he was talking about two deities, Jesus and a goddess (*Anastasis*) because Paul was preaching about the resurrection of Jesus. Regardless, they gave him a hearing.
2 Aeschylus, *Euminedes*, 647–48.
3 General revelation is the knowledge of God that is available to all persons, in all places, at all times, whereas special revelation is the knowledge of God that is available only to particular persons, in particular places, at particular times.
4 In his address Paul quotes from Greek philosophers Epimenides and Aratus, as well as showing a familiarity with Greek philosophy in knowing which philosophers to quote to make his points. By quoting Epimenides and Aratus, Paul was able to avoid having some of his message challenged directly because, were they to do so, then they would be forced to reject their own authorities and traditions. In saying "authorities," I am not suggesting that Greeks looked upon the teaching of any philosopher as Christians and Jews looked upon Scripture, as God's word. But the Greek philosophers were accorded great respect.
5 Apologists not only speak to non-Christians but also to Christians. When speaking to Christians, we should use Scripture if for no other reason than many Christians misread the Bible. Therefore, we often have to teach our own what God's word says. We have more than one audience or group to serve.
6 Gregg R. Allison, *Embodied: Living as Whole People in a Fractured World* (Grand Rapids: Baker, 2021).
7 Rudolf Bultmann, "*ginōskō*," in *Theological Dictionary of the New Testament*, ed. G. Kittle, trans. Geoffrey W. Bromiley, 10 vols. (Grand Rapids: Eerdmans, 1964), 1:692–96.
8 I recognize that with some infants, it is difficult to discern their sex because of mixed genitalia and or ambiguous genitalia, or other physical factors, but such instances are rare and not analogous to the debates of the moment and can be handled more appropriately by pediatricians and geneticists than by psychologists.
9 Notice that this analogy is not quite analogous at all points because we are not asked to back off and leave them to themselves; we are asked to accept transgenderism (which is different than accepting persons who identify as transgender) and to

celebrate it. Furthermore, if we refuse to do so, we are slandered and threatened in numerous ways. Such threats make me long for the days when our opponents proclaimed, "That's true for you, not for me."

10 Tacitus, *Annals* 15.44. Even in criticizing Nero, one clearly sees that Tacitus was no fan of Christians.

11 In a sense, this statement is false; the roots of Christian faith were at least as ancient as the election of Abraham, but when considered as something distinct from the dominant forms of Jewish religion in the first century—the forms that rejected Jesus—then its roots were indeed hardly deeper than the surface. Additionally, the majority of Peter's audience were Gentile believers.

12 I am not suggesting that there is a difference between being baptized "in Jesus' name" and being baptized with the formula that Jesus himself gave us in the Great Commission. In my view, what is intended in Acts, when baptism is said to be in Jesus' name, is that they were doing what Jesus told them to do—separating themselves from those who had chosen either through active hatred or through passive disinterest not to follow Jesus.

13 Theoretical apologetics, i.e., the writing of books, articles, or presentations at professional society, are important and needed. In this essay, I am actually walking the line between apologetics in theory and in practice because this is an article on how to practice apologetics but not actually a personal engagement with a nonbeliever or a doubting believer.

14 Blaise Pascal, *Pensees*, 131.

15 See Millard J. Erickson, *Christian Theology*, 2nd ed. (Grand Rapids: Baker, 1998), 520.

16 Augustine, *Confessions*, 1.1.

17 Apologetics is not merely about persuading nonbelievers as to the rationality and/ or truthfulness of the gospel or the Christian worldview. A secondary but still very important purpose of apologetics is to strengthen the confidence of believers.

18 Premise 1 is the major premise of the syllogism. Its antecedent is, "Christ is Lord in your hearts," and its consequent is, "you will be prepared to defend and commend your faith." ("If" is not part of the antecedent, and "then" is not part of the consequent.) Premise 1 is also a conditional statement, i.e., it is hypothetical. But if its antecedent were the case, then its consequent would logically follow. Therefore, even though the premise is hypothetical, it still has a truth value, i.e., it must be either true or false.

19 Many today, especially Protestants, disparage tradition. They do so at their own peril. We ignore the wisdom of our believing forebears at our own risk. Traditionalism is altogether different than tradition. Traditionalism is the dead faith of the living; tradition is the living faith of the dead.

Conclusion, by Daniel Darling and Lauren McAfee

1 Kenneth A. Mathews, *The New American Commentary: Genesis 1–11:26* (Nashville: B&H, 1996), 22.

2 Timothy Samuel Shah and Allen D. Hertzke, eds., *Christianity and Freedom: Volume 1: Historical Perspectives*, Cambridge Studies in Law and Christianity (Cambridge: Cambridge University Press, 2016), 21, https://doi.org/10.1017/CBO9781316408582 Leading historians uncover the unappreciated role of Christianity in the development of basic human rights and freedoms from antiquity through today. These include radical notions of dignity and equality, religious freedom, liberty of conscience, limited government, consent of the governed, economic liberty, autonomous civil society, and church-state separation, as well as more recent advances in democracy, human rights, and human development. Acknowledging that the record is mixed, scholars document how the seeds of freedom in Christianity antedate and ultimately

undermine later Christian justifications and practices of persecution. Drawing from history, political science, and sociology, this volume will become a standard reference work for historians, political scientists, theologians, students, journalists, business leaders, opinion shapers, and policymakers.

3   Tom Holland, *Dominion: How the Christian Revolution Remade the World* (New York: Basic Books, 2019).

4   Glen Scrivener, *The Air We Breathe: How We All Came to Believe in Freedom, Kindness, Progress, and Equality* (Epsom, UK: Good Book Company, 2022). "Many consider the church to be dead or dying. Christianity is seen as outdated, bigoted and responsible for many of society's problems. This leaves many believers embarrassed about their faith and many outsiders wary of religion. But what if the Christian message is not the enemy of our modern Western values, but the very thing that makes sense of them? In this fascinating book, Glen Scrivener takes readers on a journey to discover how the teachings of Jesus not only turned the ancient world upside down, but continue to underpin the way we think of life, worth, and meaning. Far from being a relic of the past, the distinctive ideas of Christianity, such as freedom, kindness, progress, and equality, are a crucial part of the air that we breathe. As Scrivener says in his introduction: "The extraordinary impact of Christianity is seen in the fact that we don't notice it. This is a book for both believers and sceptics—giving Christians confidence to be open about their faith and showing non-Christians the ways in which the message of Jesus makes sense of their most cherished beliefs. Whoever you are, you'll gain a deeper appreciation for the values you hold dear as you discover the power and profundity of Jesus and his revolution."

5   Gilbert Meilaender, *Neither Beast Nor God: The Dignity of the Human Person* (New York: Encounter Books, 2009), 90. "And therefore the reason we all ought to be treated as equals? Or is it what distinguishes some greater and more admirable human beings from the rest? What notion of human dignity should inform our private judgments and our public life? *In Neither Beast Nor God,* Gilbert Meilaender elaborates the philosophical, social, theological, and political implications of the question of dignity, and suggests a path through the thicket. Meilaender, a noted theologian and a prominent voice in America's bioethics debates, traces the ways in which notions of dignity shape societies, families, and individual lives, and incisively cuts through some common confusions that cloud our thinking on key moral and ethical questions. The dignity of humanity and the dignity of the person, he argues, are distinct but deeply connected—and only by grasping them both can we find our way to a meaningful understanding of the human condition."

6   Meilaender, *Neither Beast Nor God*

7   Oliver O'Donovan, *The Ways of Judgment* (Grand Rapids: Eerdmans, 2008), 40.

8   John F. Kilner, *Dignity and Destiny: Humanity in the Image of God* (Grand Rapids: Eerdmans, 2015), 4.

9   Derek Kidner, *Genesis*, Tyndale Old Testament Commentary (Downers Grove: IVP, 2008), 47.

10 John M. Frame, *Systematic Theology: An Introduction to Christian Belief* (Phillipsburg, NJ: P&R, 2013), 363.

11 Portions of this section are adapted from Daniel Darling, *The Characters of Creation: The Men, Women, Creatures, and Serpent Present at the Beginning of the World* (Chicago: Moody, 2022), 25–44.

12 John Calvin, *Genesis*, Crossway Classic Commentaries (Wheaton: Crossway, 2001), 25.

13 Herman Bavinck, *The Wonderful Works of God: Instructions in the Christian Religion According to the Reformed Confession* (Philadelphia: Westminster Seminary Press, 2020), 166, accessed August 18, 2022, https://www.christianbook.

com/wonderful-instructions-christian-according-reformed-confession/her-man-bavinck/9781733627221/pd/27221X.

14 Daniel Darling, *The Dignity Revolution: Reclaiming God's Rich Vision for Humanity* (Epsom, UK: Good Book Company, 2018), 34.

15 Wolfhart Pannenberg, *Systematic Theology*, trans. Geoffrey W. Bromiley (Grand Rapids: Eerdmans, 1994), 77.

16 Walter J. Burghardt, *The Image of God in Man According to Cyril of Alexandria* (Eugene, OR: Wipf & Stock, 2009), 65.

17 Orlando Saer, *Big God: How to Approach Suffering, Spread the Gospel, Make Decisions, and Pray in Light of a God Who Really is in the Driving Seat of the World* (Fearn, Scotland: Christian Focus, 2015), 76.

18 Michael and Lauren McAfee, *Not What You Think* (Grand Rapids: Zondervan, 2019), 154.

19 Kilner, *Dignity and Destiny*, 8.